How to Survive on Land and Sea

FOURTH EDITION

How to Survive on Land and Sea

By Frank C. Craighead, Jr., and John J. Craighead
Revised by Ray E. Smith and D. Shiras Jarvis

Naval Institute Press   Annapolis, Maryland

Library of Congress Cataloging in Publication Data

Craighead, Frank C. (Frank Cooper)
    How to survive on land and sea.

    Rev. ed. of: How to survive on land and sea. 2nd rev.
ed. c1956.
    Bibliography: p
    Includes index.
    1. Survival (after airplane accidents, shipwrecks,
etc.) I. Craighead, John Johnson. II. Smith,
Ray E., 1938–   . III. Jarvis, D. Shiras (David
Shiras), 1947–   . IV. How to survive on land and sea.
V. Title.
TL553.7C67   1984   613.6'9   84-4879
ISBN 0-87021-278-8 (soft)

Printed in the United States of America

To the many survivors who lived to tell their stories
and in so doing provided knowledge so that others may live.

To the many individuals and organizations working to develop
better survival equipment and techniques.

Yea though I walk through the valley of the shadow of death,
I will fear no evil, for thou art with me; thy rod and thy staff,
they comfort me.

Psalms 23

Contents

It takes an exceptional editor to turn a rough manuscript into a polished, professional publication. With authority and diplomacy, Cynthia Barry of the Naval Institute Press has accomplished this with the revision of *How to Survive on Land and Sea*. Her work on the book has been far more than that of an editor. She has contributed original writing based on her own research and on additional expert opinions that she obtained independently. We are forever indebted to Ms. Barry for the outstanding work she has done on this project.

Ray E. Smith and D. Shiras Jarvis

Acknowledgments

We enjoyed the help of many fine people in revising *How to Survive on Land and Sea*. Our thanks go first of all, of course, to the Craigheads, Frank and John, whose splendid original edition, written in the 1940s, has become a classic. It is an honor to be asked to up-date it.

We tapped the expertise of many knowledgeable people in far-ranging fields. For help with various chapters in the land survival section, we thank Mr. Ralph Odom of the Naval Air Station at Brunswick, Maine; Sgt. Curtis Ray at Lackland Air Force Base in Randolph, Texas; and Mr. John Tovrov, director of the Leadership Section of the Adirondack and Appalachian Mountain Clubs' Winter Mountaineering School. In the water survival section, we appreciate the guidance we received from Mr. John Bernhartsen, assistant branch chief and education specialist in the Office of Boating Safety, U.S. Coast Guard; Mr. Richard Henderson, author of *Sail and Power* and co-author with Adm. William J. Kotsch—to whom we also owe thanks—of *Heavy Weather Guide*; and Mr. Richard R. Hobbs, author of several books on navigation. Bringing their knowledge to the disaster survival section were Professor Gilbert White, director of the Natural Hazards Center in Boulder, Colorado, and his able staff, particularly Dr. Susan Tubbesing; Mr. Dale Brown, assistant director of the American Red Cross Disaster Service; and Mr. Richard A. Wood, program leader in the Disaster Preparedness Section of the National Oceanic and Atmospheric Administration (NOAA). We would also like to thank Mr. Oliver G.A.M. Payne, staff writer at the National Geographic Society, for his help throughout the book.

In addition, we benefited from the particular knowledge of the following people: Murray Hamlet, D.V.M. and Robert W. Hubbard, Ph.D., both of the U.S. Army Research Institute of Environmental Medicine; Dr. J. Howard Frank of the Florida Medical Entomology Laboratory; Mr. Orin Myers, national director of water safety at the American Red Cross, and his assistant, Mr. Thomas Werts; and Professor T. Theodore Fujita and his staff of the University of Chicago.

We would also like to thank Commander Alan M. Steinman, medical officer of the Search and Rescue Division of the U.S. Coast Guard; and

Ms. Louise Priest, executive director of the Council for National Cooperation in Aquatics; and Ms. Margaret McMillan for information on offshore oil survival technology.

If the readers enjoy and learn from the book's illustrations, they are indebted to the following: Ensign Elizabeth Bunker, W-VS, USNR, many of whose illustrations from the first edition are reprinted here; Ms. Melanie Barocas, free-lance photographer; Ms. Elizabeth Hooks, photo librarian at the American Red Cross; Mr. Steve Netherby of *Field & Stream*; Ms. Barbara Shattuck of the National Geographic Society, Illustrations Library; Ms. Joanne David of NOAA; Mr. Thomas A. DuRant, picture librarian at the National Park Service; Mr. Michael Logue, U.S. Army Corps of Engineers; Mr. Earnest D. Cobb, U.S. Geological Survey; Mr. Charles Recknagel of the National Aeronautics and Space Administration; Ms. Judith King of the National Zoo; Mr. Robert A. Carlisle, Department of the Navy, Office of Information; and, of course, Mrs. Patty Maddocks, photo librarian at the Naval Institute.

Also at the Naval Institute, we would like to note the generous support given us by Mr. Thomas Epley, director of the press. Mrs. Debbie Guberti, acquisitions editor, encouraged us in the initial stages. Mrs. Marge Whittington expertly typed parts of the manuscript. Ms. Beverly Baum, designer, and her assistant, Ms. Moira Megargee, are responsible for the attractive appearance of the book. To Mrs. Gee Sweetman goes the credit for a very thorough index.

Finally, and with deep affection, we would like to thank our wives, Dotty Smith and Patti Jarvis, for their patience and assistance.

Foreword to the First Edition

The first edition of this book was prepared from material used by numerous coaches and instructors in the U.S. Navy's V-Five Program during World War II, in order to provide the best possible standardized instruction in survival techniques for combat naval pilots, both on land and at sea.

Since World War II, the book has been widely used in the civilian field of instruction and reference. It is of interest and value to yachtsmen, hunters, explorers, sportsmen, Boy Scouts, and others interested in activities involving and dependent upon natural phenomena, in tropical, temperate or polar regions.

T. J. Hamilton
Rear Admiral, U.S.N. (Ret.)
Executive Director
Athletic Association of Western Universities
San Francisco, California

Preface to the First Edition

This text has been prepared to meet the need for essential yet comprehensive information on the techniques of survival under unusual conditions. It treats of survival on a global basis, emphasizing principles that can be grasped quickly and easily and practiced to the benefit of any person subjected to the hazards of nature.

This manual has been made as complete as is practical in the realization that a thorough knowledge of this subject gives confidence, aids in conquering fears of the unknown, and will serve as the foundation for making sound decisions. General and universally applicable principles formulated out of man's contact with nature throughout the ages have been set down and organized so as to enable the individual to make the maximum use of this knowledge at a time when survival may depend on the ability to apply it.

Much of the material included in this book is based on an actual survival survey by the authors of the Pacific areas during World War II.

In preparing such a text, it is impossible to rely upon information from any one source. A general acknowledgment is made to those individuals and institutions who throughout the years have recorded even the remotest of facts in order that such information might be available for the benefit of mankind. Various governmental agencies have furnished illustrations and their scientists have constructively reviewed this text. Among them are the Smithsonian Institution, the Bureau of Entomology and Plant Quarantine, the Bureau of Plant Industry, the Fish and Wildlife Service, the Special Forces Section O.Q.M.G., and the Emergency Rescue Equipment Section. The Library of Congress and the Department of Agriculture Library have also been most helpful.

Thanks are expressed to E. D. Merrill, Vilhjalmur Stefansson, and P. K. Emory whose published works were of value in preparing this book.

The sources of some of the plates were: *Wild Food Plants of the Philippines, Minor Products of Philippine Forests* by W. H. Brown; *Manual of the Trees of North America* by C. S. Sargent; and *An Illustrated Flora of the Northern United States, Canada, and the British Possessions* by Britton and Brown.

Acknowledgment is also made to the fine work of G. Donald Kepler in conducting the first Survival Training Course at the Navy Pre-Flight School, University of North Carolina.

How to Survive on Land and Sea

Introduction

In the quest for adventure and knowledge, so characteristic of the human race, some people have found themselves pitted in a struggle for survival against the obstacles of nature. Today, although the entire planet has been mapped and much of it developed, vast areas still remain where few people live and where a harsh nature rules. Even in places that seem close to safety there can occur circumstances that threaten life.

If you are sent to a foreign territory in defense of your country or if you hike or drive through untamed lands, sail the oceans, or fly a plane, you could one day come face-to-face with your ability to survive—on a forested mountainside or in a trackless desert, in the cold and snow or in a tropical rain forest, at sea, or on a coral island.

You do not have to be an adventurer to find yourself thrown back on your own will and wits to survive. Billions of people live in areas vulnerable to volcanoes, earthquakes, floods, hurricanes, tornadoes, or *tsunamis* (the Japanese word for great sea waves produced by earthquakes or volcanic eruptions).

Those individuals with a knowledge of themselves, of their environment, and of survival skills will be the ones who prevail. It is the fear of the unknown that weakens your ability to think and to act. If you prepare yourself properly for the unexpected, you will increase your chances of returning to civilization in good physical and mental trim.

Survival depends largely upon preparedness and resourcefulness. Are you mentally strong—in control and optimistic? Are you physically fit? Are you dressed and equipped for an emergency? Do you know and can you apply fundamental survival principles? Do you have some skill in living in the great outdoors? You must learn the ways of the wilderness or the sea just as you have learned those of civilization. You must know how to care for your body and how to conserve energy. You must know how to best signal for help. You must know how to procure water, and how to find or build shelter. You must know what can be used for food, where to look for it, and how to prepare it. You must know how to orient yourself at all times.

Figure I-1. Tropical rainforest

Figure I-2. Seashore

Figure I-3. Desert

Figure I-4. Mountains and cold regions. Each environment offers its own particular mix of resources and hazards that affect your chances of survival. (Courtesy of the National Park Service)

Likewise, you must know what will harm you and how to cope with it or avoid it.

The first requisite in an endurance trial is a strong mental attitude. After that, if you know your own physical capabilities and limitations, if you have prepared or can improvise the equipment you require, and if you recognize the relative importance of the various challenges, you will very likely emerge unbeaten. Mastering these principles may seem at first a formidable task, but the rigors of a survival crisis may demand that you do. This book will help you achieve a level of knowledge that will enable you to deal effectively with a dangerous situation.

The book is organized into three sections. In Part 1, various chapters discuss survival on land in terms either of tasks, such as finding and cooking food, or of environments, such as tropical rain forests or deserts. In addition, a chapter on environmental hazards alerts you to possible dangers. Part 2 examines how to survive at sea, whether for an extended period in a life raft or for hours in only a personal flotation device (PFD), or lifejacket. Because survival is not always limited to individual difficulties in the wilderness or at sea, Part 3 looks at both large-scale response to natural disasters and the actions you can take as an individual to protect yourself from nature's fury.

As we live in an uncertain and dangerous world, everyone, not just those serving in the armed forces, should know how to protect themselves and those close to them "from the thousand natural shocks that flesh is heir to." (Shakespeare; *Hamlet*. Act III, Sc. 1) Survival strategy can be summed up in two words: *preparation* and *priorities*. The rest of the Introduction elaborates on these concepts, which underlie the book as a whole. By providing a context for a "thousand natural shocks," we hope we can give you a sense of order and control to counterbalance the feelings of confusion and fear usually generated, at first, by a life-or-death situation.

PREPARATION

Mental Strength and Physical Readiness

The desire to live and a healthy frame of mind to fulfill that desire may be the critical factors determining whether you live or die. Individuals in a survival situation must battle panic and hysteria as well as loneliness and boredom.

Panic is the number-one enemy. All too often, avoidable tragedy results from the actions of one who succumbs to this killer. Panic is simply unreasoning and uncontrollable fear. Most animals, when faced with extreme danger, feel fear, which allows them to fight or flee with unusual strength and endurance. A certain amount of fear is good in that its physical changes—elevated pulse, increased respiration, and tensed muscles—

coupled with an increased tolerance for pain equip animals and humans alike with a powerful will to survive. But extreme fear or panic is self-defeating. You must allow your greatest asset, your ability to think logically, to come to the fore.

If you are to survive, you must calm yourself and carefully assess the situation. Determine the necessary actions and then execute them in a logical sequence. Although you should at all times be aware of any opportunities for rescue or escape, you should prepare yourself for a long period of just staying alive. Survivors have been known to spend many days afloat in a life raft upon the open ocean or trapped by weather in a mountain cave. If you are injured, it may be less dangerous to stay with the wreckage of a boat or aircraft and wait for rescue rather than attempt to travel to safety. Even if you're not injured, it may still be wiser to stay with your disabled vehicle. In such instances, the problems of loneliness and boredom loom very large.

As a victim of unfortunate circumstances, it is easy to feel depressed and sorry for yourself. Thoughts turn to the unfairness of the situation, and feelings of hopelessness begin to creep into your consciousness. It is vitally important to resist, for if you cease to believe in your eventual escape or rescue, you will shortly lose the will to live. One of the most powerful forces on the athletic field is the will to win; how much more important, then, is the will to live in a life or death dilemma.

Survival is a state of mind, and your life may very well depend on it. The state of mind most likely to sustain you is achieved through a combination of will and behavior. Having control of your emotions will make it easier for you to perform the necessary tasks, but likewise the action of doing what is necessary to survive will bolster your spirits. The following eight points should help you as you struggle to exert command over a life-threatening situation foisted upon you by circumstance.

(1) Study your plight—optimistically.

(2) Organize your approach to the challenge by recalling what you know of survival techniques. Set priorities.

(3) Decide upon definite goals such as setting a course, deploying survival gear, procuring water and food, or sending radio signals.

(4) Inventory your water and food and make arrangements to supplement your cache before you actually need to. Save every piece of equipment you can, as you may find a use for it.

(5) Control your fear by steadily replacing the unknown with the known. Make use of your heightened powers brought on by the biological response to fear but don't give in to panic.

(6) Hope for rescue or escape, but prepare mentally and physically for further hazards.

(7) Stay busy, to keep fear and loneliness at bay.

Figure I-5. A regimen of physical exercise stands you in good stead in a survival ordeal. (Courtesy of the President's Council on Physical Fitness)

(8)   Refuse to give in to any desire for momentary relief, and realize that your body will respond to your demands and to the rigors of your predicament. Be unyielding.

Second only to fortitude—and a close second at that—is your degree of physical readiness. Common sense dictates that the individual in good general physical condition is much more likely to survive than someone who is not. Maintaining a regular program of physical fitness will give you a headstart toward surviving an emergency in a hostile environment.

Realistic Assessment of Abilities

Worse than being in poor physical condition in a survival situation is not realizing that you are unfit. You must make a realistic assessment of your physical abilities, which should not be clouded by nostalgic recollections of earlier athletic achievements. If more than two years have passed between your moments of athletic glory and the present, chances are your capabilities have slipped somewhat. The male reaches his physiological prime in his late teens, the female in her early teens. There is a natural reduction in cardiovascular efficiency after these teenage years, and if you have ceased exercising regularly, then it is reasonable to expect a drastic reduction in overall endurance. If you are to survive, you must not try to do more than you are capable of doing. Assess your physical limitations realistically and restrict your activities accordingly. Do not compare yourself to others as you set your own limits. Some individuals may be younger, others more tolerant to cold or the sun; each must arrive at his own limits.

Your assessment of your ability is for the purpose of planning activities and not to determine your survival expectancy. Knowing what you are capable of will help prevent you from succumbing unnecessarily to the elements. In general, if you are prepared, you will be in the best physical condition possible and you will know the limits of that condition.

Medications and Other Requirements

Some individuals have to face personal handicaps. Diabetes, high blood pressure, susceptibility to severe shock, and so forth present particular problems. Travelers who prudently prepare for the unexpected will take into consideration their weaknesses. Those with poor eyesight may want to have a spare pair of glasses. Those with allergies may want a mask to screen out excessive pollen. Others may carry prescribed medicines or learn to treat themselves with what is available in the wilderness. It is not enough to be prepared in general terms, you must allow for your own special requirements.

Equipment Preparation

If you feel you are likely to experience a survival situation, you will want to prepare a supply kit that would help you respond to basic needs. In planning your survival kit you face such questions as: What situation am I most likely to confront? What type of equipment should I have? For how long might I have to survive on my own? How often should I inspect my gear? How can the gear be stored without it taking over all the space I have? How do I school myself ahead of time in the use of emergency equipment? What should be included and what can be safely excluded?

Imagine yourself in the survival context you are most likely to encounter and judge for yourself what equipment you will need. The recommendations of salespeople and books are often helpful, but don't feel you must conform religiously to them.

Unless you're backpacking, most people cross remote areas in a vehicle of one sort or another. Nearly all vehicles are equipped in some way to meet various emergencies. Motor vehicles, for instance, carry a spare tire and tools; ocean-going vessels carry lifeboats; and airplanes carry flotation devices and emergency supplies. Such equipment is often required by law, and individuals or companies not carrying these items are deemed negligent. Being prepared for an emergency is expected of normal people. If, on the other hand, you pack a two-week supply of food in the trunk of your car on the off-chance that you might break down on the way to the corner drugstore, you're in danger of being labeled slightly paranoid.

If you're wondering how to outfit your vehicle, a good place to start is with the required gear. Boating regulations, for example, require personal flotation devices (PFDs), or lifejackets, for all persons aboard. Check with

Figure I-6. Examples of a compiled survival kit. (Courtesy of Steve Netherby, *Field & Stream*)

the U.S. Coast Guard, the Power Squadron, or the Red Cross for guidance on choosing the best PFD for yourself and your family. Consumer magazines, as well as magazines on sporting, boating, and outdoor themes, offer general product evaluation. (By the way, any specific product that appears in an illustration or is mentioned in the text of this book is meant only as an example of a particular type. Such appearance is not to be construed as an endorsement of the item. Consult books or magazines whose express purpose it is to evaluate the many survival products on the market.)

Many government agencies and private concerns provide comprehensive lists of both required and suggested emergency equipment for various vehicles. Many of the items can be accommodated in a backpack. High on all lists are first aid kits and signaling flares. Other items useful in virtually any survival situation are such things as a flashlight, matches or flint and steel, and a strong knife. It is also a good idea to have some canned water, hard candy, beef jerky, and boullion cubes handy.

Much of the equipment people use in the wilderness can double as survival gear, if the need arises. Others who maintain survival gear will never use it for any other purpose. Still others who use some equipment routinely, such as a CB (citizens band) radio, may want to supplement their survival kits with, for example, a spare power source. At the end of this section is a list of useful items. To this you can add your own required items, keeping in mind the type of situation you may encounter, the equipment you normally carry, your special needs, and your budget.

No one can predict how long you may have to endure a survival ordeal. If you run into trouble near populated areas or traveled roads, you may seldom have to do more than spend the night. If you have rendered prompt first aid to injuries, you may well need only to take some shelter for the night and be virtually assured of rescue the next day. If, on the other hand, you are flying over unpopulated expanses or fishing in a boat some distance from land, you may have to survive several days to a week or more before help arrives. In that event, additional supplies beyond the basics may well prove invaluable.

Some of the supplies that one might carry are not consumable, such as a knife, signal mirror, or PFD. Some are consumable but not on a daily basis, such as first aid items, flares, and flashlight batteries. Some items such as waterproof matches, water purification tablets, and most personal medicines are consumable but can be purchased in quantity very cheaply and stored in a small space. The real decision which must be made is how much canned or bottled water to carry and how much and what kind of food. Most people carry neither of these and hope that they are either not needed or that nature will provide. Although the possibility exists that you may have to survive in the wilderness or at sea longer than you have prepared for, there is a point of diminishing returns in the preparation for an emergency.

It is not enough to merely install a survival package in some out-of-the-way place in your car, boat, airplane, or other vehicle. You must regularly inspect your gear to determine whether you have the gear you need, in the proper quantity, and in satisfactory condition. Ask yourself the following questions: Is gear available for potential survival needs? Do you have a checklist of emergency equipment required for your type of traveling? Is there anything special about the intended trip that will warrant a change in the normal survival package, such as a prolonged over-water flight? Are you dressed properly? Are there sufficient quantities of each item in the survival package? Does the first aid kit or road flare bundle require replenishing? Will a special trip require additional food stuffs? Is the emergency equipment equal to the potential task? Is the quality of the gear good? If the various items were needed in an emergency would they operate correctly? Is the equipment in good condition? Has the emergency package been sitting in the trunk of the car for several years without being inspected? Has any of the material rotted or rusted? Are the matches still good? Have any pests gotten into the powdered food? Do any of the water containers show signs of contamination? Are the batteries in various items still good? Regular inspection should reassure you regarding the type, quality, quantity, and condition of your survival equipment and supplies.

It is pointless to have the correct equipment, in good repair, and in sufficient quantity if you don't know how to use it. Precious minutes may be lost because you are fumbling through the directions to learn how to administer first aid or operate a flare. It is often well worth the slight additional expense to actually practice with the equipment. Most equipment can be used and replaced. A first aid course is strongly recommended for all people whether they travel or not. In addition, actual outdoors experience in constructing a shelter would not only be fun but also quite useful. Inflate and board your emergency life raft and practice using emergency equipment. Prepare some meals with powdered food at home to see what it tastes like. Try cutting wood with a wire saw, setting up a solar or vegetation still, purifying water, or making a snare with branches and vines. Become familiar with the equipment you carry and know how to use it properly. Periodically practice with the equipment and review its literature.

Survival Kit. When assembling a general survival kit for land or sea, refer to the items listed below. In addition, consider special protective clothing and footwear and other special tools and equipment recommended for specific geographical areas. Items marked with an asterisk (*) are considered to be the "bare bones" of a survival kit. Also included in all survival kits should be a survival manual, such as this one.

- First Aid Kit
    * (1) Sterile gauze dressings (sealed in plastic bag)
    * (2) Bandages 2" x 2"
    * (3) Compress-type bandages 3" wide roll/s
    * (4) Muslin bandage 37" x 37" x 52"
    * (5) Adhesive tape (roll/s)
    * (6) Bandaids, 25 each large
    * (7) Alcohol (in plastic container)
    (8) Sunburn prevention ointment
    * (9) Aspirin
    (10) Local antiseptic solution (such as benzalkonium chloride)
    (11) Snakebite kit
    (12) Baking soda
    (13) Insect repellent
    (14) Aromatic ampules (⅓ cc, 10 units)
    *(15) Razor blades
    (16) Antidiarrhea pills
    (17) Laxatives
    (18) Calamine lotion
    *(19) Germicidal soap
    (20) Bandana
    (21) Scissors
    (22) Tweezers
    (23) Illustrations of CPR, tourniquet placement, pressure points, and splint arrangements
    (24) Chapstick
    (25) Needles, both heavy and light duty
    (26) Rubber gloves
- Signaling
    (1) Radio, two-way voice or beacon
    * (2) Mirror
    (3) Whistle
    (4) Flashlight (batteryless)
    * (5) Flares
    * (6) Smoke signals
    (7) Illustrations of ground-to-air signals
- Drinking Water
    (1) Canned water
    (2) Solar still
    * (3) Plastic container/s
    * (4) 6' x 6' plastic material
    * (5) Purification tablets (halazone)

      (6) Illustration of land solar still or sea solar still
      (7) Sponge
      (8) Plastic bags (2' x 4')
      (9) Illustration of vegetation still
- Shelter Construction
      (1) Illustrations of shelters for survival area
    * (2) Knife (strong and sharp)
    * (3) Whetstone/file
      (4) Axe
    * (5) Wiresaw
      (6) Chemical heatpacks
      (7) Insulating blankets (wool)
      (8) Space blankets
    * (9) Candles
   *(10) Line
    (11) Mosquito netting
- Food
    * (1) Glucose sweets (hard candy)
    * (2) Beef jerky
      (3) Boullion cubes
      (4) Flint and steel
      (5) Waterproof matches
      (6) Fishing gear
      (7) Gill net
    * (8) Aluminum foil (one square yard, 2 each)
      (9) Gun and ammunition
    (10) Slingshot
    (11) Wire (for snares)
- Navigation (see page 289 for navigation equipment at sea)
    * (1) Map of area
    * (2) Compass/wrist compass
      (3) Illustrations of improvised footwear
      (4) Rope
      (5) Mountain-climbing gear
      (6) Machete.

THE PRIORITIES OF SURVIVAL

Survivors of life or death situations report that initially many thoughts raced through their minds and they felt a tremendous thirst. It is very important to avoid succumbing to diverse impulses and to execute a well-planned program for dealing with the emergency. Each survival situation is different, and you must analyze yours and determine your course of ac-

tion. In this book, we will address the demands of survival in the order they occur in most, but not all, cases. Although there is no one predetermined set of priorities that applies to every situation, the following order applies to many:
(1)   Render first aid
(2)   Prepare signaling devices
(3)   Procure water
(4)   Find or build a shelter
(5)   Procure food
(6)   Prepare to travel, if necessary.
In addition, you should be aware of dangers presented by particular environments and how to avoid them. The above ordering will not, of course, prevail on all occasions. Sometimes you will decide to alter the set of priorities, changing their ranking or subsituting other tasks. At sea, for example, the need for flotation will come first, perhaps followed closely by the need to protect against hypothermia, or lowered body core temperature.

First Aid

The first order of business is to meet the vital requirements for life. This usually consists of rendering first aid to yourself or your companions. Do not allow a driving thirst or an intangible fear to prevent you from stopping severe bleeding or treating wounds promptly to prevent infection. Mouth-to-mouth resuscitation and cardiac massage may also be tremendously important in saving the lives of others. These lifesaving skills can be carried out in the water or in the life raft as well as on land. Because first aid is a complex subject, we devote an entire chapter to it.

Signaling

The quickest way out of a life-threatening predicament is usually by rescue, and you will want to do all you can to help search and rescue teams pinpoint your location.
   Experienced travelers make sure that someone knows where they are going, what route they are taking, and when they are due. Pilots file flight plans with the Federal Aviation Administration, fishermen file trip plans with the local marina, truckers follow assigned routes—all so they might be missed quickly should a mishap occur and found quickly because rescuers know where to look. Radio contact en route enables those monitoring the traveler's progress to know promptly if something goes wrong. Rescue forces can be mobilized as soon as an emergency is reported.
   Pilots are required by law to carry an emergency locator transmitter (ELT) on board their aircraft. The equivalent device for mariners is called an emergency position-indicating radio beacon (EPIRB). These small,

Figure I-7. An emergency locator transmitter (ELT). (Courtesy of NASA)

relatively inexpensive, shock-resistant, self-energizing beacons are capable of forty-eight hours of continuous broadcasting on 121.5- and 243 MHz channels, which are reserved worldwide for distress signals.

For ELTs and EPIRBs to be effective, their signals must be picked up by passing aircraft, and therein lie their limitations. Aircraft must be within 200 miles of the distress site and their distress monitors have to be turned on. Given these drawbacks, therefore, it is clear that a great deal of the earth's surface will be unmonitored much of the time. Survivors, on the ground or at sea, can by no means be confident about their prospects for rescue.

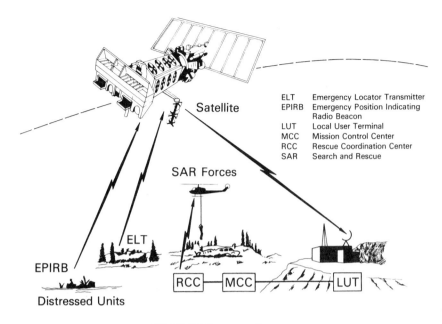

ELT	Emergency Locator Transmitter
EPIRB	Emergency Position Indicating Radio Beacon
LUT	Local User Terminal
MCC	Mission Control Center
RCC	Rescue Coordination Center
SAR	Search and Rescue

SARSAT System Concept

Figure I-8. SARSAT system concept. (Courtesy of NASA)

In response to these deficiencies, a new system called Search and Rescue Satellite-Aided Tracking (SARSAT) has been devised. In 1983, a two-year program in part administered by the National Aeronautics and Space Administration (NASA) began to test the effectiveness of SARSAT. A low-orbiting satellite has been launched which will be capable of receiving signals from ELTs and EPIRBs operating on 121.5- and 243-MHz and from experimental ELTs and EPIRBs using the 406-MHz band.

During the early phase, emergency signals from ELTs and EPIRBs using 121.5 and 243-MHz channels can be detected only if emitted from parts of North America and Western Europe and adjoining coastal areas (see maps). Locational accuracy is within five to ten miles and the system can handle about ten signals simultaneously. When the more powerful 406-MHz transmitter comes into use, coverage will be worldwide, accurate to within one to three miles, and capable of handling from two hundred to four hundred distress signals at a time. Complementing the SARSAT system—a joint effort by the United States, Canada, and France—is the Soviet Union's COSPAS project. With international cooperation and coordi-

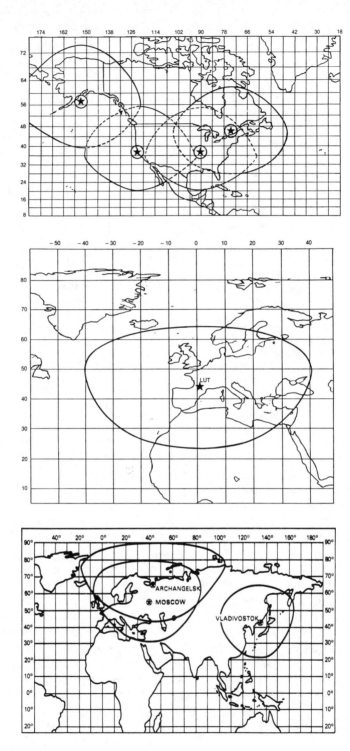

nated launching of satellites, SARSAT and COSPAS may put an end to the time when people could disappear from the face of the earth without a trace.

In the meantime, though, what can you do to make sure that the search and rescue teams find you? Knowing the different types of equipment that are available and selecting the one that is right for you is a start.

Pilots must understand the differences between the four types of ELTs:

- The *automatic fixed* is meant for permanent attachment to the airframe.
- The *automatic portable* can be easily removed from the aircraft in the event of a survival situation.
- The *automatic deployable* detaches itself from the airframe at an appropriate time during the plane crash.
- The *personnel* or *survival* type is designed to be carried out of the aircraft and has only an ON/OFF switch.

Be sure that your ELT is securely installed. Know how to operate your ELT and replace batteries and run tests regularly. After testing, be sure the switch is on the "ARM" position. Finally, just before you leave your plane, listen to the 121.5-MHz channel on your airplane to make sure that your ELT is not accidentally on.

Sailors have similar responsibilities with regard to their EPIRBs. There are three classes. Class A, mounted externally, floats free of the vessel and begins to operate automatically when the craft sinks. Class A EPIRBs are required on commercial vessels. Class B EPIRBs are stored in a handy place. They can be taken aboard a life raft and operated manually. Class C signals will *not* be picked up by SARSAT. They operate on channels 15 and 16 in the FM marine band and are intended for use within twenty miles of a coastline.

With either an ELT or an EPIRB, you can conduct tests within the first five minutes of any hour. These tests are limited to three audio sweeps. Do not rely solely on either the ELT or EPIRB. Have flares, signaling lights, marine or CB transmitters, mirrors, and so forth available.

In the absence of space-age technology, you may have to signal rescuers with more primitive methods. Also, ground signals will help draw rescuers to your exact spot, not just your general area. Signal fires are easily spotted. Less visible but still highly effective are messages that contrast with the surrounding foliage in both color and shape. Be sure they are large enough for an aircraft to see. On land, prepare signal fires and messages as soon as possible, and be prepared to start the fires or make

Figure I-9. (a) North American geographical coverage with ground stations at Kodiak, Alaska; Point Reyes, California; Scott Air Force Base, Illinois; and Ottawa, Ontario. (b) Ground coverage contour for French ground station. (c) Ground coverage contours for USSR ground stations. (All Courtesy of NASA)

Figure I-10. Flares are used both on land and at sea to signal rescuers. (Courtesy of the Defense Audio-Visual Agency)

Figure I-11. Ground-to-air signals in a clearing: (*top*) an SOS made of rocks; (*bottom*) signal fires prepared for lighting.

whatever effort is indicated if rescuers come within range. You should always have flares, mirrors, lights, reflective materials, and so forth close to hand. Flares are highly visible but not long lasting and should not be wasted. Lights are not seen during the day unless the rescue party is close, but at night they may be seen from great distances.

If the potential for a quick rescue is great and little energy is required for signaling, then communication should be high on your list of priorities.

Water Procurement

Because many people experience a tremendous thirst in a survival emergency, military pilots carry plastic bottles of water in their survival vests. Canned water should be included in all survival kits, especially if you are

Figure I-12. Vines are often a good source of water in the jungle.

traveling over desert areas. Plastic containers for collecting and storing water should also be included.

Water is one of the basic necessities of life. Humans can last many days without food but only a short time without water. In fact, food shouldn't be consumed without water since digesting requires a considerable amount of water. Water taken immediately after an accident will help alleviate shock.

Obtaining water can be very easy—you may be able to drink from a mountain stream or melt snow—or it can be very difficult, as anyone who has been lost in a desert knows. In most areas, however, water is plentiful but may require treatment such as boiling to make it safe. The resourceful survivor knows how to obtain water by many means: digging at the foot of cliffs or in dry stream beds; melting snow or ice; distilling sea water by use of a solar still; trapping rain; producing and capturing condensation; and tapping plants.

In addition to knowing how to procure water, you must know what not to drink and how to conserve water. Seawater must never be drunk because, while it may satisfy the immediate thirst, its salt will further dehydrate you. Water is lost by perspiration, urination, diarrhea, and regurgitation. You must take every precaution to avoid this loss, especially if fresh water is not plentiful.

If it looks as though you will have to survive on your own for several days, you must attend to the task of water procurement as soon as you have taken care of the vital requirements of life and have prepared signals. The chapters on specific climatic regions will discuss how to find water, given the geographical conditions.

Shelter Construction

Protection from hostile elements is very important. Extreme hot or cold temperatures make you think immediately of the need for shelter. In some circumstances, it may be more important than anything else. In cold climates, you could succumb to hypothermia (lowered body core temperature) long before you feel thirsty or hungry. In the desert, you could suffer from dehydration and heatstroke without adequate protection. In the tropics, you would need protection from insects and would have to remain dry to prevent the excessive growth of bacteria and fungi. Even in relatively mild temperatures, prolonged exposure to the elements will have bad effects. You must evaluate your situation and give shelter its proper priority as you try to survive. Because your need for shelter and the available materials depend to a large extent on the immediate ecology, shelter is discussed in those chapters dealing with survival under certain climates. A few general comments, however, are possible here.

Natural shelters. Shelters should be prepared with the least possible

Figure I-13. (a) Windbreak shelter. (b) Tarpaulin shelter. (c) Log shelter. (d) Lean-to.

expenditure of time and energy. Look for caves; large rocks; advantageous formations of bushes, rocks, or trees; logs; and ravines, hills, or depressions that will either provide shelter or make construction less difficult. In selecting your shelter, consider safety, adverse weather, and wildlife. If you think you're going to be there for several days, consider also the availability of water and food.

Improvised Shelters. Survival kits should include items for the construction of shelter appropriate for the area you're most likely to become stranded in. In cold regions, carry space blankets and chemical heaters; in tropical areas, mosquito netting and insect repellant.

Materials that could be used in constructing shelter may be at hand because of the nature of the emergency: parachutes, life rafts, or parts of a disabled vehicle could be used alone or, preferably, in combination with tree branches, palmetto leaves, rocks, and the like. Knowing the basics of lashing and building in the outdoors will stand you in good stead. If the survival experience becomes extended, additional comforts may be added after more pressing concerns have been met. Engaging the mind in such efforts goes a long way toward fending off loneliness and boredom. With imagination and common sense, you can construct a serviceable shelter in all but the most dire of situations.

Figure I-14. Improvising a shelter. (Courtesy of the Defense Audio-Visual Agency)

Figure I-15. A good bed is warm and dry. Note the branches and ground cloth that provide insulation.

Beds. You need a good bed. It allows the body to relax completely, and it insulates you from ground chill.

A good bed is warm. A cold person can't relax and will wake up fatigued. The ground is cold at night and conducts body heat away. To sleep warmly, place insulation—salvaged clothing, plants, trees, sod, grass, etc.—between yourself and the ground or the floor of the raft. In the desert, however, a good bed is cool. In the heat of the day, which you may want to sleep through, the temperature will be several degrees cooler just one foot above the ground. Alternatively you could dig eighteen to twenty-four inches below the surface to reach cooler temperatures, but remember to conserve energy.

A good bed is dry. Keeping dry is a challenge in a jungle during the wet season. If it is not raining but the ground is damp, you can make a hammock or a platform from vines and leaves or a parachute. If you need a roof to protect yourself from rain, you can split and shingle palm fronds. Banana leaves "rubberized" by heating on a hot stone also repel water.

A good bed is smooth. Hard, level ground is more comfortable than soft, uneven ground. Avoid hillocks, small depressions, sticks, and stones. Sand is deceptive; if you are restless, it soon becomes very uncomfortable. To make a good smooth bed, clear away rocks, sticks, or other debris. Make hollows to fit the contours of your body, especially your hips.

A good bed is preferably level, although you may have to accommodate a small slope. Do not, however, sleep with your head downhill, and don't choose a slope that is too steep or you will be sliding and rolling all night.

A good bed is, finally, free of insects. You might want to surround your bed with mosquito netting or apply an insect repellent to your skin. A smudge produced by burning wet or green wood, leaves, or grass will help keep away mosquitoes, flies, and other insects.

Food Procurement

You can go without food for many days. In fact it would take several months to starve to death, but you could die in minutes from injuries or within days from dehydration or overexposure. For these reasons, the acquisition of food rates a relatively low status in the hierarchy of survival priorities.

Food is, of course, mandatory for the maintenance of health and strength, and as your stay in the wild lengthens, it will rise in importance up through the ranks. Yet you can go for, say, two weeks without food, before the energy necessary to carry on the fight begins to diminish.

Fortunately, food is available in most places. Wild plants are stocked with edible parts such as nuts, berries, fruits, leaves, stems, buds, roots, tubers, seeds, grains, sap, and bark. You must know what edible plants look like and where they grow. The best way to learn about plants is to have someone identify them for you and point out the edible parts. But because you may not have a nature specialist at your side, this book includes illustrations to aid you in identifying plants.

For survival purposes, there are three general groups. The first group contains those that are edible and nutritional. The second group consists of those plants that are edible but contain little or no nutritional value. Finally, there are the poisonous plants. Your success may well depend on being able to classify plants into one of these three groups with passing accuracy. Chapter 2 will help you.

Other abundant sources of food include fish, mollusks, birds, crustaceans, snakes, mammals, insects, reptiles, frogs, and so on. Wild animal food, the subject of Chapter 3, is usually more nourishing than wild plant food and is often more abundant and easier to identify. It may, however, be harder to obtain. Considerable energy goes into hunting or trapping wild animals. Although almost any living thing found in the wild may be used for food, it is better to restrict yourself to familiar animals that are easily obtained and plentiful. Imagination, ingenuity, resourcefulness, and the will to live may all figure in food procurement.

Training in food identification, procurement, and preparation is available from many sources, for example, the Boy Scouts, the Girl Scouts, and the Outward Bound Society. The military is another good source of training. Many colleges also offer classes in woodsmen's skills.

Survival gear carried in vehicles and backpacks should have sufficient quantities of nutritional food for a brief survival experience. Emergency food packets containing hard candy, beef jerky, or condensed (dried) food-stuffs are commercially available.

Traveling

One of your earliest decisions is whether to wait for rescue or to attempt to find your way back to civilization. Not only is this one of the most important decisions, but it can be frustrating, because there is a tremendous urge to do something, anything, rather than sit and wait. There are often many very good reasons, however, to remain where you are. In fact, staying put is usually the best choice. Search and rescue parties have a much greater chance of finding you if you have remained with your disabled vehicle or in the general vicinity of your shipwreck. You save energy if you wait rather than travel. You run less risk of injury if you stay put rather than traverse rough terrain. If you travel, you must find new sources of water and food and new sites for shelter. If you or any of your companions are injured, the stress will be tremendous. Additionally, the problems of navigation at sea or in unfamiliar territory are not slight. Before you charge off, sit down and think the situation through.

You must weigh the chances of being rescued in your present location against your ability to travel safely through wilderness or sea to a point of refuge. Some of the factors to consider are:

(1)   Your physical condition and that of your companions

Figure I-16. A stream provides water, attracts wildlife for food, gives you a baseline, and, if followed downstream, will lead you to civilization.

(2)   The availability of water, shelter, and food
(3)   The safety and comfort of the present location
(4)   The distance you must travel to safety and the terrain you must cover
(5)   The appropriateness of your equipment for either traveling or staying
(6)   The probability of losing your bearings.

If you decide to travel to safety, take care to plan the trip first. On land, decide what to take and what to leave behind and leave a sign of the direction you took, should rescuers locate your disabled vehicle before they find you. Check periodically to ensure that your course is relatively straight and as planned. At sea, collect all debris and plan your course. All factors of a given survival situation may dictate that traveling is warranted, but it should never be undertaken lightly.

The possibility of travel should be considered when you are buying emergency equipment. You should, of course, educate yourself regarding the basics of wilderness travel or navigation at sea. Many colleges and universities, as well as the military, teach courses on this subject, and organizations such as youth groups and outdoors clubs offer training and practical experience. For further information on travel, see the chapter on it in this book. The section on water survival contains directions on how to navigate.

Environmental Hazards

Every environment presents hazards of one sort or another. The demands of living for any length of time in an unfamiliar place will be stringent enough. The more you know beforehand about the possible dangers of a beautiful lagoon or a splendid mountain, the better off you'll be. Hazards can be divided into two main types: physical and biological, but the possibilities are so myriad that we've given an entire chapter to the topic.

A positive attitude is the first step in a successful survival situation. You must be prepared for anything, expect the worst, and never give up. Realize that in conditions of high stress you have increased strength, super endurance, and a tremendous ability to tolerate pain. You must be mentally tough, however, and constantly evaluate the situation in light of the priorities of survival contained in this book.

PART 1

LAND SURVIVAL

CHAPTER 1

First Aid

When assembling your survival gear, you should give highest priority to your first aid kit, as you will very likely find yourself administering basic medical care, either to yourself or to others, in any struggle for survival. Some survival situations come about as a result of an accident—your plane crashes into a mountainside or your truck goes off the road in a remote area. In those cases, you may have to deal with lack of respiration or heart beat, heavy bleeding, wounds, fractures, burns, or shock. Other survival situations begin less dramatically—you simply wander away from your hiking companions in the wilderness and become lost—but the medical complications are no less life-threatening. You should be aware of ways to prevent or, if necessary, to treat hypothermia (low body core temperature), heatstroke, dehydration, and poisoning. Although included in the chart at the end of this chapter, they are discussed more fully in the environmental hazards chapter.

The American Red Cross and other organizations offer both basic and advanced first aid courses. We highly recommend such courses, whether you plan on traveling over vast uninhabited areas or whether you simply want to be prepared in case of a natural disaster. This chapter briefly reviews basic first aid procedures and applications. We emphasize principles rather than specific treatments, but a chart at the end summarizes particular health problems, their cause and symptoms, and the recommended treatment when professional help is not available.

PREVENTION

The adage, "An ounce of prevention is worth a pound of cure," is especially true in survival situations. In the wilderness, there are no hospitals or doctors to call. It is imperative that you make every effort to prevent injuries and their complications such as blood loss, infection, and shock. In addition to completing first aid training courses and preparing a suitable first aid kit, you can immunize yourself against some diseases. Preventing health problems must be paramount in your mind.

Good personal hygiene, fitness, and common sense will help prevent

Figure 1-1. A prepackaged first aid kit. (Courtesy of Cutter)

many of the diseases associated with the stress of surviving, such as diarrhea, dysentery, and malaria. Do not become careless in personal cleanliness or proper hygiene in the shelter area. Prevent poisoning by being careful in your selection and storage of food, and try not to let certain types of plant life come in contact with your skin.

Protective clothing will prevent cold-related problems such as frostbite, trenchfoot (a painful foot condition resembling frostbite), and hypothermia. Mosquito netting in tropical regions and sunglasses in the high glare of snow or desert may be necessary. Light-colored clothing will reflect the heat, protect from the ultraviolet sunrays, and retain moisture in very hot, dry areas. Not only will these preventive methods and others help head off many health problems but they will also significantly increase your comfort.

TRAUMATIC INJURIES

The accident that triggered the survival crisis may have caused some injuries of varying severity and type. Victims may be bleeding, their bones may be broken, or their bodies burned. Undoubtedly, all will suffer some degree of shock. First aiders must identify the injuries that exist, not only to others but to themselves as well. They must not become so involved in the treatment of others that they allow their own injuries to go unattended. Problems should be treated in the order of their seriousness, generally as follows:

(1) Lack of respiration or heart beat
(2) Severe external bleeding
(3) Wounds
(4) Fractures
(5) Burns
(6) Shock.

Heart or Respiratory Arrest

Regardless of the cause of heart or respiratory arrest—whether a sudden traumatic incident or the strain of a prolonged survival test—a person whose heart is not beating or who is not breathing must be revived quickly to prevent irreversible brain damage. When a person is unconscious and lying flat out on his back, the lower jaw may drop backward, possibly carrying the tongue with it and causing it to obstruct the air passage. Sometimes all that is necessary to clear the passage is for you to gently tilt his head backward as far as possible and to lift the neck or chin (see Figure 1-2). This position of the head must be maintained at all times. When the victim is in this position, you should look, listen, and feel for whether he is breathing. If he does not seem to be breathing and does not respond to a tap on the shoulder or a shout, that person is a prime candidate for cardiopulmonary resuscitation (CPR), or mouth-to-mouth resuscitation and cardiac compression.

CPR. Cardiopulmonary resuscitation combines mouth-to-mouth breathing, which supplies oxygen to the lungs, with chest compressions, which squeeze the heart and artificially pump blood to the vital organs of the body. We strongly recommend courses in CPR, as problems may develop with the naive individual that can possibly lead to tragedy, while the fully trained first aider will know exactly what to do.

To remember the correct step-by-step method of initiating CPR, the American Red Cross advises memorizing the phrase "A Quick Check."

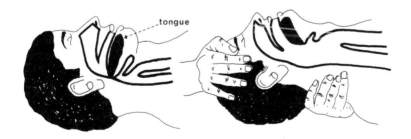

Figure 1-2. Airway: (*left*) obstructed; (*right*) opened.

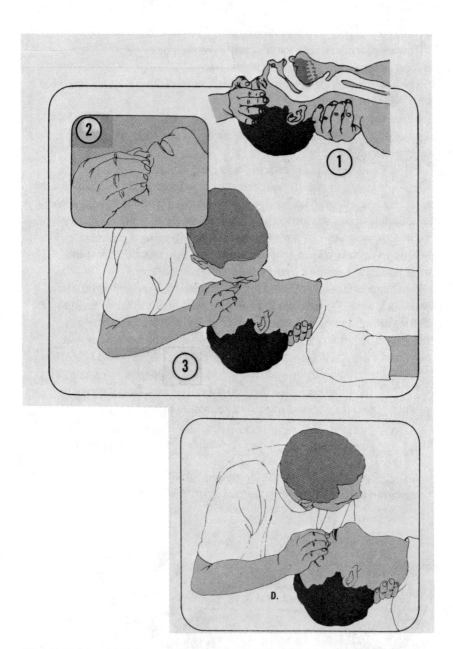

Figure 1-3. (*above*) Mouth-to-mouth resuscitation; (*opposite page*) One-rescuer CPR. The steps in Figure 1-3 (*above*) may be remembered by the phrase, "A Quick Check": "A"— opening the airway and determining if there is breathing; "Quick"—providing four quick, full breaths if there is no breathing; "Check"—checking for a pulse and breathing. (Cardio-pulmonary Resuscitation © 1981 by The American Red Cross, reprinted with permission.)

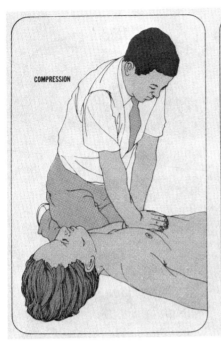 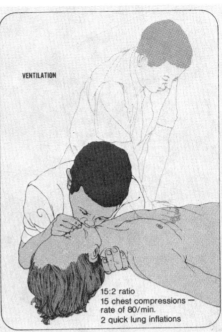

A-Airway: Tip the head and check for breathing. Look, listen, and feel for signs of breathing for five seconds.

Quick: If the victim is not breathing, pinch his or her nose and place your mouth over the victim's mouth, or place your mouth over the victim's mouth and nose together; give four quick full breaths. Do not allow victim's lungs to completely deflate. Babies and small children should receive gentle puffs.

Check: After administering the four quick breaths, check the pulse and respiration. Check the pulse on the closest side of the neck by feeling the carotid artery. Check the respiration by placing your ear close to the victim's mouth and listening. This check should last five seconds. The pulse of babies and small children may be checked on the inside of the upper arm by feeling the brachial artery.

(1)   If the victim is not breathing but has a pulse, give mouth-to-mouth breathing at a rate of twelve to fifteen breaths per minute (fifteen to twenty breaths per minute for children). Again, babies and small children should receive gentle puffs.

(2)   If there are no signs of either pulse or respiration, then full CPR must be administered.

(a) Ensure that the victim is horizontal and on a firm foundation.

(b) Locate the lower one-third of the victim's sternum.

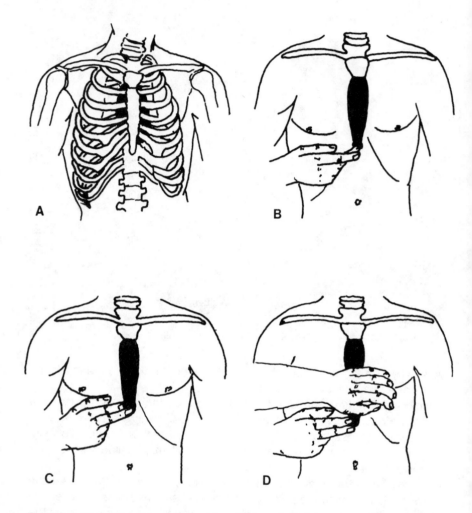

Figure 1-4. (a) Position of heart in chest beneath lower half of the sternum; (b) locate tip of xiphoid; (c) measure up two finger-widths from tip of xiphoid; (d) place heel of other hand over lower half of sternum above base of xiphoid.

(c) Place the heel of one hand on the sternum and the other hand over the first hand.

(d) Compress an adult's sternum one and one-half to two inches at the rate of sixty to eighty compressions per minute. Proportionally smaller compressions are required for babies and small children (as little as one-half inch for babies) and the rate must be increased to eighty to one hundred compressions per minute.

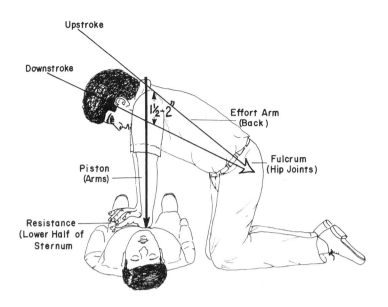

Figure 1-5. Cardiac compression

Figure 1-6. While full CPR can be administered by one person, two are better. (Courtesy of the U.S. Coast Guard)

(e) Provide both mouth-to-mouth and chest compressions by establishing a cycle of fifteen compressions and two inflations. If two first aiders are available, a more effective cycle can be administered if one first aider compresses the chest and the other gives mouth-to-mouth on a five to one ratio. The person giving mouth-to-mouth should impose a breath on the fifth upstroke so that the rhythm of chest compressions is not interrupted. Cardiac massage and mouth-to-mouth may be given simultaneously on babies and small children by one first aider.

(3)   If there is an obstruction in the airway, you will feel the resistance as you attempt to inflate the victim's lungs through mouth-to-mouth.

(a) Recheck the position of the victim's head. Tipping the head back prevents the victim's tongue from blocking the airway.

(b) If the airway is still blocked, roll the victim on his side toward the rescuer and hit the upper middle back four times. Return the victim to his back and administer four abdominal thrusts. Finally, clear the victim's mouth by probing with your finger.

Again, let us emphasize that this is only a description of CPR; there is no substitute for taking a course in first aid and CPR.

External Bleeding

Severe bleeding from any major blood vessel is extremely dangerous. Loss of two pints of blood, for example, can produce moderate shock, while loss of four pints can lead to severe shock and loss of six pints or more can result in death.

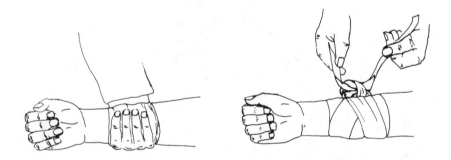

Figure 1-7. Direct pressure is the best way to stop most bleeding.

Types of Bleeding. The type of bleeding may be defined by its source: arterial, venous, or capillary. Arterial bleeding is the most serious and is recognized by its bright red color and distinct spurts or pulses which correspond to the heartbeat. A large volume of blood can be lost in a short time because of the high pressure in the arteries. Venous bleeding is blood that is returning to the heart and is recognized by its dark red or maroon color and steady flow. It is usually easier to control than arterial bleeding. Capillary bleeding results from cutting the very small vessels that actually supply blood to the tissues of the body and is recognized by its slow, oozing flow. All external bleeding must be cared for immediately in a survival situation.

Control of Bleeding. Direct pressure over the wound or broken blood vessel is the primary method of stopping external bleeding. No time should be lost in attempting to locate a sterile dressing if the bleeding is severe. The first aider should immediately press directly on the severed vessel using his or her bare finger or hand. While firmly pressing directly on the wound, attempt to locate a sterile dressing. If a sterile dressing is not available, use the cleanest cloth you have. Place the cloth firmly over the wound as you remove your hand.

Apply the dressing firmly with even pressure directly over the point of blood loss until the bleeding no longer shows through the dressing. Do not remove any dressing once it has been applied. If bleeding continues to permeate the dressing, apply a tighter bandage directly over the first one. The bandage is too tight, however, if the skin, fingernails, or toenails beyond the bandage start showing a bluish tinge, and the bandage should be loosened.

Bleeding may also be controlled by elevating the affected extremity as high above the heart as possible. Do not do this, however, if a fracture is involved. Pressure points may also be used to help control arterial bleeding. Pressure points are identified as those anatomical locations where the arteries are near the surface of the skin or directly over a bone. By locating the pressure point pertaining to the artery that supplies blood to the injured limb, you can apply pressure and control bleeding, especially arterial bleeding, in the entire limb. Do not use a pressure point for an arm or leg wound unless direct pressure and elevation will not stop the bleeding.

A common mistake is to think of a tourniquet as the primary means of arresting severe bleeding. In fact, a tourniquet is a last resort and should only be used if all other methods of controlling blood loss have failed. An improperly applied tourniquet may obstruct venous blood flow without totally stopping arterial flow, resulting in more profuse arterial bleeding than before the tourniquet was applied. Improperly applied tourniquets can also cause nerve damage.

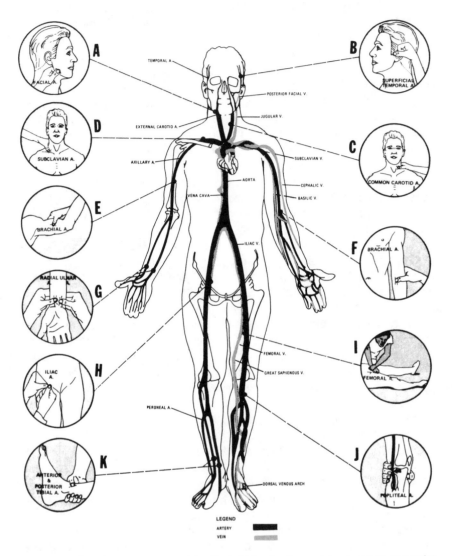

Figure 1-8. The eleven pressure points. Control bleeding by applying pressure at a point where the main artery lies near the surface and over a bone.

A tourniquet is a wide constricting band placed around an extremity between the wound and the heart (two to four inches above the wound) and pulled just tight enough to stop the bleeding. A tourniquet that has been properly applied will stop the blood flow both to and from the wound. To correctly apply the tourniquet, follow this procedure:

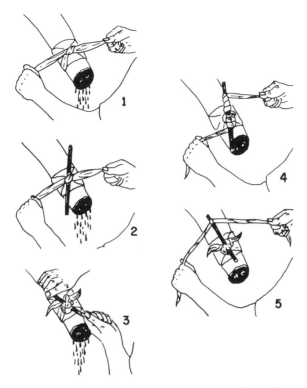

Figure 1-9. Apply a tourniquet only as a last resort. Tie the bandage with an overhand knot, tie a square knot over the stick, and twist the stick to tighten the tourniquet. The tourniquet must be tight enough to stop arterial blood flow, but no tighter than necessary.

(1) Place a dressing or pad, three to four inches wide, over the major artery leading to the wound.

(2) Wrap the tourniquet material (three to four inches wide before tightening) around the extremity, directly over the pad.

(3) After two wraps, tie the ends together, then tie the material using a square knot around a stick.

(4) Slowly tighten the tourniquet by rotating the stick until the bleeding stops. Check to see that no blood is flowing from the wound.

(5) Secure the stick by tying one end of it to the limb with another bandage. The tightened tourniquet should be at least one inch in width.

(6) If you've applied the tourniquet to your own body, do not release once it has been applied. There is a possibility you may go into shock and be unable to resecure it. If, however, you have applied the tourniquet to another, then it should be loosened every ten minutes for a period of one or two minutes to reduce the danger of losing a limb.

Wounds

The care of open wounds is extremely important not only because of the potential for loss of blood but also because of the likelihood of infection. Infection results from contamination by and growth of bacteria, which may enter a wound at the time of injury or by contact with unsterile materials such as clothing or bandages. Unwashed hands will undoubtedly introduce bacteria into the wound as you attempt to control the bleeding. Although speed is the primary consideration, you should try to wash your hands and, if possible, to sterilize your instruments and materials.

Water to wash both the wound and your hands can be purified by boiling for three minutes at sea level and an additional minute for each one thousand feet thereafter. To sterilize instruments, hold them over an open flame and follow with an alcohol rinse.

If severe bleeding is not a problem, gently wash the wounds prior to dressing. Remove the clothing around the wound and cleanse the whole area thoroughly. The wound itself, unless it is abdominal, should be irrigated—that is, pour sterile water over it—to remove any foreign matter. More infections are caused by foreign matter left in the wound than by the use of unboiled water. If necessary, irrigate with unboiled water. A pair of rubber gloves in your survival kit (be sure they are not packaged with talcum powder) makes a good syringe for washing wounds.

Do not apply solutions such as Merthiolate, iodine, and Mercurochrome directly to open wounds. Rather carry an antiseptic solution such as benzalkonium chloride in your first aid kit and use that on open wounds. If sterile water for cleaning or benzalkonium chloride is not available, fresh urine may be used. After cleaning, the wound should be covered with a sterile dressing and bandage.

In the case of abdominal wounds, cleaning will probably introduce more infection than it prevents. Do not push organs back into the abdomen. Simply apply a dressing and keep it moist.

Open chest wounds often mean associated respiratory difficulties, which can be recognized by the victim's difficulty with breathing and perhaps hissing or sucking sounds coming from the wound. This type of wound should be made airtight immediately to restore normal respiratory function. Check both front and back before bandaging. Place plastic or rubber material directly over the open wound and cover with a sterile dressing. The dressing should not be removed once it has been applied.

Fractures

Fractures are classified as either open or closed. In an open fracture, the broken bone protrudes through the skin, while a closed fracture is a break in the bone without an associated break in the skin. Although recognizing

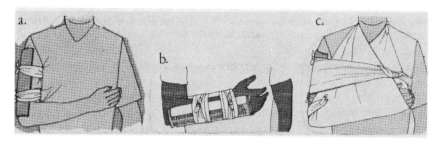

Figure 1-10. Arm fractures with splints and sling: (a) upper arm break with splint; (b) lower arm break with splint; (c) sling for break in either upper or lower arm.

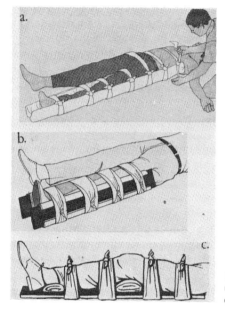

Figure 1-11. Leg fractures with splints: (a) upper leg break; (b) lower leg break; (c) knee or knee cap break.

a closed fracture is often difficult, pain, swelling, and disfiguration are some indications. If you are not sure whether a fracture exists, treat the bone as if it were fractured.

The first aid for a fracture is to immobilize the affected area and the joints at either end. A splint carefully applied with bandages is the most common way to immobilize fractured bones. Any straight, firm piece of wood or metal can function as a splint; for a neck or foot fracture, use a rolled up blanket. Pad the splint with soft material such as cloth rags. Tie the splint to the body both above and below the fracture.

Cracked ribs will give a sharp sensation of pain in the chest when moving, breathing, or straining. If a simple fracture, apply a snug bandage to restrict movement of the rib cage. If a compound fracture, immobilize the victim and treat for shock.

If medical help is not expected within a few hours, it is advisable for the first aider to set the bone before applying the splint. This should be done as soon after the accident as possible because swelling and muscle spasms will make it more difficult later. To set a broken bone, pull on the bone to straighten it. To set your own broken arm or leg, use the good arm or leg to apply traction, or, if additional traction is needed, make gravity work for you. Tie the limb to a fixed object and pull back. Alternatively, wedge a wrist or ankle into the fork of a tree or the niche of some rocks and then lean back with the full weight of your body until you feel the bone snap into place. Then apply the padding and splint, which you have arranged for beforehand. If mobilization is not necessary, continued traction would help ensure correct alignment of the bone.

The first aid is similar for an open fracture except that the open wound must also be treated. Examine the ends of the broken bone for any dirt or debris, and, if dirty, rinse them with a saline solution of one-fourth teaspoon of salt per quart of sterilized water.

Burns

The aim of first aid treatment for serious burns is to control fluid loss and to prevent infection and shock. Minor burns (no broken skin) can be run under cold water. Check the first aid kit carefully for instructions and supplies for treating burns.

Burns can have a number of different causes. For chemical burns, quickly and thoroughly wash to remove all traces of the chemical. Remove any material such as clothing from in and around the burn.

Burns caused by steam or hot water (scalds) should be cooled immediately by immersion in cold water, as should burns caused by open flames or hot materials. Pieces of burned material such as clothing should not be removed from this type of burn because it would likely cause additional fluid loss.

All burns should be covered with a dry sterile dressing to prevent infection. Those with serious burns or burns over a large area of the body should be treated to prevent shock. Give aspirin to reduce the pain, keep the victim quiet and comfortable, lying down with feet elevated. Give plenty of fluids. Immobilize the burned limb by using splints or slings.

One burn that is unnecessary and easily prevented is sunburn. Keep the body clothed and cover open skin with a sunscreen. Sunburn can become severe if you lie unprotected under the sun's rays.

Shock

Injury-related shock is commonly called *traumatic shock* to differentiate it from other forms of shock, such as electric or insulin. Traumatic shock, which can result from any serious injury, is a reduction in the flow of oxygenated blood to the vital organs of the body. First aiders should make every effort to prevent shock when the situation indicates that it is likely. Severe stresses on the body, such as loss of blood, pain, poor circulation, or change in body temperature, cause shock and should be treated and, if possible, eliminated as soon as possible. Keep victims quiet, warm, comfortable, and lying down with their feet slightly elevated. If the victim's injuries permit, you may give water in small doses.

OTHER HEALTH CONCERNS

Some threats to health may develop slowly. You should be aware of the dangers and act to prevent them. If you are not prepared for them, they may lead to unsuspected tragedy.

Figure 1-12. Steps to achieve a firefighter's lift—the recommended way for lifting and carrying an injured person.

Strenuous Exertion

In any climate, severe headaches are common after strenuous, unaccustomed exertion. An aspirin will ease the pain, but the best relief is sleep or rest. If hungry, eat moderately of hot broth or sweets. Nibble at food more or less continually. If you're not hungry, don't force yourself to eat but wait until you are rested and your appetite returns. This may be as long as twelve hours. Try not to exert yourself over a long period of time without eating.

Care of the Feet

If you are going to be doing a lot of walking, you will have to take care that your feet do not develop blisters and sores that could impede your progress. Try to be sure that you are properly shod for any contingency when there's a chance that you may find yourself in harm's way.

As you travel, bathe and massage your feet daily, if possible. Examine your feet for tell-tale redness or blisters. Do not puncture blisters, as this may cause infection. Apply an adhesive bandage for protection.

Care of the Digestive System

It is important that under the general stress of survival conditions, you strive to purify your water and cook your food. These two actions should help you considerably in your fight to ward off digestive problems.

If you develop diarrhea, rest and fast but continue to take water. Overeating of fruit, especially green fruit, often leads to diarrhea and simply changing your diet will often make you feel better.

If the opposite problem—constipation—afflicts you, do not be overly concerned. Provided you have plenty of water, your bodily functions will soon return to normal.

FIRST AID CHART

Below is a quick-reference chart describing the symptoms and treatments for various health problems in a survival situation.

Survival First Aid

Injury	Cause	Symptoms	Treatment
Blindness	Exposure to bright sunlight reflecting off snow, sand, or water	Burning pain in eyes	(A) Provide complete darkness by bandaging eyes with thick dressing (B) Give aspirin

Survival First Aid (*continued*)

Injury	Cause	Symptoms	Treatment
Burns (chemical)	Contact with chemicals (acids or alkalies)	Pain Redness of skin Swelling	(A) Remove irritant (1) remove clothes (2) wash with lots of water (B) Cover with thick dry sterile dressing (C) Treat for shock (D) Check for respiratory distress
Burns (sun)	Exposure to direct sunlight	Redness Hot skin Blisters	(A) Cool affected area (1) small area: bathe with cool water (2) large area: cool with wet packs (B) Elevate area (C) Give aspirin (D) Treat severe cases for shock (E) Apply fluid of aloe plant on burn
Burns (thermal)	Contact with open flame or hot materials	Redness (1st degree) Blisters (2nd degree) Charred flesh (3rd degree)	(A) Reduce pain and prevent infection (1) bathe 1st & 2nd degree burns with cool water (2) give aspirin (B) Cover with thick dry sterile dressing; *Do not* remove charred material from the burn area (C) Treat for shock

Survival First Aid (*continued*)

Injury	Cause	Symptoms	Treatment
Cardiopulmonary distress	Heart disease Stroke Drowning Blocked airway Shock Severe bleeding Electrocution Toxic gasses	No breathing No pulse	(A) Open airway, tip head back (B) Give four quick full breaths (C) Check pulse and breathing (D) Start CPR as required (E) Treat for shock
Dehydration	Loss of too much body fluid (from, for example, Diarrhea Vomiting Drinking sea water Eating "protein foods" without sufficient amounts of water for digestion) Inadequate drinking water	Light-headedness Dizziness Headache Difficulty in breathing Tingling in arms and/or legs	(A) Give drinking water (B) Do Not Give: Blood Urine Salt Water Alcohol
Dysentery	Poor hygiene Contaminated drinking water	Diarrhea Weakness Fever Bloody stools	(A) Boil all drinking water (B) Wash all eating utensils in boiling water (C) Increase intake of solid starchy foods such as roots, bark, etc.
External bleeding	Wounds suffered in accident or during survival period	Blood spurting out (cut artery) Blood oozing out (cut veins)	(A) Direct pressure over wound (bandage, hand, etc.) (B) Elevation (C) Pressure points (D) Tourniquet (E) Treat for shock

Survival First Aid (*continued*)

Injury	Cause	Symptoms	Treatment
Frostbite	Prolonged exposure to extreme cold Poor blood circulation	Skin stiff or numb Redness turning to pale or white Possibly no pain in later stages	(A) Immobilize area of body; move carefully if necessary (B) Warm with water approximately 100°F or place next to warm body (C) Cover with dry sterile dressing (D) Do not massage or apply ice or snow (E) Do not break blisters
Heatstroke	Overheated body Severe loss of body fluids through strenuous labor Insufficient water	High temperature Hot dry skin Strong rapid pulse Unconsciousness	(A) Remove victim to cool area (B) Sponge body with cool water (C) Do not give stimulants
Hypothermia	Lowering of body core temperature through exposure to cold air or water	(In order of severity) Shivering Cold pale skin Dilated pupils Rapid respiration changing to labored Slow, irregular pulse Muscular rigidity Unconsciousness	(A) Apply hot towels to body trunk (B) Immerse trunk in hot water (100° to 115°) (C) Treat for shock (D) If respiratory distress, start CPR. (E) Do not immerse limbs (F) If unconscious, do not give anything orally (G) If not unconscious, give warm, sweet drinks

Survival First Aid (*continued*)

Injury	Cause	Symptoms	Treatment
Infections	Bacteria growing in open wounds	Pain Swelling Fever Nausea Headache Swollen lymph glands Redness Red streaks running from wound	*Prevention:* Keep all wounds clean, dry, and covered (A) Clean wound with soap and water (do not reopen wound) (B) Keep victim lying down with affected area elevated (C) Restrict movement (D) Apply hot or warm compresses every 30 minutes and dry dressings every 30 minutes alternately
Injuries—head, neck, and/or internal	Wounds suffered in accident or during survival period	Unconsciousness Dizzy Bleeding from mouth, nose, and/or ears Pupils dilated Headache	(A) Keep lying down flat (B) Check pulse and respiration (C) Treat for shock (D) Move body as a unit
Poisoning (animal puncture wounds)	Wounds from sting rays cone shells certain fish sea urchins	Local pain Swelling Bleeding Tingling Numbness Paralysis	(A) Remove material from wound (B) Wash wound area (C) Soak in hot water (D) Apply constricting band between wound and heart (E) Treat for shock (F) Control bleeding

Survival First Aid (*continued*)

Injury	Cause	Symptoms	Treatment
Poisoning (by contact)	Contact with toxic plants or animals	Rash Blisters Swelling Burning Itching Trouble breathing	(A) Wash with soap and water (B) For severe cases apply a constricting band between affected area and heart (C) Reduce pain by giving aspirin
Poisoning (food)	Ingesting toxic foods	Abdominal pain Cramps Nausea Diarrhea Convulsions	(A) Give lots of water or milk to induce vomiting (B) Or put finger down throat (following a drink) (C) If unconscious, check for respiratory distress
Exception	Ingesting petroleum products	As above plus smell of petroleum on breath	(A) Do Not Induce Vomiting
Poisoning (by inhalation)	Breathing toxic gasses	Sudden unconsciousness Lightheadedness Dizziness Possibly none	(A) Remove source (B) Check for respiratory distress
Snakebite	Bites from poisonous snakes (look for fang marks) *Neurotoxic venom—* sea snakes and elapids	Neurotoxic venom affects nervous system and impairs blood circulation. Numbness Respiratory distress Dizziness Muscle spasms	(A) Keep victim calm (B) Keep victim lying down with head lower than heart (C) Immobilize bite area lower than the heart

Survival First Aid (continued)

Injury	Cause	Symptoms	Treatment
Snakebite (cont.)	Hemotoxic venom— pit vipers, true vipers and black-fanged snakes	Hemotoxic venoms attack the blood cells. Excruciating pain Swelling within 3 to 5 minutes	(D) Suck the venom from the wound with the mouth or suction cup (E) For small fang marks on fleshy parts of the body make ½ inch skin-deep incisions along the long axis just over the fang marks before suction (F) Apply suction for 30 minutes (G) Avoid all physical activity until symptoms are relieved (H) Restrict food intake to reduce the chances of vomiting (I) Give aspirin for pain
Trench foot or "immersion foot"	Prolonged exposure to cold and/or wetness	Aching Coldness Tingling Redness Swelling	(A) Dry, rewarm, and restore circulation by warming feet with 100°F water or a warm body

CHAPTER 2

Wild Plant Food

After you have tended to the more pressing demands of survival, such as first aid, water, and shelter, your mind will turn to the question of food. Plants are one of the most valuable food sources. To use them intelligently in an emergency, you must have some practical knowledge of what the edible ones look like and where they grow. In this chapter we'll discuss some of the different plants available around the world in various climates. For a closer look at tropical seashore plants, see the chapter on seashore survival.

RECOGNITION AND USE OF PLANTS

There are thousands of edible plants distributed throughout the world. Descriptions and pictures will help you identify them, but the best way to learn about the appearance and use of edible plants is to have someone point them out to you. Each time someone shows you a plant, make a mental note of the kind of place (the habitat) where it is found. Without any particular effort you will soon find that you know just where to look for the best food plants of a region. Mastering a few principles and facts beforehand will help you find specific food plants in any part of the world—coconuts, breadfruit, and plantains in the tropics, for example, or cranberries, salmon berries, and crowberries in the Arctic.

Many groups of plants that are found in your home locality may be widespread throughout the world. Some North American plants also grow in the Philippines, Malaya, Africa, India, China, Europe, the Arctic and other widely dispersed areas. Although the different species which comprise a group may be limited in distribution and habitat and may vary in minor details, all are similar in general appearance. The persimmons of the Philippines or China, for example, differ somewhat from American ones, but they have characteristics by which they can be recognized as persimmons.

Almost everyone has picked and eaten raspberries or blackberries from thorny brambles near the edges of woods, fences, roads, and trails. They will look similar whether found in the Philippines, Pacific Islands, Africa, Australia, Siberia, Alaska, or the Arctic. Likewise, many people have

Figure 2-1. Gathering wild grapes

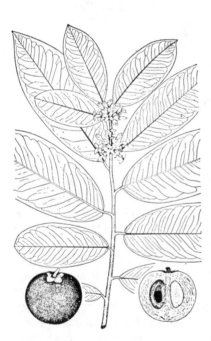

Figure 2-2. Philippine persimmon (*Diospyros*)

Figure 2-3. Philippine blueberry (*Vaccinium*)

picked and eaten the round, dark blueberries that grow on low bushes in areas where the soil is acid, such as on the borders of bogs and swamps or on sandy mountains or coastal plains. Blueberries and their close relatives are found in practically all parts of the world except Austrialia. When you find a plant that appears to be familiar, use it as that kind of plant would be used at home.

The appearance and availability of berries, fruits, nuts, and so forth vary according to time of year. In temperate zones fruit of some kind can be found the year round, although most of them are available only in summer or fall. In the tropics some plants flower and fruit continuously, and some fruits are available at all times. Arctic fruits, on the other hand, ripen only during a short summer period.

In addition, edible portions of plants vary greatly in their food value. Buds are very nourishing. The stems of some plants are excellent, furnishing starch, sugar, oils, and greens. A diet of leaves alone is at best like eating only spinach. Select young, tender leaves in preference to old ones, and boil them. Change the water if they are bitter and boil again. This is called *leaching*. Bitter-tasting substances are boiled briefly, then put into new water and boiled again. The process repeats until the bitter taste is "leached out." Usually, the early boilings produce discolored water; the later water remains relatively clear. Acorns, leached about seven times, can be pulverized and made into a type of flour. Dandelions are improved immensely by leaching.

Many plants, especially aquatic plants, store food (starch) in underground parts. Tubers, of which the potato is an example, are a source of food in all parts of the world and are often available throughout the year. In cold climates, when plant food appears completely absent, you can find bulbs and roots by digging at the base of dried plant stalks.

EDIBILITY TEST

A safety test should be conducted on all unfamiliar plant food. Before beginning the edibility test, be sure the plant is available in enough quantity to warrant the time and effort.

The first step is to check that the plant is not a contact poison. Rub the leaf, juice, or sap on the inner wrist and wait fifteen minutes, looking for any signs of itching, swelling, burning, or blistering.

If no negative reactions develop, then, if it is possible, cook the plant. Boil it for thirty minutes to an hour, with at least two changes of water. You can also proceed with this test using raw food.

Take a pea-size portion and chew it. There should be no bitter, burning, or soapy taste. Spit out the pulp, but swallow the juice. Wait eight hours. If no ill effects (nausea, pain, dizziness, drowsiness, stomachache, cramps) are felt, eat a teaspoonful and wait another eight hours. Again, if no negative signs occur, consume perhaps half a cup and wait another eight hours. If there are no negative effects on this last test, the plant can be considered safe for consumption in large quantities. *This test does not apply to mushrooms*. (The death angel mushroom [*Amanita phalloides*], for example, may prove fatal after a couple of spoonfuls. Avoid all mushrooms; it is too difficult to tell the safe ones from the dangerous.)

You should have at hand, as you conduct an edibility test, some activated charcoal, which acts as an antidote for all known food poisons, with two exceptions—mushroom and ergot poisoning. There are no known antidotes for either of those. A fire is a good source of activated charcoal. Scrape off fresh burned wood, pulverize it into a powder, and place it in an airtight container. If needed, use a handful with some water to wash it down into the stomach. It will neutralize all but the above two poisons.

Try to vary your food intake, but not excessively so. Acceptable food, when eaten to excess or to the exclusion of other foods, can result in vitamin deficiencies, weakness, boredom, and other ill effects. On the other hand, if you begin to develop feelings of illness, you'll want to be able to determine the source fairly easily. A balance between two extremes is desired.

FERNS

The roots and young curled fronds of many ferns are edible and none are known to be poisonous. Their food value is not great, but they will help sustain life. The brake fern is eaten all over the world. A fern called Pakó furnishes edible young fronds which are eaten either raw or cooked by Philippine natives. It grows in wet ground, on gravel bars, and along the banks of streams. The young shoots of the high climbing fern are eaten cooked or raw by the people of the South Pacific and India. This fern grows in thickets near brackish or salt water. The young leaves and terminal buds of the tree fern are edible. These huge ferns may be twenty or more feet high and are found in wet jungle areas. The succulent foliage of the common swamp fern, which is boiled and eaten as a vegetable, is found either floating or attached to the soil in shallow, still, or slightly moving fresh water in the subtropical and tropical regions of Asia, Africa, America, and Australasia.

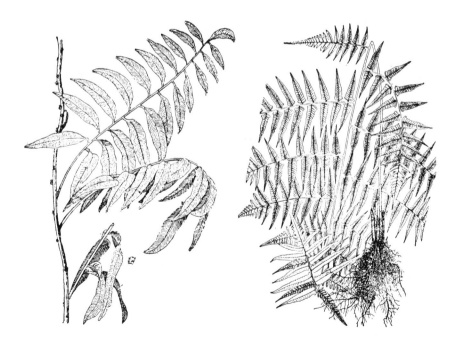

Figure 2-4. (*left*) High climbing fern (*Stenochlaena palustris*); (*right*) Pakó fern (*Athyrium esculentum*)

Figure 2-5. (*left*) Swamp fern (*Ceratopteris*); (*right*) Tree fern (*Cyathea*)

NUTS

Edible nuts are the most sustaining of all raw forest foods and are found throughout the world. Many American nut trees are found throughout the North Temperate Zone and closely related trees of similar appearance grow in the Tropic and South Temperate zones. Familiarity with some of the common North American nut trees will help you in recognizing and locating nut-bearing trees in other regions. Pine trees, for example, grow throughout the North Temperate Zone and seeds from the cones of many of them are edible and very sustaining. They are a principal article in winter diets from the American Southwest to Russia's Siberia.

The single leaf pine, the sugar pine, the limber pine, the nut or piñon pine, and the Coulter pine of the American West produce cones containing seeds or nuts that are both tasty and nourishing. The seeds from the Nepal nut pine and the Emodi pine of the Himalayas; the Swiss stone pine of Europe and Asia; the Korean pine of China, Japan, Korea, and Kamchatka—all produce edible nuts. You do not need to be able to differentiate between pines. Shake or break seeds out of the cones and try eating them.

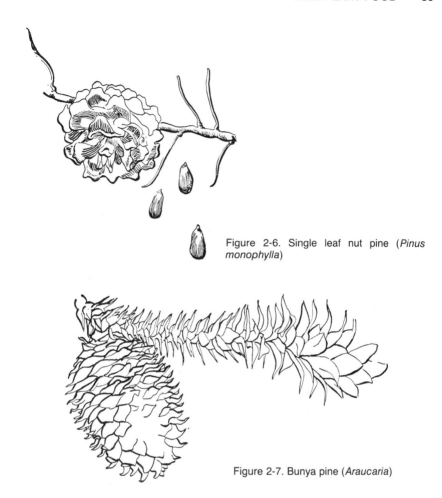

Figure 2-6. Single leaf nut pine (*Pinus monophylla*)

Figure 2-7. Bunya pine (*Araucaria*)

Recognizable members of the pine family bearing edible seeds also grow in the Tropic and South Temperate zones. Nuts from the *Araucarias* of Australia and New Zealand, Brazil, Chile, Norfolk Island, and New Caledonia furnish excellent food. These are lofty evergreens bearing globular cones containing large, chestnutlike nuts which may be eaten either raw just before ripening or boiled or roasted.

Nut-producing members of the beech family, represented in North America by the oaks, beechnuts and chestnuts, are found in many parts of the world. Chestnuts, hazelnuts and walnuts are found in North America, the West Indies, Europe and all of Asia including the Philippines and the East Indies.

Some Nut Trees with Wide Distribution

Beech
Characteristics: Large forest trees producing triangular nuts. Bark smooth, varying from light to dark gray.
Distribution: North Temperate Zone.
Eaten: Raw.

Oak
Characteristics: Trees and shrubs producing acorns; leaves either evergreen or deciduous (falling).
Distribution: Edible species found in Java, India, China, Mexico, North and South America, northern Africa, Mediterranean area.
Eaten: Sweet acorns raw. Bitter acorns boiled in changes of water, or dried and roasted; or ground into flour, soaked in water, and baked or roasted in cakes.

Chestnut and Chinquapin
Characteristics: Oaklike trees or shrubs containing nuts in burrs lined with soft, leathery covering.
Distribution: North America, West Indies, Europe, Asia including Philippines and East Indies.
Eaten: Raw, boiled, roasted.

Walnuts and Butternuts
Characteristics: Large trees with alternate compound leaves. Nuts with fleshy husks which do not split into regular divisions when ripe.
Distribution: See chestnut and chinquapin.
Eaten: Raw

Hazelnut
Characteristics: Small trees or bushes with nuts in clusters and covered by leaflike husk.
Distribution: See chestnut and chinquapin.
Eaten: Raw.

Figure 2-8. (*left*) Beech nut (*Fagus grandifolia*); (*right*) Oak (*Quercus alba*)

Figure 2-9. (*left*) Chinquapin (*Castanea pumila*); (*right*) Bush chinquapin (*Castanopsis sempervirens*)

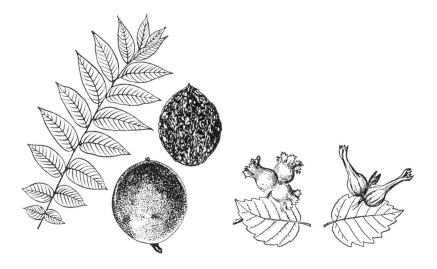

Figure 2-10. (*left*) Walnut (*Juglans nigra*); (*right*) Hazelnut (*Corylus americana* and *Corylus cornuta*)

Nuts Restricted in Distribution

Many nut trees will furnish food in relatively restricted areas of the world, such as the hickory nuts and pecans of North America.

Australian Nut Trees
Characteristics: Grow 25 to 30 feet tall, hard-shelled nuts grow in bunches and are encased in husks like hickory nuts.

Distribution: Australian jungles.

Eaten: Raw.

Panama Nut Tree

Characteristics: Immense forest tree with thick trunk of buttressed roots and huge crown with large hand-shaped leaves. Fruits in five pods containing black, peanutlike seeds, covered with irritating hairs.

Distribution: Central and South America, with other species in various parts of the tropics.

Eaten: Raw or toasted.

African Walnut or Gabon

Characteristics: Desert nut resembling a walnut.

Distribution: Liberia and adjacent regions.

Eaten: Raw, boiled, roasted.

Pili Nut

Characteristics: Large forest tree. Hard inner nuts are triangular in cross section and pointed at each end.

Distribution: Philippines, other Pacific islands, Malaya.

Eaten: Raw, but much improved by roasting.

Brazil Nut

Characteristics: Grows in immense forests with trees attaining 150 feet in height and 4 feet in diameter.

Distribution: Brazil, the Guianas, Venezuela.

Eaten: Raw.

Figure 2-11. (*left*) Panama nut tree (*Sterculia apetela*); (*center*) Pili nut (*Canarium*); (*right*) Brazil nut (*Bertholletia excelsa*)

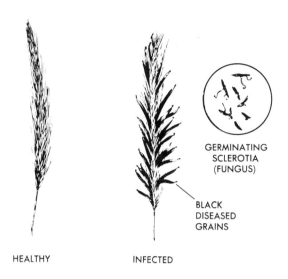

GERMINATING
SCLEROTIA
(FUNGUS)

BLACK
DISEASED
GRAINS

HEALTHY   INFECTED

Figure 2-12. Ergot infection in rye

GRASSES

By far the largest part of human food comes from such grasses as oats, wheat, corn, and rice; and the seeds of all grasses are edible. Grasses are distinguished by their joined and usually hollow stems.

You must watch out for ergot infection in grasses. It is revealed by black spurs in place of normal seed grains. It is poisonous, and there is no antidote. Avoid all grain heads that show a fungus or rust.

Wild rice, one of the staple foods of the American Indians, is distributed widely, with both wild and cultivated rice particularly abundant throughout the tropics. Many kinds of sorghums and millets are found in the tropics. Wild oats grow in Europe, Asia, North America, Australia, and the upland regions of South America. Their grains can be eaten either raw or parched, or they can be pounded into flour and roasted. At long intervals bamboo produces edible seeds, and the young shoots of most varieties can be eaten safely.

MUSHROOMS

Although many mushrooms are edible and may furnish a source of food, several species are deadly poisonous. For this reason, all mushrooms should be avoided. The nutritional value of edible mushrooms is questionable and the risk of tragedy is far too great to take any chances.

BEVERAGES FROM PLANTS

Some plants that have little food value can be used for making refreshing beverages. The bark from sassafras roots, spicebushes, black birch, the leaves of wintergreen, Laborador tea, spruce, hemlock, many of the mints, and other plants produce palatable drinks when steeped or boiled.

BARK AS FOOD

The inner barks from numerous trees can be eaten raw or cooked. In famine areas people make bread from flour derived from the bark of trees. The thin, green outer bark and white, innermost bark are normally usable for food, but brown bark ordinarily contains too much tannin. Among trees whose bark is used as sources of food are the poplars (including the cottonwoods and aspens), birches, willows, and the inner bark of a few species of pine, including the Scotch pine of northern Europe and Asia and the lodgepole or shore pine of western North America. Outer bark of these pines is scraped away and the inner bark stripped from the trunk and eaten fresh, dried, or cooked. It is most palatable when newly formed in the spring.

POISONOUS OR IRRITATING SUBSTANCES

Some plants may be eaten only after poisonous or irritating substances are removed. Among these are a large group known as the Aroids, of which the taro root, a staple food of the Polynesians, is a good example. It is pungent and bitter when raw, but perfectly palatable after cooking.

Jack-in-the-pulpit, found in the United States, and Badu or Coco of the West Indies or Central America are edible when the roots are cooked, but even prolonged cooking may not make elephant ear or skunk cabbage edible. When eaten raw, these plants' needle-shaped crystals of calcium oxalate puncture the tongue and cause a stinging sensation. Drying (roasting) so rearranges the crystals of some of them as to make them harmless. One taste of skunk cabbage or jack-in-the-pulpit will enable you to recognize this irritating principle when found in other plants. Skunk cabbage should never be confused with false hellebore, which is poisonous. The young hellebore plant looks something like the young skunk cabbage, but the false hellebore contains a central stalk, which skunk cabbage does not.

Roots of the bitter manioc of South America contains small quantities of the poison hydrocyanic acid. The root is prepared as food by crushing, pressing and washing the juice containing the poison and then heating to drive out the last traces.

Some fruits and seeds are poisonous at certain stages of growth but not at others; while many plants contain some edible and some poisonous parts. An example is the poke weed, whose young shoots and leaves are edible, but whose root is poisonous.

SOME EDIBLE PLANTS OF THE UNITED STATES
FOUND ELSEWHERE

The following groups or genera of food plants are widely distributed. Some contain numerous edible species. By learning a few plants from each group an individual will be better able to recognize and use the same or related species in any area of the world. Instead of attempting to learn them all in a short time, learn a few well, adding to the list from time to time.

Roots and Other Underground Parts

Wild Onion
Found: Small plants, North America, Asia, Europe. Year round but difficult to locate in winter.
Eaten: Bulb, boiled, or raw.

Spring Beauty
Found: Small plants, Africa, Europe, Australia, southern Asia, North America. Year round but difficult to find in winter. Common in moist woods of North America.
Eaten: Bulb raw or cooked.
Note: Leaves only of some species are eaten.

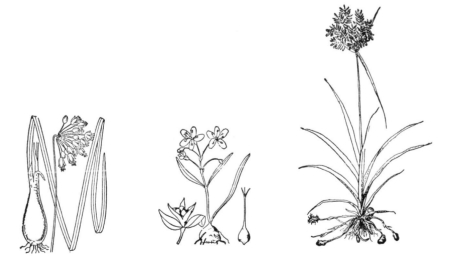

Figure 2-13. (*left*) Wild onion (*Allium cernuum*); (*center*) Spring beauty (*Claytonia virginica*); (*right*) Nut grass (*Cyperus esculentus*)

Nut Grass
Found: Sedge, worldwide, common in open ground and along river banks. Available in the United States summer, fall, winter.
Eaten: Small hard nutlike tubers, raw or cooked.

Water Chestnut
Found: Many parts of the world, particularly in southern Asia and Pacific Islands. Plant grows wild in some freshwater swamps of the United States.
Eaten: Tubers, raw or cooked.

Water Lilies, Lotus
Found: Worldwide, year round.
Eaten: Fleshy rootstock, tubers and seeds, raw or cooked, but rootstock of bitter varieties require long cooking.

Wild and Sweet Potatoes
Found: Trailing plants, in all warm climates of the world.
Eaten: Large tuberous roots, chiefly cooked (baked, roasted, boiled). Leaves and stems as greens.

Solomon's seal
Found: Small plants, North America, Europe, northern Asia, Jamaica. Available in the United States in spring and summer.
Eaten: Fleshy roots boiled or roasted, taste like parsnips. Young shoots also edible.

Figure 2-14. (*left*) Water chestnut (*Eleocharis tuberosa*); (*center*) Water lilies (*Nymphaea, Nelumbo*); (*right*) Wild potato (*Ipomoea pandurata*)

Figure 2-15. (*left*) Solomon's seal (*Polygonatum commutatum*); (*center*) Brake fern (*Pteris aquilina*); (*right*) Arrowhead (*Sagittaria latifolia*)

Brake Fern
Found: Nearly all temperate and tropical regions, year round. In the United States in spring or summer.
Eaten: Preferably roast and chew starch out of roots, raw if necessary. Stalks and coiled young fronds as greens, but first remove woollike covering.

Arrowhead
Found: Small plants, North America, Europe, Asia. In the United States year round. Follow threadlike root down to the bulb. Grows in wet ground and shallow water.
Eaten: Boil or roast. Tastes like a potato.

Bulrush
Found: Tall plants, North America, Africa, Australia, East Indies, Malaya. In the United States year round, in wet and swampy areas.
Eaten: Roots and white stem base, raw or cooked.

Wild Potato
Wild potatoes (and other species related to the white or Irish potato, tomato).
Found: Small plants, worldwide, numerous in tropics. Berries of some species reported as poisonous.
Eaten: Raw or cooked.

Figure 2-16. (*left*) Bulrush (*Scirpus validus*); (*right*) Wild potato (*Solanum Jamesii*)

Figure 2-17. (*left*) Cattail (*Typha latifolia*); (*right*) Wild rice (*Zizania aquatica*)

Cattail
Found: Tall plants, Europe, northern Asia, North America, Africa, Australia, and some Pacific Islands. Available year round, always near water.
Eaten: Bake or roast roots and chew out starch, discarding fiber. May also be eaten raw. White portions of the new shoots and the flowering spike edible (before blooming).

Wild Rice
Found: Tall grasses, North America and Asia along swampy streams, rivers, bays. Base of stems and root shoots, in the United States best in spring or summer, grain in late summer and fall.
Eaten: Lower stem and root shoots are sweet. Remove tough covering and chew central portion. Grain is excellent.

Fruits and Berries

Juneberry
Found: Small trees, North America, northern Asia, Europe, in forest and mountain areas. In the United States summer and early fall.
Eaten: Small purplish fruit, fresh or dried.

Papaw
Found: Trees, North American papaw in fall. Along streams. Related custard apple family found throughout tropics.
Eaten: Bananalike tasting fruit, skinned and eaten raw. Black or yellowish-green when ripe.

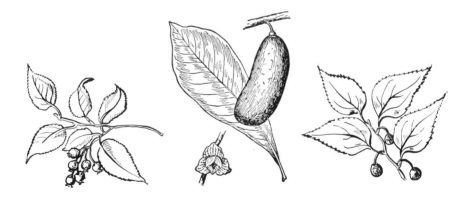

Figure 2-18. (*left*) Juneberry *Amelanchier canadensis*); (*center*) American papaw (*Asimina triloba*); (*right*) Hackberry (*Celtis occidentalis*)

Figure 2-19. (*left*) Hawthorn (*Crataegus*); (*center*) Persimmon (*Diospyros virginiana*); (*right*) Mulberry (*Morus*)

Hackberry
Found: Trees, North America, temperate Asia, northern India, Europe, either in arid or moist habitats. In the United States in fall, winter.
Eaten: Raw or cooked.

Hawthorn
Found: Bushes, open wastelands of temperate Asia, Africa, Europe, North America, Mexico, East Indies. In the United States in fall and winter. In winter, look on ground beneath the bushes.
Eaten: Tiny red or yellow apples, raw or cooked.

Persimmon
Found: Trees, North America, South America, Asia, Africa, Australia, Pacific Islands.
Eaten: Ripe (soft) fruits only, eaten raw or cooked.

Mulberry
Found: Trees, North Temperate Zone and subtropics. In the United States in summer.
Eaten: Raw or cooked.

Cherries, Plums, Apricots
Found: Trees and bushes, North and South Temperate zones. In the United States in summer and fall.
Eaten: Fruit containing single seed, raw or cooked.

Currants and Gooseberries
Found: Low, sometimes prickly shrubs throughout the Americas and in Europe, Asia, North Africa, Australia, and elsewhere.
Eaten: Berries, raw or cooked.

Figure 2-20. (*left*) Wild cherry (*Prunus virginiana*); (*center*) Golden currant (*Ribes aureum*); (*right*) Wild raspberry (*Rubus strigosus*)

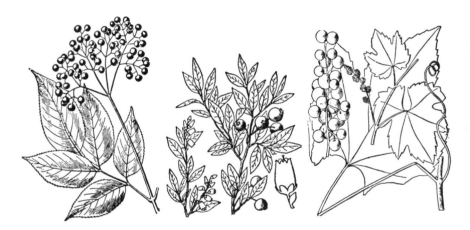

Figure 2-21. (*left*) Elderberry (*Sambucus canadensis*); (*center*) Blueberry (*Vaccinium angustifolium*); (*right*) Frost grape (*Vitis bicolor*)

Blackberries and Raspberries
Found: Shrubs, nearly worldwide, the United States in summer, in open land and forest margins.
Eaten: Raw or cooked.

Elderberry
Found: Bushes, North America, South America, Europe, Asia, Australia.
Eaten: Reddish or purple berries eaten raw or cooked.

Blueberries and Cranberries
Found: Shrubs, the Arctic, North Temperate and Tropic zones. In the

United States in summer and fall with some berries remaining through winter. Abundant in burned-over areas of the north.

Eaten: Raw or cooked.

Grapes

Found: Climbing vines, nearly worldwide. In the United States in fall and winter.

Eaten: Raw or cooked.

Leaves, Stems, and Shoots

Burdock

Found: Worldwide, particularly in open wasteland. Stems available in the United States in spring and summer.

Eaten: Tender leafstalks of this weed peeled and eaten raw or cooked as a green. Root is edible.

Sorrel

Found: Small plants, nearly worldwide.

Eaten: Leaves raw as a salad. Tubers of some species cooked.

Goosefoot

Found: Weeds, all temperate and tropic regions. In the United States in spring and summer.

Eaten: Leaves cooked as greens, seeds roasted.

Figure 2-22. (*left*) Burdock (*Arctium lappa*); (*right*) Sorrel (*Oxalis violacea*)

Figure 2-23. (*left*) Goosefoot (*Chenopodium album*); (*right*) Plantain (*Plantago major*)

Figure 2-24. (*left*) Purslane (*Portulaca oleracea*); (*center*) Dock (*Rumex crispus*); (*right*) Dandelion (*Taraxacum officinale*)

Plantain
Found: North and South America, Europe, Asia, New Zealand, some Pacific Islands. In the United States in spring and summer.
Eaten: Young leaves of this common weed may be boiled or eaten raw.

Purslane
Found: Fleshy plant, worldwide. In the United States in summer and fall.
Eaten: Fleshy leaves and stems boiled.

Dock
Found: Weeds, North and South Temperate zones. In the United States in spring and fall.
Eaten: Young basal leaves boiled or raw.

Dandelion
Found: Weeds, most of the civilized world.
Eaten: Young leaves, cooked. Roots may be eaten raw.

CORD, LINE, AND ROPE FROM PLANTS

Throughout the world there are numerous plants whose roots, outer and inner barks, and leaf and stem fibers can be twisted and used as cord or rope for fishing, lashing, and climbing. Fiber from palms, rattans, bamboo, and various vines are common in the tropics. The tough inner or outer bark of trees is the easiest and simplest material to use. Soaking often helps to separate the fibers.

Some Plants from which Cord, Lines, and Ropes May Be Made

Name	Part Used	Where Found
1. Leather wood (*Dirca*)	Strands of split bark	Eastern North America
2. Basswood or Linden (*Tilia*)	Shredded layers of inner sapling bark	Temperate countries of northern hemisphere; rich humus soil
3. Mulberry (*Morus*)	Inner bark of trunk and roots	Temperate regions of northern hemisphere
4. Spruce (*Picea*)	Barked rootlets	Cold climates of northern hemisphere; southern mountainous country
5. Hemlock (*Tsuga*)	Fibers of roots and the roots themselves	Northern North America and southern mountains

Name	Part Used	Where Found
6. Tamarack (*Larix*)	Fibers of roots	Cold climates of northern hemisphere; swampy wet region
7. Elm (*Ulmus*)	Shredded bark of trunk and roots	Temperate climate of northern hemisphere
8. Indian Hemp (*Apocynum*)	Bark fibers	Temperate regions of northern hemisphere; open land
9. Yucca (*Yucca*)	Fibers in leaves	Southern United States, Mexico, tropical America; many are semi-desert plants
10. Breadfruit (*Artocarpus*)	Strands of inner bark	South Pacific Islands, Malaya, Southern Asia
11. Plantains & Bananas (*Musa*)	Fibrous tissue in mature leaf stalks Musa produces manila hemp	Throughout tropical and subtropical countries
12. Coconut palm (*Cocos*)	Fibers of coconut husks and midrib of the leaves	Throughout tropical countries
13. Liana (*Entada scandens*)	Whole smaller stems and fibers of large stems	Native of tropics of both hemispheres; South Pacific Islands; also furnishes drinkable sap
14. High climbing fern (*Stenochlaena palustris*)	Wiry stems, very durable under water	India and South Pacific Islands; another species in Africa and Madagascar; found in swamps or near the sea
15. Climbing Cane (*Flagellaria*)	Stems	India, Australia, and South Pacific Islands
16. Climbing or scrambling aerial plants (*Freycinetia*)	Flexible stems	Indian Archipelago, New Zealand, Pacific Islands
17. A climber of open country (*Pachyrhizus erosis*)	Stem fibers	Tropical America, East and West Indies, South Pacific Islands; found in thickets in open country

Name	Part Used	Where Found
18. Common tropical weeds (*Urena sinuata and lobata*)	Fiber from inner bark	Common in tropics
19. Shaw trees (*Stercula*)	Fibrous inner bark. Rope not affected by wetness	Tropics of both hemispheres
20. Wild Hibiscus (*Hibiscus cannabinus*)	Stem fibers	South Pacific Islands
21. Screw pine (*Pandanus*)	Leaf fibers	South Pacific Islands

CHAPTER 3

Wild Animal Food

Animal food is any food not derived from plants. It may be in the form of fish, birds, mammals, crayfish, insects, mollusks, and so on. It is in general more nourishing than wild plant food and often more available; thus a knowledge of the animals you can eat, where to look for them, and how to catch them will increase your chance of surviving.

FISH

Learn to look upon bodies of fresh water as food reservoirs, and when lost or stranded, try to strike a river or stream. Generally speaking, animal life is more abundant in the water than on land, is concentrated in a more limited area, and is quite often easier to get. The chance of surviving alongside a body of water is excellent. You can catch fish with crude equipment or with none at all if you know when, where, and how to fish.

When and Where to Fish

Different species of fish feed at different times of the day and night, but on the whole early morning and late afternoon are the best times to fish with bait. Fishing is usually good just before a storm breaks. Signs that fish are feeding are jumping minnows and fish rising to the surface.

Pick a good place to fish so your efforts won't be wasted. It is usually easier to locate fish in small shallow streams than in large streams, lakes, or rivers where they can find suitable habitats over a much wider area. Peer into the water away from the sun, or reflections will make it impossible to see fish.

In streams, fish usually congregate in pools and deep calm water. The heads of riffles, small rapids, the tail of a pool, eddies below rocks or logs, deep undercut banks, in the shade of overhanging bushes, wherever submerged logs and rocks are seen—all are likely places to fish.

Fish the mouths of small tributary streams when the main rivers or streams are high or muddy. Fish seek shelter here at such times.

When streams are low and the weather is hot, fish congregate in the deepest pools and at places where cool underground water enters the

Figure 3-1. A good meal, caught with fish line and an improvised rod. (Courtesy of Steve Netherby, *Field & Stream*)

main stream. At such times fish are much more likely to hide under rocks, where you can often catch them with your hands.

In the cool spring weather of temperate climates, fish keep to the shallow water that is warmed by the sun.

Methods of Catching Fish

Experiment with baits. Look for bait in the water, for this is the source of most fish food. Insects, crayfish, worms, meat of shellfish, wood grubs, immature forms of aquatic insects, small minnows and fish eggs are all good. So are the intestines, eyes, and flesh of other fish. Fruit is seldom good bait. After catching the first fish, open it and examine the stomach and intestines. See what it was feeding on and try to duplicate it. If it is crayfish, turn over rocks in the stream until you find one. Usually the other fish will be feeding on the same food. Meat will attract crayfish.

Make live bait appear to act natural and try to conceal the hook. Don't let the bait remain still. Move it slowly from time to time. When fish are scattered or are feeding near the surface, allow the bait to drift with the current. If fish are breaking water and feeding, work the bait down to them. In all probability they will continue to feed at that spot, unless disturbed.

In clear shallow water, approach fish upstream as they lie heading into the current. Move slowly when the water is clear. If fish are shy, try fishing for them at night.

You can increase your catch if, instead of using just one fishing pole, you rig up a signaling device to a few others. The signaling device need be

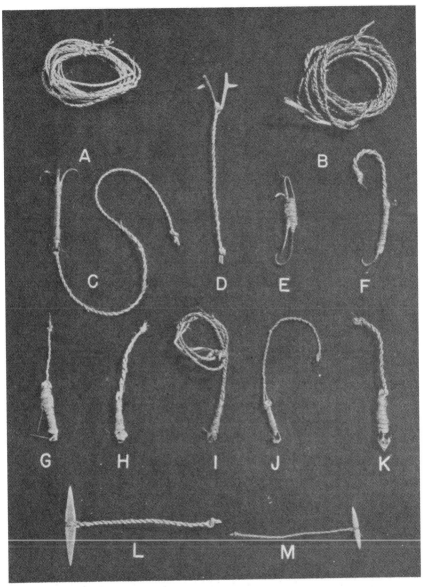

Figure 3-2. Makeshift Fish Hooks: (a) and (b) Bark lines; (c) Triple thorn hook; (d) Gorge hook made from a thorny vine; (e) Latch barb hook; (f) Plain thorn hook; (g) Straight thorn hook with latch; (h) (i) (j) and (k) Variations of thorn hooks made from rattans and trees; (l) and (m) Wooden gorge hooks.

nothing more than a simple trip pole. Prop the fishing pole on top of another short pole. When the fish bites, the pole will fall.

There are many ways of catching fish. The hook and line is the common method, but others can be more effective, depending on the conditions.

Using Hooks and Lines. Hooks can be made from pins, needles, wire, or any piece of available metal; out of wood, coconut shell, bone, thorns, flint, sea shells, tortoise shell; or a combination of these.

Lines may be made from a great variety of plants. The inner bark of trees is best. Plant fibers and bark may be rolled into a line by twisting the fibers together. This is done by securing the knotted ends of two strands of fibers to a solid object. Holding a strand in each hand, twist them clockwise and then cross one above the other counterclockwise. Continue adding fibers to lengthen the cord and when necessary to keep it a uniform thickness. Two strands twisted in this manner are four times as strong as one strand, and a twenty- or thirty-foot line can be made in an hour with the more easily worked materials.

Setting Lines. If there are extra hooks and lines, bait and set them overnight. A skewer or gorge hook is excellent for overnight sets, as the fish have ample time to swallow the baited hooks. Fasten the lines to low-hanging branches that will bend when a fish is hooked; otherwise the hook, line, and fish may be lost.

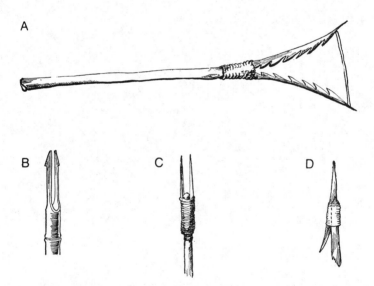

Figure 3-3. Improvised Fishing Equipment. (a) Fish Spear Trap. When a fish is speared the trigger stick is released and the barbs clamp tight. (b) Bamboo spear point. (c) Thorn spear point. (d) Bone spear point.

Figure 3-4. Weaving rope from vine. As one strip runs out, add another.

Fishing with Hands. Catching fish with your hands is most successful in small streams with undercut banks, or in cut-off channels or sloughs where clear shallow ponds are left by receding flood waters. Reach under the bank or rocks and move your hands slowly. When you feel a fish, work your hand gently toward its head, grasping it firmly just behind the gills.

Spearing Fish. Where fish are large and numerous, spearing works well. Any straight sapling with a solid core will serve as a spear. Fashion a point and harden by lightly charring it in fire. Bamboo, though hollow, is excellent. Two points should be shaped just beyond a joint. A wooden spear must often be repointed, so if time and facilities are available, spearheads of bone, shell, or stone should be shaped, or heavy thick thorns may be utilized. A knife or bayonet tied to a long straight shaft, or a large fish hook, heated and straightened, is good. A fish spear trap is often effective. Spearing is most efficient if the fish are the kind that lie on or near the bottom or rise to the surface for air. Many species of fish can best be speared at night with the aid of a torch or flashlight. The light dazzles the fish, reflects from the scales, and shows the bottom clearly. Be sure to aim well below the fish to compensate for the refraction of light which will make the fish appear higher than it really is. This aiming technique should also be used when shooting fish with a firearm.

Knifing Fish. In shallow water, fish can be caught by slashing them with a knife or bayonet. Clubs or machetes can be used to dispatch fish that were attracted by torchlight at night in shallow water or driven from pools over shallow riffles.

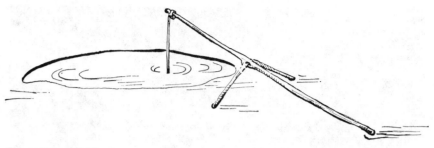

Figure 3-5. Ice fishing

Netting Fish. A scoop net for catching small fish or bait can be made from a piece of mosquito netting, a perforated parachute, underwear, clothing such as a T-shirt, clothlike material at the base of coconut leaves, or a knotted mesh of hibiscus or coconut fibers. Stitch or tie these along a circular frame made by bending together the ends of a forked sapling. If no fish are visible, hold the net on the downstream side of rocks or submerged vegetation. Muddy the water upstream and as it flows over the net, strike the rock or vegetation with a downstream stroke of the foot. At the same time, scoop upstream with the net.

It is often possible to catch fish in small pools by trampling about until the water is muddy. The fish will come to the surface, and you can scoop them out with a net, spear them, or even grab them with your hands.

Swimming to Catch Fish. Fish seek concealment and shade, so if the water is clear and there are large rocks on the bottom, swim down and feel under them just as might be done in catching fish under a bank. Slip into the water quietly and swim slowly beneath the surface until you can get close enough to strike a large fish with a hook or gaff attached to a wooden handle and line. Drop the gaff after striking the fish and haul in the catch when you have regained the bank.

Ice Fishing. When ice is clear enough for fish to be seen, you can stun them by striking the ice above them with a large rock or the butt end of a log. Chop a hole and pick up the fish. This method is most effective in shallow water. When water is deep and the ice thick, cut a hole and fish through it. If possible, build a brush shelter and fire nearby. Rig up an automatic signaling device so several lines can be watched at once.

EELS

Eels, found throughout the world in both fresh and salt water, are fish with a snakelike appearance. They are smooth-skinned and swim under water. Snakes, on the other hand, are scaled and usually swim on top. Eels are excellent eating and can be caught in muddy water or at night by using many of the methods described for fish. They are easily speared at night under a torchlight. After catching them, strike them a sharp blow toward the end of the tail to stun them. Eels, like catfish, should be skinned before cooking.

FROGS AND OTHER AMPHIBIANS

Skin frogs before cooking them, as many species secrete irritating and poisonous fluids from their skins. Particularly avoid those marked with yellow and red. Frog legs are a real delicacy, but there is no reason you can't eat the entire body. Frogs are widely distributed throughout the world in warm and temperate climates and are found along the banks of streams, lakes, ponds, swamps, and marshes.

At night frogs may be located with a light or by their croaking. Approach slowly. In warm weather when frogs are active, club them with a stick. Snag the larger ones with a hook and line. Frogs are very tenacious of life and frequently escape after they are stunned. Stick a knife through the spinal cord just behind the head.

Newts, salamanders, and other amphibians are found in many of the places where you find frogs. They can be seen swimming in the water or crawling on the forest floor at night. In the day they can be caught by looking under rocks in streams, in damp woods, and under rotting logs. All of them are harmless. They inhabit fresh water only. The best way to catch them is with a dip, or scoop, net. Skin and gut them, but avoid eating parts that contain glands.

MOLLUSKS

Mollusks, such as terrestrial and aquatic snails, and bivalves similar to North American fresh water mussel are found the world over under all water conditions. All of them are edible, but they should never be eaten raw. They may carry parasites which cause serious diseases or be contaminated from polluted water. You can usually pick them up in your hands or locate them by feeling around in the mud with your feet. Streams and rivers are the best places to look for them. Seek out the shallow water with a sand or mud bottom in which mussels can bury themselves, and look for the narrow trails they leave in mud, or for the dark elliptical slit of their open valves.

CRUSTACEANS

Crabs, crayfish, lobsters, shrimps, and prawns are found in fresh water throughout the world. All of them are probably edible, but they spoil rapidly and some contain parasites harmful to man. They should always be cooked. The saltwater forms can be eaten raw with little danger provided they are fresh.

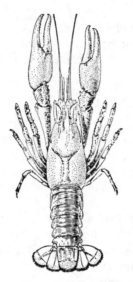

Figure 3-6. Crayfish

Figure 3-7. A crab caught by a student during a survival exercise. (Courtesy of the Defense Audio-Visual Agency)

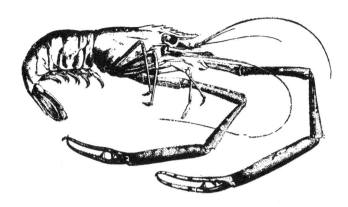

Figure 3-8. Fresh water shrimp

Freshwater crabs and crayfish can be scooped up in a dip net or picked up from moss beds under rocks and brush in streams. Many species of crabs and lobsters are nocturnal and can be most easily caught at night. This is particularly true of the landcrabs. All the meat within the skelton of crabs, crayfish, and lobsters can be eaten, but the gills are usually discarded, since they are the first to spoil.

Freshwater shrimps are abundant in tropical streams. You can see them swimming or find them clinging to branches or vegetation in the water. Look for them along a stream where the water is shallow and sluggish. The shelled tail is the part most commonly eaten.

Prawns will rise to a light at night and can be scooped off the surface of the water.

REPTILES

This category includes lizards, snakes, turtles, and alligators. Freshwater snakes frequent sluggish water; rocky, muddy, and vegetation-covered banks; piles of driftwood; and overhanging bushes. In such places they bask in the sun when it is not too hot. All of them are edible, some delicious, but caution should be used in securing them as the bites of some are fatal. Landsnakes, including the poisonous species, are also edible.

Lizards are found almost everywhere, but they are most abundant in the tropics and subtropics. You can club them or snare them easily with a grass or bark noose on the end of a stick. Remove their scaly skins and broil or fry the meat. There are only two poisonous lizards and they are confined to the American Southwest, Mexico, and Central America; their flesh, however, can be eaten. Many of the lizards such as the monitors, inhabiting southern Asia, Africa and Austrialia, look exceptionally fierce and dangerous. In spite of their appearance, however, they are good to eat. The flesh of iguanas is much like white chicken meat. Crocodiles and alligators are also good to eat. Skin them by first heating over a fire to loosen the plates.

Turtles are found over most of the land areas of the temperate and tropical zones and in nearly all the waters of the earth. The marine, freshwater, and land forms are all edible. Small freshwater ones can be grabbed or clubbed on the bank or caught on hook and line. Most of them are slow swimmers. In clear water, you can catch a turtle by swimming under water. Grip well to the rear of the shell, but don't try this technique on the large forms such as the snappers. They can inflict a serious bite.

INSECTS

Insects are abundant throughout the world and the larvae or grubs of many are edible and nourishing. Insect forms of one kind or another live in practically every conceivable habitat. Grubs are found in rotten logs, in the ground, and under the bark of dead trees. They should be boiled or fried, but they can be eaten raw. Grasshoppers should always be cooked, as some contain harmful parasites. Termites are a native delicacy, cooked or raw, and in jungle country they are generally available. Be cautious about eating caterpillars, as many are irritating and some are poisonous.

BIRDS AND MAMMALS

Birds and mammals are edible and easily seen, but they are usually the least abundant or available form of animal life. First seek the lower animals such as fish, reptiles, insects, crustaceans, and mollusks for food. They are far more abundant and much easier to obtain. When you have quieted starvation pangs by eating them, you may consider ways and means of catching birds and mammals. This is only a very general rule and of course there are many exceptions. In the far north, mice and rabbits are often the most numerous and available source of food, and at nesting colonies birds may be caught by the hundreds. As all birds and mammals are edible, it is not necessary to recognize specific ones, but it is necessary to know their general, and where possible, their specific habits in order to obtain them for food. They are of great benefit for any prolonged stay in the wilderness.

General Principles of Hunting and Trapping

A few general principles concerning birds and mammals will prove helpful in hunting or trapping them.

Land animals leave conspicuous signs, such as tracks, feces, runways, trails, dens, and feeding marks that indicate their presence and relative abundance. Look for such signs. They will tell you whether it is worthwhile to stop or to continue to a more favorable place.

Many mammals large and small travel on trails and runways. This is especially true of small rodents such as mice, ground squirrels, rabbits, and groundhogs. By hunting and trapping along these trails, you eliminate large areas of less suitable ground.

Birds and mammals are creatures of habit. Their normal daily activities of eating, sleeping, drinking, and traveling are fairly regular and continuously repeated. If you observe them, you can anticipate their movements. They can be hunted or trapped most successfully during their periods of activity.

Birds are less fearful of man during the nesting period than at any other time, and with patience you can catch them. Their nests and young are generally well hidden, but they can be located by watching the parent birds, which return often and regularly. Birds nest in every conceivable habitat—rocky cliffs, sandy beaches, marshes, on trees, in the woods, and in the fields. Some live in colonies. In the tropics, some birds are nesting all year round. Spring and early summer are the seasons to look for bird eggs in temperate or arctic regions.

Birds and mammals tend to congregate in the most favorable habitats. Some of the places to look for them are in the edges of woods and jungles; on trails, in glades, and at forest or jungle openings; near streams and on river banks; and on lake and ocean shores. In some environments such as tropical rain forests and desert regions, more mammals are active at night than during the day. A country seemingly destitute of life during the daytime may "become alive" at night. Two things to keep in mind are (1) that hoofed animals forage both day and night and (2) that many rodents and carnivores are active only at night. Birds and mammals, however, are most active early in the morning and late in the evening and are generally quiet during the middle of the day. In general, using early morning or late afternoon shadows usually enables you to approach more closely your quarry.

Birds detect danger by sight and hearing but rely little, if any, on a sense of smell. Most mammals, in addition to good eyes and ears, have a keen sense of smell.

Animals have natural camouflage, but movement makes them visible. Stop often when hunting for food. By doing so you become less visible and the animal that has "frozen" at your approach may begin to move. It is possible to see more animals in one hour of sitting than in several hours of hiking.

A few examples will help illustrate how some of these general principles can be specifically applied. When you enter an area of open country where mice, moles, and lemmings are abundant, look for trails and ground tunnels that crisscross the grass and weeds. If the vegetation is matted or snow covered, you may have to kick under it to observe these signs. Watch also for tiny droppings in the trails or places where the bark has been gnawed completely off and the bases of bushes and trees are white.

Here is a place to stop and get food. Upon closer observation, you will probably see mice scurrying ahead as you walk. Lift up logs and kick into all matted or dead grass. These small mammals can be clubbed or stepped on. They don't move about more than a few hundred feet. In the woods, knock open hollow logs and standing hollow dead stubs and investigate all round grass or leaf nests in trees or on the ground.

Wherever rabbits or hares are fairly abundant, you will jump seven or eight in an hour's walk. During the day, you will find them "bedded down" in grass on a sunny hillside, in brambles, or among vegetation at the base of trees or logs. Approach it slowly and shoot or club it. Before you retire for the night, set snares in runways. If snow is on the ground, these runways will be clearly evident by the tracks. In the north, rabbits and hares seek out the swamps during the winter and are concentrated in these habitats. If a rabbit is jumped, don't shoot at it on the run. Whistle shrilly and the chances are that it will stop just before disappearing into the brush. That's the chance for a still shot. These are only a few of the countless ways in which you can make use of animal habitats in your search for food.

Trapping Principles

To be effective, a trap must be constructed and set with a knowledge of animal habits. There is no "catch all" among traps. A trap set at random to catch whatever chances to come along is worthless. Decide upon the kind of animal to be trapped, bait the snares with the kind of food it eats, and keep the surroundings as natural as possible.

The fundamental principle of successful trapping is to determine what the animal to be trapped is going to do and then catch him doing it. It is easier to determine this for some animals than others. Small mammals such as mice, rats, rabbits, or squirrels are most easily trapped, because their activities are confined and regular and thus more easily anticipated.

Remember that wherever birds and mammals are naturally abundant, or for one reason or another are congregated or follow very definite and observable habits, trapping will prove effective.

Hanging Snares. A snare is a noose that will slip and strangle or hold any animal caught in it. It is fastened to the end of a bent pole or sapling, and spread open in a well-worn runway or in front of an animal den or bird nest. The size of the loop will vary with the kind of animal to be trapped. Make it large enough to admit the animal's head, but not its entire body. On a rabbit trail the loop should be about four inches in diameter and hang 1½ inches to 3 inches above the ground. The trigger or crosspiece holds the sapling down until an animal puts its head in the noose and with a jerk frees the trigger. The bent sapling lifts the animal off the ground where it soon strangles.

Figure 3-9. Running bowline

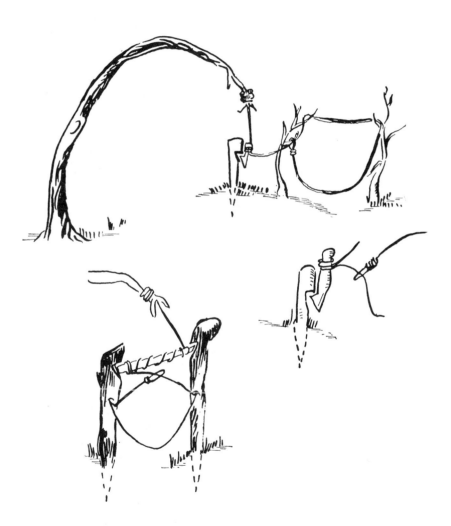

Figure 3-10. Hanging snares set on trail. Closeup of triggers.

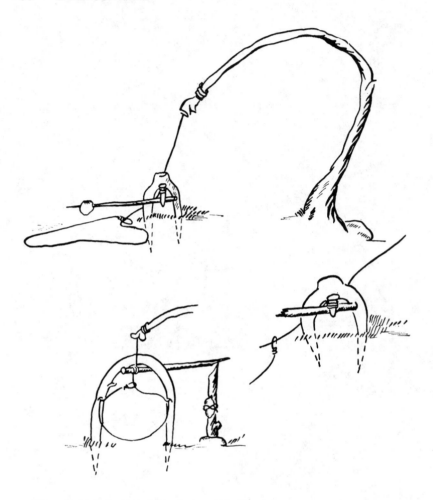

Figure 3-11. Baited hanging snares and triggers

Fixed Snares. Fixed snares are fastened to stationary objects such as logs, trees, or a forked stake. To be most effective, the snare should be set near a bush or limb where the animal will get tangled and strangle itself while struggling. This is particularly useful for catching rabbits and hares.

In the jungle, small mammals and especially birds such as pheasants and jungle fowl are more readily snared by building a low fence of sticks on either side of the runway to lead them to the trap. The treadle spring snare is very effective for such a set. A spear trap should be used for large mammals.

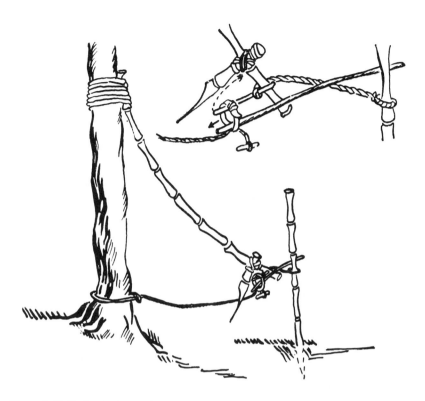

Figure 3-12. Spring and spear trap

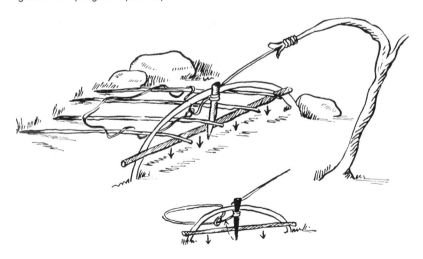

Figure 3-13. Treadle spring snare. Treadle should be covered with leaves or grass.

Figure 3-14. Deadfall with figure four trigger

Deadfalls. Deadfalls will trap both birds and mammals, and the basic principles can be infinitely varied to meet specific conditions. The trigger should be long and the weight tilted at a steep angle. Place a small flat stone under the upright so that it will not sink into the ground. Bait the trigger and the trap will fall when the bait is disturbed. The bait should always be tied on before the trap is set.

These traps can also be sprung with a long string or strip of bark. If they are placed in front of a den or over a regularly used trail, no bait is necessary.

Trapping with Bird Lime. Bird lime is any strong adhesive (generally made from the sap of plants), used to catch birds just as flies are caught with flypaper. This method of trapping is common in many parts of the world. The adhesive is usually smeared on slender sticks that adhere to the wings of birds and prevent flight.

When using bird lime, study the habits of the bird you wish to trap so you can set the sticks where they will come in contact with its wings. A tripod of sticks baited with an insect is often effective.

The sticky qualities of bird lime are neutralized by dust. Try to place the sets in dust-free areas, but if this is not possible, lose no time in grabbing the entangled bird.

Bird lime can be used in either jungle or desert, but not in cold climates. It can be made by boiling the sap of various *Euphorbias* or, in many places, the sap of fig trees. The sap of the breadfruit tree swells when exposed to air and forms a glutinous substance utilized as bird lime. In parts of South America it is made from the milky sap of the sapodilla tree which furnishes chicle for chewing gum. Heated chewing gum makes a good substitute and may be added to your survival kit.

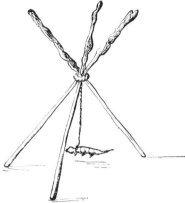

Figure 3-15. Tripod smeared with bird lime and baited with a mole cricket

Figure 3-16. Noosing wand

Trapping Tricks. The best way to attract mammals to a trap or to within shooting distance of a hide is to place salt along a trail or at a water hole. Squirrels, coons, opossums, and other mammals that live in hollow trees can be extracted by inserting and twisting a short forked stick. Pin the animal against the side or bottom of the hollow and then twist the stick. The fur and loose skin will twist around the fork and the animal can be pulled out. Keep tension on the stick when withdrawing. A short fork takes a secure hold, a long fork does not. These same mammals can be smoked or flushed out of dens and clubbed as they emerge.

A noose fastened to the end of a long pole can be used to snare an animal as it comes out of its burrow. If there is more than one entrance to the burrow, block all but one. Roosting and nesting birds can also be noosed in this manner. Some birds can actually be touched while incubating eggs or brooding young; others are more wary. All will return to their nests or roosts provided the surroundings have not been too greatly disturbed. Conceal yourself by building a blind of vegetation and remain still and quiet within. Drop the noose over the bird's head and pull it up and back against the bill.

Birds that nest in hollow trees such as woodpeckers, owls, hornbills, and so forth, can be blocked in the hollow tree or noosed as they go in or out.

A tethered live bird acts as a decoy for other birds of the same species. Imitation distress sounds and calls will lure some birds within striking or noosing distance. A very effective distress sound can be made by kissing the back of your hand.

A fish-baited hook placed along the beach or in the water will catch shore birds, herons, and fish-eating ducks. Gulls, terns, albatross, and other ocean birds can sometimes be caught by trolling slowly with a minnow or piece of fish.

If you learn a few trapping techniques, are resourceful, and, above all, have observed the habits of the wildlife, you should be able to obtain enough wild meat to sustain yourself. In the wilderness, resourcefulness and observation are the greatest tools.

Hunting Principles

Game animals rely upon their senses of sight, hearing, and smell to detect danger. Some have only one or two of these senses highly developed, while others have all three. An experienced hunter takes advantage of the shortcomings of his quarry; the novice, however, when hunting unfamiliar game should proceed on the assumption that they are naturally wary and that they possess keen senses of sight, sound, and smell. Be overcautious until experience indicates the best hunting technics for the quarry at hand.

To be consistently successful in hunting, one must know how to *approach* game and where to *shoot* it. In a tough spot you may have only one chance. Learn a few dos and don'ts of hunting. Some of the hunting principles that follow can be applied to almost any type of mammal shooting but are especially applicable to large game such as deer, antelope, caribou, sheep, goats, buffalo, and wild boar.

Approaching Game.

(1) The greatest advantage you can have in hunting is to see the quarry before it sees you.
(2) Look for fresh signs that indicate the recent presence of game such as tracks, beds, and warm or moist droppings.
(3) Whether in the woods or in the open, peep cautiously over ridges, examining first the distant and then the closer ground.
(4) In the woods move slowly and stop often. A motionless man has an immense advantage over a moving animal.
(5) One of the surest ways to get a shot is to locate a waterhole, feeding ground, or well-traveled trail and wait quietly for the game to come to that spot.
(6) In dense forested country where the range of vision is limited and the game must be closely approached to be seen, silence is essential. Avoid treading on dry sticks and leaves or brushing against bushes.
(7) In open or mountainous country, game is generally seen and shot at a distance. Silence is not such an important factor as in the woods, but you must keep under cover.
(8) Whether looking for game or stalking it, move up or across wind, never downwind. This applies equally in open or forested country.

Go out of the way to utilize cover and contours even if it requires a wide circuit.

(9)   In open country, keep the sun behind you, as it is difficult to shoot into the sun. You will be less visible to the game and it will be more visible to you.

(10) If the quarry has sighted you but has not fled, do not approach it directly; tack back and forth across the line of approach. Move when the animal is feeding and freeze when it looks up or ceases the activity that is absorbing its attention.

(11) Get above mountain game; it seldom suspects danger from above.

(12) Never become silhouetted on a skyline, as it makes one immediately visible and suspicious to game.

(13) Camouflage all clothing so it blends with the landscape.

Shooting game.

(1)   Never make a shot unless it is the very best shot available. Take plenty of time, for a miss will scare the game and increase the difficulties manyfold.

(2)   Many animals are curious about strange noises and objects. You can make them stand for a good shot or to linger while you come within range by attracting their attention with a whistle or moving cloth.

(3)   Aim for the head, neck, or just back of the shoulder, which are vulnerable spots on many animals.

(4)   Don't follow a wounded animal too closely; give it time to bleed and weaken, otherwise it may run for miles.

The principles of hunting set down here will prove invaluable to the novice, but remember that a knowledge of the habits of the game and the locality are equally important factors in successful hunting. The chances of success increase with each day spent in hunting an area or a particular animal, so keep hunting until you are successful.

Skinning and Dressing

You should drain the blood from the animal as soon as possible after killing, as this will retard spoilage. Cut the jugular vein on the side of the neck. Have a container ready to collect the blood as, after thorough cooking, it is a valuable source of salt and nutrients. Use in broth or soup. Fish and birds are also improved by immediate bleeding; the flesh keeps better and feathers become easier to pluck.

To prepare large game, hang it up by its hind feet. This can be done by tying the feet to a short stick and hanging it across two branches. A short stick can also be run between the large tendons and bone of the lower hind legs, eliminating the need to tie the feet to the stick. Do this by feeling for the tendons and then slit the skin, taking care not to cut the tendon.

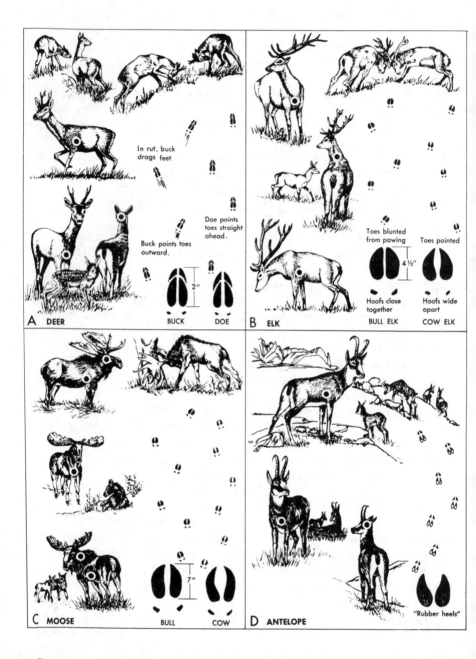

Figure 3-17. Vital Spot

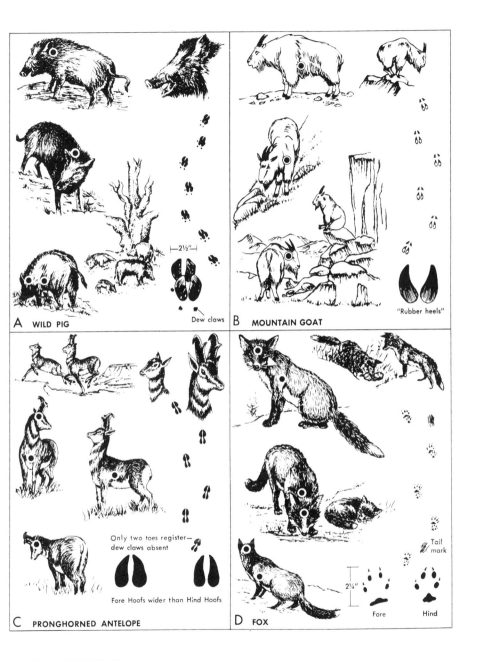

A **WILD PIG** — 2½" — Dew claws

B **MOUNTAIN GOAT** — "Rubber heels"

C **PRONGHORNED ANTELOPE** — Only two toes register—dew claws absent — Fore Hoofs wider than Hind Hoofs

D **FOX** — Tail mark — 2¼" — Fore — Hind

Figure 3-17. Vital Spot (continued)

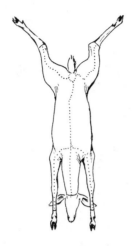

Figure 3-18. To make preliminary cuts, follow dotted lines.

The stick should be at least one foot longer than the distance between
the feet.

You can skin and gut the animal either as it hangs or as it lies stretched
out on the ground on its back. It is easier to work with it hanging. To remove the skin and gut the animal, take a sharp knife and begin cutting
through the skin in a straight line. If the animal is hanging, begin at the top
and work down. If it is lying on the ground, begin at the end of the tail bone
and work up to just under the neck.

To ensure the correct depth of cutting, place the index and middle fingers of one hand inside the first incision and, as you proceed, lift the skin.
Use the fingers as a guide so as to cut only the skin and not the thin membrane enclosing the guts.

If the animal is male, cut the skin parallel to, but not touching, the penis.
Carefully avoid the tube leading from the bladder. If it is cut, you'll have a
mess and unclean meat will result. Also take care not to cut the gall bladder (a purplish-blue organ attached to the liver) or the urine bladder (a yellowish organ). If you inadvertantly do, wash the meat. Otherwise it is preferable to allow the meat to form a protective glaze rather than wash it.

In opening the membrane to get at the internal organs, again use your
fingers to guide the knife between the membrane and the intestines. To
see better, you can cut away the membrane from the ribs and sides. The
large intestine, which passes through an opening in the pelvis, must be
disengaged from the bone by the knife. Tie a knot in the bladder tube,
which you can trace from the bladder, to prevent the release of urine. Having done these things, you can then remove the entrails, glands, and blad-
ntact from the carcass. Wipe the body cavity clean with a dry cloth.

Some animals such as beavers, muskrats, opossums, raccoons, squirrels, and woodchucks have a small gland—white to brownish in color and oblong in shape—on the inside of each leg just under the skin, usually encased in fat. Some animals—again, for example, opossums, raccoons, and woodchucks—have as many as nine glands nestled in the small of the back. These glands should be removed after skinning to preclude giving a strong taste to the meat. Rabbits and porcupines do not have these glands. Rabbits, however, may be sick with Tularemia or "rabbit sickness" which is revealed by white or yellow spots on the liver. It is transmitted to humans through skin contact. Wear gloves or cover your hands with cloth when skinning rabbit until you are sure the rabbit did not have Tularemia. Deer have scent glands, located on the inside of the hind legs at the hock joint, which must always be discarded.

Generally speaking, you should eat first the liver, heart, and kidneys of animals, followed by the tenderloin. True to the name, the long strips of meat on each side of the backbone are usually very tender. Areas around the head, brisket, ribs, backbone, and pelvis will also yield edible meat.

CHAPTER 4

Fire Making and Cooking

Fire will sustain you indefinitely in the wild by warming you, cooking your food, and destroying the harmful germs commonly found in food and water.

FIRE MAKING

You should be able, with matches, to build a fire under any weather condition. No one who may have to shift for himself in a remote area should ever be without matches carried in a waterproof case. If you remember and practice a few basic principles of fire building, you can always make a fire:

(1) Select a dry sheltered spot.
(2) Use only the driest of tinder to start the fire.
(3) Have a good supply of kindling on hand before striking the match.
(4) Start with a tiny fire and add fuel as the flame grows.
(5) Fire needs air. Add fuel sparingly.
(6) Blow lightly on the burning wood. This helps the flame along.
(7) Fire climbs. Place fresh kindling above the flame.
(8) Use dry deadwood.

Fire Site

Use judgment in selecting a fire site. Don't select a windy spot. Don't build on damp ground if dry is available. Pick a spot where the fire won't spread. In rainy weather, build under a leaning tree or rock shelf. If snow is on the ground, build the fire on a platform of logs, or metal salvaged from vehicle wreckage; but one can build or keep a fire going on bare snow or ice.

Tinder

Tinder may consist of dry grasses or plant stems, dry inflammable bark such as birch, or dry leaves. The most available tinder in dry weather is the tiny, brittle branchlets from dry, dead limbs. Twigs not much thicker than a straw should be broken in lengths of several inches and arranged in a wigwam pile three to four inches high, the shortest and thinnest twigs being underneath. Touch a match to these and add kindling as the flames. A fuzz stick, or shaving clusters, may be used in place of small twigs.

Figure 4-1. In addition to its practical benefits, a fire imparts a feeling of warmth and, to some degree, a feeling of security. (Courtesy of the U.S. Coast Guard)

Figure 4-2. Use small dry tinder.

Select some dry branches the diameter of a dime and shave them halfway through for most of their length to form a cluster of shavings. Stand these in a wigwam with curls down, and light them.

Kindling

Have plenty of kindling at hand to keep the fire burning. Soft woods make the best kindling as they light easily and burn rapidly. Split wood burns faster than round branches. Branches lying flat on the ground are generally damp. Select dead branches off the ground. Most dead branches snap when broken. Live ones bend and are usually not brittle.

Fuel

All woods do not burn alike. Some scarcely burn at all; others burn quickly and make a hot flame. Some burn slowly and make good coals; some smoke, others don't. Use whatever is at hand, but where there is a choice, select the best fuels for the purpose. In general, hardwoods make a slow-burning fire with lasting coals, and soft woods make a quick, hot fire with coals that are soon spent.

In the Arctic fire is essential. Dried lichens, moss, heather, scrub willow, and driftwood all make good fuel. The resinous white heather is the most valuable Arctic prairie fuel. Willows and alders grow along practically all Arctic rivers, and their stems and roots alike serve as fuel. Even in mid-winter, you can find willows in wind-swept spots.

Seal blubber is the most abundant natural fuel. To obtain, kill a seal—usually by clubbing or by drowning one in a water hole—and remove the skin. Blubber is the one-to-four-inch thick layer of fat next to the skin. Just cut it off. Seal blubber can be burned in a shallow stone lamp or tin can with a wick of thoroughly dry powdered moss, grass, or decayed wood. Another method is to soak a small piece of cloth in seal grease, which can be made by cooking the blubber. Then place a small pile of dried bones or other noncombustible material on top of the rag. Lay several strips of blubber on top of the bones and light the rag, which will burn like a wick and start the blubber frying. The blubber oil will trickle down on the bones and flare up as soon as they become hot. Fat and hides of land animals are also usable fuel.

Lubricating oil will not light with a match unless first vaporized by dripping on a piece of hot rock or metal. It can, however, be burned in a container with a wick of rope, cloth, dried bark or moss. If you're stranded in the wild with your vehicle, drain the oil before it congeals (if in the Arctic, drain it quickly). Mix it with gasoline, pour it into a container, and burn it with an improvised wick.

Banking a Fire

It is essential to bank a fire properly if you expect to have it burning the next morning or the next week. For a slow-burning fire, use green logs or the butt of a decayed punky log (wood so decayed as to be dry, crumbly, and useful for tinder). Eliminate as much draft as possible. The coals or the charred backlogs can be blown into a flame when needed. Dry coconut husks, punk, and fungus on a stick are excellent for keeping a fire ʼg and for carrying it from place to place. It requires less work to keep a ʼing than to start a new one.

Fire in Wet Weather

The trick of making a fire in wet weather is to find enough dry tinder and wood to get it started. Once you've got a good fire going, even wet wood will burn. Look for dry wood under overhanging rocks, in caves, on the underside of leaning trees and logs, and in hollow trees. Rain does not soak far into a standing dead tree; split it open and use the inside. Cut away the wet exterior of small dead limbs to get dry wood. If matches become wet, dry them by rotating them rapidly between the palms of your hands.

In wet weather, a fire can be started with certain inflammable tinders that will ignite even when damp. The resinous pitch in pine knots or dried stumps burn like an oil torch. Slivers of dry pitchy pine make excellent tinder and kindling. The loose bark from living birch trees contains a resinous oil that is easily ignited and burns fiercely.

Fire without Matches

Sun and Glass. Sunlight focused on a pile of tinder through the lens of a flashlight, binoculars, telescopic sight, or camera will produce heat that can be fanned into a flame. It may be necessary to take the lenses apart and use a single element.

Flint and Steel. Sparks struck from a piece of flint, quartz, or pyrite into a pile of tinder can start a fire. Use the back of a knife blade or any piece of hard steel to strike the sparks. Let the sparks fall on a spark-catcher of shredded cloth, dry moss, bird and seed down, dead fungi, punk or pulverized bark. Once the spark catches, blow it gently until it flames. Experiment with the driest tinders available. Charred rags catch better than anything else; so if matches are running short, char some clothing by burning it without air in a closed container such as a tin first aid kit or a ball of clay.

Wood Friction. Choose dry, well-seasoned wood to make a fire by friction. Dead branches slightly punky are the best, and, in general, soft-grained woods are better than hardwoods. Resinous, gummy woods are worthless. The best woods include balsa, yucca, elm, and the root of willow and cottonwood. The right kind of wood makes a fine carbon dust with the formation of an ember. If a coarse, gritty powder results, discard the wood and try another.

Fire with Bow and Drill. The bow and drill is the easiest method of making fire by friction. When a dry, soft shaft of wood is spun into a block of the same material, a black powdered dust will form and eventually catch a spark. To make a fire, draw the bow, made of wood and a leather thong, back and forth causing the drill to spin in the block. Start slowly with long full strokes and work faster. When a volume of smoke begins to rise through the fire pit, there is a sufficient spark to start a fire. Lift the block,

FLINT AND STEEL

Waterproof matchbox

This is the easiest and most reliable way of making a fire without matches. Use the flint fastened to the bottom of your waterproof match case. If you have no flint, look for a piece of hard rock from which you can strike sparks. If no sparks fly when it is struck with steel, find another. Hold your hands close over the dry tinder; strike flat with a knife blade or other small piece of steel with a sharp, scraping, downward motion so that the sparks fall in the center of the tinder. The addition of a few drops of gasoline before striking the flint will make the tinder flame up — FOR SAFETY, KEEP YOUR HEAD TO ONE SIDE. When tinder begins to smolder, fan or blow it gently into a flame. Then transfer blazing tinder to your kindling pile or add kindling gradually to the tinder.

BURNING GLASS

A convex lens can be used in bright sunlight to concentrate the sun's rays on the tinder. A 2-inch lens will start a fire most any time the sun is shining. Smaller lenses will work if the sun is high and the air clear.

ELECTRIC SPARK

If you have a live storage battery, direct a spark onto the tinder by scatching the ends of wires together, to produce an arc.

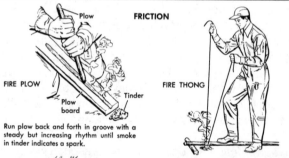

FRICTION

FIRE PLOW

Plow

Tinder

Plow board

Run plow back and forth in groove with a steady but increasing rhythm until smoke in tinder indicates a spark.

BOW AND DRILL

Tinder and wood dust

Hand holding drill socket is braced against left shin. Wood dust piles on tinder as drill spins.

FIRE THONG

Use a thong of dry rattan or other long, strong fiber, and rub with a steady but increasing rhythm.

FIRE SAW

Fibrous tinder

Notch

NOTE:

Split bamboo or soft wood makes a good fire saw. Dry sheath of coconut flower is a good base wood.

Figure 4-3. Fire making without matches. If you have a vehicle with you, don't overlook its cigarette lighter or battery.

add tinder, and blow gently until there is a flame. Fire has been made with a bow and drill in less than seven seconds.

Fire Thong. Fire can be made by drawing a dry rattan thong back and forth on a soft, dry piece of wood. Wedge tinder into a split in the hearth log to catch the embers.

Fire Saw. The fire saw, commonly used in the tropical rain forest, consists of two pieces of wood and plenty of "elbow grease." Split bamboo or a soft wood will serve as a rub stick, and the dry sheath of the coconut flower makes an effective base wood. Good tinder is the brown, fluffy covering on the trunk of the Apiang palm, the dry, fabriclike material found at the base of coconut leaves, and the fine, skinlike membrane lining the bamboo cavity.

These methods, however, are always a last resort and should be tried only as such. Fire with matches is infinitely easier; always carry them in a waterproof case.

Fires for Warmth

A small fire is better than a large one for nearly all purposes. A very small fire will warm you thoroughly if you sit or kneel over it, draping your coat or blanket so as to direct all of the heat upward.

Figure 4-4. A small fire will serve you better in most cases than a large one. (Courtesy of Dr. Murray Hamlet, U.S. Army Research Institute at Natick, Mass.)

Figure 4-5. A wall of logs will reflect the heat of a fire back to you.

Figure 4-6. Stone, tin can, and log fireplace

A reflector fire will keep the victim warm while sleeping. The base of a tree, a large rock, or a log are ready-made reflectors. Lie or sit between the fire and reflector, as this will prevent "baking" on one side and "freezing" on the other. A reflector can be constructed of logs, snow, boughs, or sod.

Cooking Fires

When fuel is scarce, make a hobo stove from an empty tin. Such a stove will conserve heat and fuel and is particularly serviceable in the Arctic.

The criss-cross fire is the best all-round cooking fire, as it burns down to a uniform bed of coals in a short time (see the subsection "Fuel"). The simplest fireplace consists of two rocks, two logs, or a narrow trench on which a vessel can rest with the fire below. Arrange the fireplace so that it will have a draft. If the fire does not draw well, elevate one edge of the log or stone. Replenish a fire by stacking the wood on criss-cross. It will burn to coals much sooner.

COOKING TECHNIQUES

Cooking renders most foods more palatable and digestible and destroys bacteria, toxins, and harmful plant and animal products. Cook your food whenever possible.

Preparing Food with Fire

Cooking is best done over a bed of glowing coals, not flames. If you use containers, construct an "A" frame over the fire to support the cooking vessels.

Boiling requires a container. When meat is tough or food requires long cooking, it is often a wise procedure to boil it first and then roast, fry, or bake it. In the Arctic, boiling is not the easiest method, but it should be used whenever it is desirable to save the juices. Generally speaking, boiling is the best method of cooking as it saves nourishing vitamins and minerals and provides a broth as well. Roasting is easier but you lose the vitamins and minerals and fats.

At high altitudes, food has to be boiled longer than at low altitudes. Do not try to boil food above 12,000 feet; it requires too much time and fuel.

Water in a scooped-out log or clay pit can be boiled by dropping heated stones into it. In the tropics, half a green coconut or a bamboo stem cut well above and just below the joint can be used for containers. They will not burn completely until well after the water boils. After placing food and water in a freshly cut bamboo joint, tie green leaves over the open end and support the vessel against a stone.

Water can be boiled in vessels made of bark or leaves. The container will not burn below the water line, but it may catch fire above unless moistened. If a small fire is used, keep the flames low and you shouldn't have any problems.

Figure 4-7. (*left*) Broiling fish; (*right*) Boiling water and heating soup.

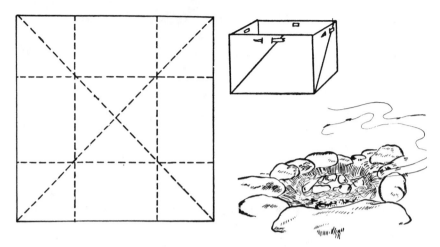

Figure 4-8. Diagram for
making a back container

Figure 4-9. Steam or baking pit

Birch bark and banana leaves make excellent containers. Cut out about a twelve inch square of bark, make two diagonal folds between all four corners, open them up, turn the bark over, and fold it in thirds. Open again and fold in thirds the other way.Then pinch up each corner so that the triangle is pointing out. Fold this along the side and pin in place with a thorn or sliver of wood. Make sure your bark contains no holes.

Roasting or broiling is a quick way to prepare wild plant foods and tender meats. Simply run a stick through the piece to be cooked and hold it over the coals. Keep the piece as close to the coals as possible. This hardens the outside quickly and holds the juices in.

Baking is cooking with moderate, steady heat in an oven. The oven may be a pit, closed vessel or a wrapping of clay or leaves. Without cooking equipment, most of your fish and meat must be either broiled or baked. To bake in a pit, get a good bed of coals, then drop in a covered shell vessel containing water and meat, tubers wrapped in leaves, or fish or bird wrapped in wet leaves and mud. Cover whatever is baking with coals, and then fill the pit with a few inches of earth. A stone-lined pit will hold more heat and cook more quickly than an earthen pit.

Steaming is slower than boiling but can be done without a container. Dig a hole and fill it with stones. Build a fire to heat the stones. Cover the stones and coals with leaves, then put in the food. Cover this with more leaves and then a layer of dirt. Punch a hole down to the food and pour in some water. Close the hole and the food will steam. This method is suitable for foods such as shellfish that require little cooking.

Large leaves, a slab of bark, turtle, coconut or sea shells will serve as plates. Some kind of container is necessary for carrying water. An excellent one can be made by punching out all but the last node from a convenient length of bamboo. Fit with a wooden plug for a stopper and it can be slung over the shoulder on a piece of vine. A water belt can be made of short bamboo nodes strung together.

Fruits. Succulent fruits are best boiled. Large, tough, or heavy-skinned fruits are best baked or roasted.

Potherbs (Leaves, Stems, and Buds). Boil until tender; several changes of water with subsequent rinsing will help eliminate bitter juices or undesirable tastes.

Roots and Tubers. These can be boiled, but are more easily baked or roasted.

Nuts. Most nuts can be eaten raw, but some such as acorns are better cooked. Acorns should be broken up, boiled with ashes from the fire to eliminate tannin, molded into cakes, and then baked. Chestnuts are good roasted, steamed, or baked.

Grains and Seeds. Parch grains and seeds. They are more digestible and tasty that way.

Sap. The sap of plants containing sugar can be dehydrated to a syrup or sugar by boiling to remove the water.

Large Game. Larger animals may be cleaned and cooked. Remove the entrails and the glands in the anal and reproductive regions, as they will impart an objectionable taste to the meat. Animals the size of a domestic cat or larger should be boiled first, then roasted or broiled. If meat is very tough, stew it with vegetables. Broil meat as quickly as possible over hot coals. Slow roasting makes tough meat tougher. Cook small pieces at a time.

Small Game. Small mammals and birds may be cooked whole or in part. If tough, or if the flavor is strong, boil first and then broil. If fruit is available, stuff the animal and bake or roast.

Fish. Fish can be roasted on a grill of green sticks or baked in leaves and clay. Fish wrapped in leaves should be placed on green logs on the fire to keep the flesh free of ashes. Fish with scales should be scaled or skinned after cooking.

Reptiles and Amphibians. Frogs, small snakes, and salamanders can be roasted on a stick. Large snakes and eels are better if boiled first, then roasted. Turtles should be boiled until the shell comes off. Then cut up the meat and cook with tubers and greens to form a soup.

Crustaceans. Crabs, crayfish, shrimps, prawns, and the like can be steamed, boiled, roasted or baked. They require very little cooking, but they spoil quickly. The safest way to cook them is to drop them alive in boiling water.

Mollusks. Shellfish should be steamed, boiled, or baked in the shell. They make excellent stews in combination with greens and tubers.

Insects. Insects such as large grubs, locusts, grasshoppers, ants, termites, and so forth, can be fried, boiled, or roasted, but they are generally more palatable if disguised in a stew containing other foods.

Eggs. Eggs can be hardboiled with the shell on and carried for days. They can be poached in a bark container or fried on a hot rock. Turtle eggs don't get hard with boiling. Fresh eggs are among the safest of foods, and they are edible at any stage of embryo development.

Salt. Salt is necessary for proper functioning of the human body. It can be obtained by boiling sea water. The ashes of burned nipa palm boughs, hickory, and some other plants, contain salt that can be dissolved out in water. Evaporate the water and a black-looking salt remains.

Preparing Food without Fire

Fresh papaya leaves contain papain that renders meat soft and tender in a short time. It is especially useful when freshly killed meat must be eaten raw or cooked.

The citric acid in limes, lemons, and other citric fruits can be used to pickle fish and other flesh. Dilute two parts lime juice with one part sea water, add raw fish, and allow the mixture to stand for half a day or more. The citric acid will "cook" the fish.

PRESERVATION OF FOOD

Wild food is scarce in some localities and abundant in others. Whenever more food is procured than immediately required, preserve it, especially if it looks like it may be difficult to get more.

Freezing

In cold climates, meat will be the principal food you will get in excessive quantities. It will keep indefinitely when frozen. To defrost it place it next to fire.

Drying

Drying food not only preserves it but decreases its weight without losing any of its calories. Dry foods can be eaten uncooked when necessary. Food can be dried by wind, air, sun, or fire with or without smoke, or by a combination of these. The main object is to get rid of the water. In hot, dry climates the sun and air will be sufficient, but in humid climates fire must be used and the dehydrated product kept dry. Cut the food to be dried in small strips so that a maximum area will be exposed to dry.

Smoke-Drying Meat. To smoke-dry meat, build a stick grate three to four feet above a slow-burning fire, and lay strips of lean meat one-fourth inch thick on this lattice. Do not let the fire get hot enough to cook the meat or draw out the juices. The smoke which rises naturally from the burning wood is sufficient. Continue the smoking until the meat is brittle. The meat

Figure 4-10. Preserving food: (*left*) drying strips of meat; (*right*) smoking strips of meat. (Courtesy of the Defense Audio-Visual Agency)

will then keep for long periods and can be chewed while traveling or cooked in a stew if time permits. Avoid using resinous or oily woods to smoke meat; they will blacken it and give it a disagreeable flavor.

Drying Fish, Birds, and Fruit. To dry fish, cut them in strips or split them down the back. Leave the heads on small ones and hang them over the fire by threading a stick through the gills. Small birds may be gutted and dried whole. Plantains, bananas, breadfruit, apricots, cherries, grapes, potatoes, tubers, leaves, figs, dates, apples, berries—in fact most wild fruites—can be dried. Cut them into fine slices and place them in the sun. A fire may be used if necessary.

CONCENTRATED RATIONS

Two of the best concentrated foods are pemmican and pinole. These keep indefinitely, contain a maximum of calories for their weight, are easy to prepare, and do not require cooking when used.You could live entirely on either one for long periods. Pemmican, for example, contains nearly every necessary nutrient save vitamin C. You can make pemmican by pouring hot suet (fat) over shredded dried meat and mixing the two to attain a sausagelike consistency. Keep in a waterproof container and cook or eat raw.

Pinole is prepared by parching corn grains in hot ashes, on heated rocks or in an oven. The browned kernels are then ready to eat or can be pounded to a fine meal. A small handful of this in a cup of cold water has a pleasant flavor and will keep you going all day. Most grass seeds can be prepared in this way, though few of them will have the same nutritional properties as corn.

POISONOUS ANIMAL FOODS

No birds or mammals are poisonous to eat, though the liver of polar bears and sea lions may cause serious sickness. In South America, some mammals may have flukes. Snake flesh is generally safe if cooked.

Some sea foods are poisonous at certain times and places. Only along tropical shores, especially in the vicinity of coral reefs, is there any real danger. The alkaloids in the flesh of poisonous fish are not destroyed by cooking.

Spoiled meats and fish are far more dangerous to eat than animals that are themselves poisonous. Poisoning from such food is common in the tropics and constitutes a real hazard. Seafood is especially likely to spoil and should be eaten when fresh. Fish should be gutted at once to prevent spoiling. Good fish will be firm; spoiled fish soft and flabby.

Meat and the flesh of all *freshwater* fish should be *cooked* whenever possible for they may contain flukes and other parasitic worms harmful to humans. Saltwater fish are generally free of harmful parasites.

In populated parts of the tropics, cholera, typhoid fever, and dysenteries can be contracted by eating raw foods that have been touched by unclean hands. Flies carry these diseases, too, and are more dangerous in villages than in the open country. Protect food from flies. Sterilize it by cooking.

VITAMIN DEFICIENCIES

When living off the land or sea, there is often little choice of food. If the diet is restricted to a few foods over a period of at least a month, vitamin deficiency diseases are likely to develop. Under extreme conditions, especially at sea, nothing can be done but grin and bear it. Although these diseases are painful and appear serious, they disappear almost miraculously when the survivor gets fresh fruit and vegetables.

Vitamin deficiencies often occur through ignorance where proper food is available. You cannot live on lean meat alone, but you can remain active and healthy for long periods on fat and lean meat.

Vitamin A deficiency causes night blindness, followed by extreme muscular weakness and, in late stages, blindness. Carotene, which supplies vitamin A, is found in yellow fruits and vegetables. Vitamin A in pure form is found in fat, egg yolk, liver, and in oily fresh and saltwater fish.

An absence of vitamin B_1 or thiamine causes fatigue, headache, and finally beriberi, a degenerative disease of the nerves, digestive system, and heart. Vitamin B_1 occurs naturally in egg yolks, grains, and lean meat.

Lack of vitamin B$_2$ (riboflavin) causes irritations of the digestive tract. A wide variety of foods, such as lean meat, liver, eggs, and grains, contain this vitamin.

Scurvy is the result of a deficiency of vitamin C and is characterized by irritability, lethargy, soreness and stiffness of the joints, loosening of the teeth, nose bleed, and hemorrhages under the skin. Vitamin C is abundant in liver, citrus fruits, green vegetables, and wild herbs such as sorrel, purslane, and dock.

Vitamin D deficiency causes rickets. This vitamin is produced in the skin by sunlight and is found in liver oils.

Pellagra is a vitamin deficiency disease caused by a lack of vitamin B$_1$ and complicated by other dietary deficiencies. It is charcterized by skin lesions, digestive disturbances, nervousness, and paralysis.

If the symptoms of any vitamin deficiency diseases should appear, make a special effort to vary your diet. You can generally obtain an adequate supply of vitamins by eating a variety of foods. If you survive for a month on land, chances are that you have eaten enough different kinds of foods to keep yourself supplied with all the necessary vitamins. If you begin showing any symptoms of deficiency, get busy and experiment with some new foods. Green grass contains vitamins A, B, and C. Try it.

CHAPTER 5

Traveling

The decision to travel through wild, unpopulated regions under survival conditions should be made only after much thought. Evaluating whether your chances for survival are better if you move on or stay put will be among the most important calculations you will have to make. Although your instinct may be to rush off, that could be very much against your best interest. Rescuers will more likely spot the wreckage of your vehicle before they will a single human amid vast acres of forest or brush.

After tending to the requirements for first aid, you may want, as part of your preparations for communications and signaling and if no other priority is pressing, to determine your location. Eventually this information will be a factor in your decision about navigation and travel. Even if you decide not to move, getting your bearings will help give you confidence in your abilities and may increase your hopes for rescue. Among the other factors to consider as you decide whether to travel are safety; water, shelter, and food procurement; and signaling.

Wilderness travel is risky business. We use the word *wilderness* to refer to any large area essentially undisturbed by human activity, whether it be a forested mountainside or a desert wasteland. Crossing unfamiliar terrain opens you to unpredictable dangers and increases the risk of injury or exhaustion. Unless you feel strongly that there is something to be gained by traveling, you would probably do better to remain in one place. Establish a base, and deal with the priorities of survival, as you see them, from one location.

If, after thoughtful weighing of all the circumstances, you decide to travel, you must do so only after making the proper preparations. And as you travel, you must go slowly and carefully to avoid complicating an already hazardous situation.

GETTING YOUR BEARINGS

If you find yourself stranded, you will want to determine as precisely as possible your present location, the place you want to reach, and the inter-

Figure 5-1. Traveling means constantly finding new sources of water and food. (Courtesy of Dr. Murray Hamlet, U.S. Army Research Institute at Natick, Mass.)

vening distance and terrain. Climbing a tall tree or hill will give you a vantage point from which to observe, for example, drainage patterns, trends of mountain ridges, and the characteristics of the local vegetation, as these will be factors in your choice of a route. Maps, charts, or aerial photographs, if available, will further guide you. Compare natural features with the map, and you may very will learn where you are. Knowing how to use a compass will verify and supplement information gleaned from your own observations and maps. And the sun and stars have served humans as navigational aids for millennia.

Observing the Landscape

Traveling means constant alertness. As you attempt to find your way out of a life-threatening situation, your skill in observing and interpreting information about an unfamiliar, hostile environment may be your lifeline. The simple phrase—*use your eyes*—belies a complex process.

From a vantage point, look for the general direction of the flow of large rivers, note features of a shoreline, and pinpoint the location of landmarks. Following rivers downstream or hiking along the shoreline will usually lead to human communities and safety. Marking the position of prominent natural features will orient you as you travel.

Watch for signs of civilization such as power lines, lights, trails, tracks, roads, cultivated fields, or buildings. Observe the direction in which aircraft fly.

When you have related your position to permanent landmarks and have decided on the place you want to reach, the best route is as straight a line as possible. If, as you travel, you observe signs that may indicate that civilization lies in other than the direction you thought, revise your route accordingly.

Reading a Map

How often have you looked at a map and become confused because markings on the map didn't seem to match the surroundings? The first thing you must do is study the map. Look at its markings, read the legend, and understand the scale. Check the date. If the map is old, there may be changes, especially in manmade features.

Once familiar with the map, orientate it with the real world by aligning north on the map with true north. (The sections in this chapter on "Using a Compass" and "Using Celestial Bodies" will help you do this.)

Identify on the map where you are and where you must go. In planning the best course for traveling consider efficiency, in terms of time and effort; safety; and the potential for rescue. Plan when and where you will stop and what arrangements you will make for water, shelter, and food. Don't overestimate your endurance nor underestimate the difficulty of the terrain. The best speed in this situation is usually a slow, deliberate pace.

Using a Compass

A compass, even a cheap one, is a sensitive instrument that must be handled correctly or it will give erroneous readings. The compass is a magnet that should align itself with the magnetic field of the earth, but a metal object close to the compass will attract the magnet needle and distort the compass reading. Also, you must realize that the compass points to "magnetic north" rather than "true north".

Accounting for Variation. True north is the direction toward the North Pole, which is the north axis about which the earth spins. This is the direction used by all maps unless otherwise noted. The magnetic north pole, however, is in Canada's Northwest Territories. It drifts slowly, and navigational charts are periodically updated to account for this movement. The difference between the magnetic compass reading (which points to the

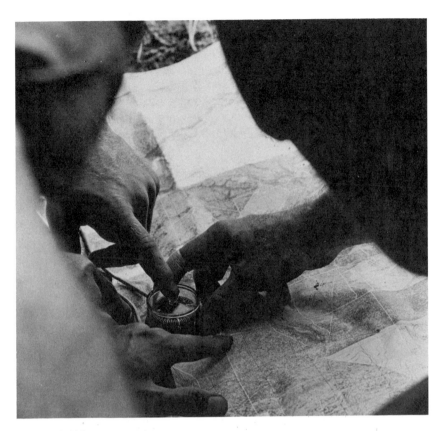

Figure 5-2. Using a map and compass

magnetic north pole) and the true direction is known as *variation*. You must be able to accurately calculate true direction from the magnetic compass reading. This is done by adding or subtracting the variation noted on the map. If the variation is *east*, then the variation is *added* to the compass reading to determine true direction. If the variation is *west*, then the variation is *subtracted* from the compass reading to arrive at true direction.

Example 1. Compass reading from present location to mountain is 120°. Map says the variation is 25° east. What is the true direction to the mountain?

120° magnetic + 25° east variation = 145° true.

Example 2. The desired direction of travel is 270° true. The map says the variation is 15° west. What should the compass reading be to get the desired true direction?

Desired compass reading − 15° = 270° true
285° magnetic − 15° west variation.

Taking a Reading. To get a proper reading, be sure the compass is level and not affected by any metal objects. Allow the compass needle to settle down. Adjust the compass so that the needle aligns to north or 360°. (To read true headings directly, the needle may be aligned to the variation noted on the map. Degrees of west variation are to the left of north, while degrees of east variation are to the right.) Sight desired landmark and note compass reading.

Using Celestial Bodies

Humans have been using the sun and stars for navigation for thousands of years, and they will serve you too.

The Sun. Although our planet spins on its axis each day, on earth it appears that the sun is going around the earth. It is easy to imagine a path on the earth's surface above which the sun travels. Since the earth's axis is not perpendicular to the sun, this path changes as the earth goes around the sun in the course of a year. During the summer, this path moves northward to 23½ degrees north latitude, while during the winter it moves southward an equal amount. With a conventional watch set to local time, you can use the sun to find rough true headings any time of the day. By pointing the hour hand of the watch toward the sun, south can be found by bisecting the angle between the hour hand and 12:00. On cloudy days, if you hold the watch so that the shadow of a matchstick held upright at the center of the watch falls along the hour hand, north will be one half the distance between the shadow and 12:00 on the watch. In the Southern Hemisphere, the directions must be reversed. Point 12:00 at the sun and true north will be halfway between that and the hour hand. If the sun is so close to overhead that this method is not productive, a stick rising from the ground will cast a shadow roughly westward in the morning and roughly eastward in the afternoon.

The Stars. In the Northern Hemisphere, the two end stars on the bowl of the Big Dipper point to the North Star (Polaris), which is the last star in the handle of the Little Dipper. The stars of the Little Dipper are quite dim and may not be visible. Polaris, fortunately, is the brightest star of the Little Dipper. You can make a rough determination of your latitude because it is approximately the same number of degrees as the height of the North Star above the horizon.

In the Southern Hemisphere, a line through the long axis of the Southern Cross points to the South Pole. There is no guiding star above it—only a blank space in the sky so dark by comparison that it is known as the Southern Coalsack.

East of the Southern Cross are two very bright stars. By using these

Figure 5-3. Big Dipper

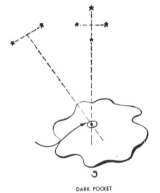

DARK POCKET

Figure 5-4. Stars of the Southern Cross that point due south

Figure 5-5. Southern Cross

and the Southern Cross as guides, you can locate a spot within the Southern Coalsack which is approximately above the South Pole.

Extend a line along the long axis of the Southern Cross, to the south. Join the two bright stars east of the Cross by a line. Bisect this line with one at right angles. The point at which this line intersects the line through the Cross is approximately above the South Pole.

Near the equator, a star rising directly east of you will pass directly overhead and set directly west. In the Northern Hemisphere, that part of the horizon where the low stars move horizontally across the sky, is the southern horizon. In the Southern Hemisphere, it is the northern horizon.

In open country you can hold a reasonably accurate course at night by selecting a fairly bright star near the horizon in your direct line of travel and continuously lining it up with trees and other skyline landmarks ahead. Since stars appear to move from east to west because of the earth's rotation, you should check your direction frequently by the North Star or Southern Cross and choose a new guide star when the old one moves out of position.

If you have a compass, check the magnetic bearing of your guide star every fifteen minutes if the star is in the general direction of north or south, or every thirty minutes if it is east or west.

ON THE MOVE

The hazards inherent in any survival situation are increased when you begin to travel. You can to some extent mitigate them by careful and thorough planning beforehand. Nevertheless, the problems you faced originally—first aid, signaling for rescue, sustenance, and shelter—accompany you even as you try to walk out of your predicament.

Traval adds to your burden, because of the constant change of a "home" base. While on the move, you must maintain the priorities of survival. You must attend promptly to injuries. You must be prepared to signal rescuers quickly. You must procure water nearly every day. Each night you must find a safe and dry place to rest. Somedays you will have to take time out from traveling to find and prepare food. Your first consideration must be to maintain physical and mental fitness.

Your best hope for a successful outcome lies in the preparation you put in before setting out. Leave a message at your point of departure, so that rescuers know in what direction to look if they find your abandoned vehicle first. Make it easy for rescuers to track you by arranging signs along your trail. Consider the terrain you will have to cross and salvage clothing and equipment that will make it easier for you. Plot a course and try to anticipate possible detours. Plan on traveling during daylight hours, although you may opt to travel at night for navigational or climatic reasons.

Leaving a Message

Before you leave the place where your plane went down or your car went off the road, or whatever, construct some sign that rescuers may follow, should they find that site before they find you. The message should be able to withstand the weather. Such a message could be scratched into the wreckage of a vehicle or on a large rock, carved in a tree, or made on the ground with rocks or debris. The more information provided in such a message, the better, but at the very least it should indicate your direction. Other information might include the date and time you left, the intentions of your group, and whether anyone was injured. Leaving a message may well cause rescuers to continue a search they might otherwise have canceled. Arrange signs en route also, so potential rescuers will be able to pick up your trail. Remember, a well-made sign will be (1) permanent, that is, not easily obliterated by weather or animals; (2) easily seen from all angles, but especially visible to potential trackers; and (3) informative, if time allows telling the number of survivors, their physical condition, direction, and destination.

Trekking through Various Terrains

Whether you choose to travel on ridges and divides or follow valleys or streams; whether you choose to follow trails or cut across country—these and many other decisions will be determined by your situation and by the vegetation and topography of the area.

Ridges and Divides. Traveling on a ridge or divide is often easier than traveling in a valley or along a stream. Vegetation is usually less dense, the ridge itself serves as a guide, outlooks are frequent, and tributary streams or swamps are few. On divides, be careful not to stray onto an intersecting ridge going in the wrong direction.

Streams and Valleys. Following a stream generally requires much fording, detouring, and penetrating of thick vegetation. In mountain country there will be falls, cliffs, and side canyons. In flat country, the stream will meander, the vegetation will be dense, outlooks rare, and swamps common. Even so, streams and valleys present many advantages in strange country, giving you a definite course that may lead to inhabited areas and providing you with a source of water and food. If you can rig up a boat or raft, you will overcome many of the disadvantages of traveling by foot along streams. Travel *down* streams to the main river course.

A strong pole can greatly help you in fording a swift stream. The pole should be about five inches in diameter and about seven or eight feet long.

Use the pole on your upstream side to break the current. Do not use it on your downstream side where the current tends to push you down on the pole and to lift your feet from under you.

Figure 5-6. Traveling along ridges or divides usually makes for easier going. (Courtesy of Melanie Barocas)

Keep the pole grasped firmly on your upstream side and firmly plant your feet with each step. Lift the pole a little ahead and downstream from its original position but still upstream from you.

Step below the pole. Keep the pole well slanted so that the force of the current keeps the pole against your shoulder.

The pole is used differently when there is more than one person. The

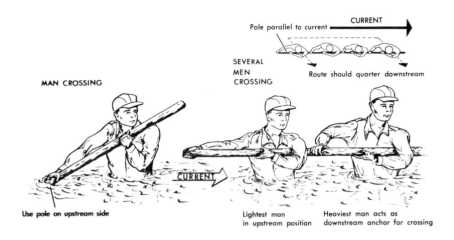

Figure 5-7. Fording a swift stream

heaviest person forms the downstream anchor with the pole held parallel to the current. The lightest person is placed at the upstream end of the pole where he breaks the current; those below move in the eddy formed by his body.

If the current comes from the right, grasp the pole under the left armpit with the right hand extended for balance. If the current comes from the left, grasp the pole under the right armpit and extend the left hand for balance. At times the upstream person may be temporarily swept from his feet, but the eddy formed by his body enables those below him to move with comparative ease.

As in all fording, the route should quarter downstream. Currents too strong for one person to stand against usually can be crossed safely in this manner.

Experience can enable you to judge water and the swiftness of its flow with greater accuracy, but there is always danger in fording. Take all possible precautions for your safety and that of your equipment. Do not worry about having a heavy pack on your back, since nothing helps more in swift water than weight—if you can release it quickly. Remember that the weight of a pack is a help and not a hindrance.

If you have a pack with you, deal with it in the following way.

(1) Remove your pants and underdrawers and lash them to the top of your pack. The water will then have less grip on your bare legs.

(2) Keep your shoes and socks on to protect your feet and ankles from boulders and to give you firmer footing.

(3) Tie important articles securely to the top of your pack. If you are forced to release your pack, you will probably find it again but you would seldom find individual articles.

(4) Shift your pack well up on your shoulders; be sure the slipnooses are working in case it is necessary to drop your pack. Prepare yourself and your gear so that, if swept off your feet, you can quickly release your pack. Unencumbered, you can then hold onto one end of the packstrap and, half-swimming and half-wading, fight your way to the far bank. Many competent swimmers have drowned because they could not get out of a heavy pack quickly enough.

Shorelines. Travel along shorelines may be easy or difficult but almost certainly will be long and circuitous. Nevertheless, a shore provides an excellent baseline (discussed below) and source of food, and it is a good place to "stick to" until you can orientate yourself and lay a course for a known objective.

Jungle Brush or Dense Woods. Move through dense vegetation in one direction but not necessarily in a straight line. Avoid obstructions instead of fighting them. Keep alert, watching your surroundings generally and the ground in front of you closely. Stop and remain motionless now and then to listen, check your bearings, and locate animals. Rest frequently. A slow, steady rate of travel with rest as needed will get you much farther than a rate that will exhaust you in a short time.

Keeping a Course

The sun by day and the stars by night are valuable guides for maintaining a course. Additionally, outstanding features of the landscape can serve as aids in keeping on course.

If possible, choose a prominent landmark in your desired direction that you can keep in sight as you move. Relate the position of the sun to yourself and the distant landmark. As you approach this landmark, line up another one farther away. In dense forests where distant landmarks can't be seen, you can hold a course by lining up three trees. As soon as you pass one of these, line up another beyond the next two. Look back occasionally to note the relative positions of landmarks and the slope and contour of the ground, for country looks entirely different when viewed from different points.

Streams, ridges, trees, and bluffs will generally guide you in open country and enable you to retrace your route if necessary. On cloudy days, in dense vegetation, or wherever the country presents a sameness of appearance, mark your trail with blazes, bent bushes, overturned logs, or rocks. Bushmarks are easily made, and should be cut or bent in such a manner that the under and lighter side of the leaves is uppermost. Such a sign is conspicuous in dense country.

Use trails when they are going in your general direction. You must look carefully for them as they may be well hidden, particularly in tropical rain forests. At a fork, take the most traveled path. Keep a lookout for traps and pitfalls on game trails.

If you lose your course or trail, stop and try to remember when you were last sure of your position. Mark the spot where you were with a pile of rocks, a bent bush, or blazes on four sides of a tree—marks you can see from some distance and any direction. Then you can start hunting or "back tracking" for your trail with the assurance that you can at least recognize the spot from which you started, should you circle or choose the wrong direction.

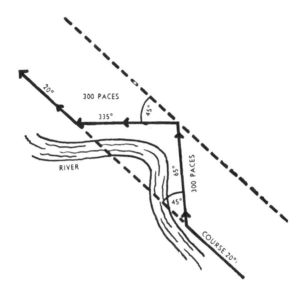

Figure 5-8. Averaging angle of departure and angle of return

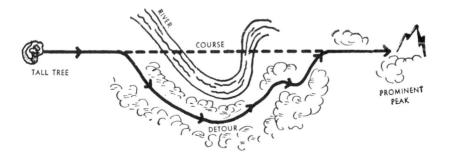

Figure 5-9. Use of landmarks

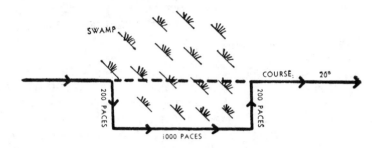

Figure 5-10. Paces and right angles

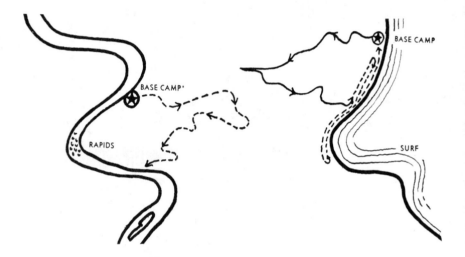

Figure 5-11. (*left*) Stream baseline; (*right*) Shore baseline

Detouring. In rough country you will have to make frequent detours, and you should know how to compensate for them to get back on your course. One way, if the detour is short, is to estimate the distance and average the angle of departure. On your return, gauge the angle and distance so as to strike your line again. For greater accuracy, count paces and use a compass.

Another method is to select a prominent landmark ahead of you and one behind you on your line of travel. On returning from your detour, walk until you are again "lined up" on the two landmarks, then follow your original course.

A third way, and very easy, is by counting paces and turning right angles, although it requires more walking.

Baselines. A baseline is a well-defined demarcation such as a river, shoreline, ridge, or well-marked path from which you can easily find your campsite or starting point. To establish a baseline, explore the intended demarcation extensively in either direction, leaving signs to help you recognize the baseline and the direction to camp from any point on it. Once the baseline is established, you may venture away from camp in any direction in search of good signaling areas, water, food, and so forth, and return by heading for the baseline. You may not know exactly where you are, but you will have a good idea as to the direction of the baseline (you either went to one side of it or the other). When you hit the baseline, the signs you've arranged will easily guide you to camp.

Traveling at Night

In most circumstances, travel at night is not advised, especially in strange wooded country. Humans are normally active during the day and sleep at night. Our senses and physiology are geared to this schedule. Unless the geography indicates it, travel at night only in an emergency. In open or desert country, however, the moon and stars may make navigating easier and the ground presents less dangers. In fact, nighttime might be the only time to travel in a desert.

Use a light at night only to read a map or compass or in particularly rough or dangerous spots. Your eyes will adjust to darkness in a short time, while with a light you are blinded to everything outside the small area of illumination.

CHAPTER 6

Environmental Hazards

Physical and biological hazards can take a heavy toll of stranded persons, even when water and food are available. The ability to evaluate and surmount these hazards will give you confidence, diminish your hardships, and help you survive a longer time.

PHYSICAL HAZARDS

Physical hazards are those dangers posed by the geographic features of a place. Sun, heat, cold, snow, and water are aspects of nature we often take for granted, but when we are stripped of the normal accoutrements of civilization, they can often make their presence felt in no uncertain terms. Nevertheless, there are ways to circumvent their dangers, even with limited resources.

Effects of Sunlight and Heat

Sunburn. Sunburn prevention is much easier than treatment. Many people do not realize that sunburn is not felt until several hours after the exposure. If you wait until your skin turns pink or red or feels hot before covering it, it will already be too late. Hazy, overcast days are sometimes worse than sunny days because there is much reflected light yet little warning warmth from the sun. Cool breezes blowing off the water can also keep you from realizing how burned you're getting. Danger of severe sunburn is greatest on mountain snowfields, open water, desert sands, and beaches. Special care should be taken during the middle hours of the day when the sun's rays are strongest.

A "sunburn powder" of lime can be made by burning seashells or coral in an open fire and then crushing them. Mix the powder with water or oil and apply it as a paste over your face and body—for protection, not as a cure. Coconut oil (made by exposing coconut meat to the sun) is also a good sunburn preventive. The best preventive is to keep covered as much as possible with clothing or a makeshift covering.

For sunburn treatment, use the burn ointment and dressing in the first aid kit. Tannic acid is effective in treatment of severe sunburn. Gather the

Figure 6-1. When you enter a harsh environment, such as a desert, be prepared to counter the region's physical and biological hazards.

Figure 6-2. Improvised glasses protect eyes from glare.

dark brown bark from a tree, boil it, and then apply the solution to the burn. Inner bark of oak, hemlock, or chestnut wood and all parts of the mangrove tree are particularly rich in tannic acid. Boil betel nuts. They contain a high percentage of tannin. Also, the aloe plant is effective in treating sunburn and other burns. Cut the stalk or stems and rub them on the burn.

Eye inflammation. Extended exposure to the sun can adversely affect your eyes. Wear sunglasses, or improvise shading for the eyes. Small slits cut into a headband and soot rubbed beneath your eyes will help reduce light reflection. Glare affects your depth vision and can hinder your adaption to night vision. Severe headaches are often indirectly due to excessive glare and exposure to sun. Eye inflammation often occurs among survivors at sea. It may be caused by exposure to wind, cold, water glare, saltwater, or a combination of these. Protect the eyes at the first sign of soreness. For more information on eye inflammation in specific environments, see the appropriate chapters.

Heatstroke. Also called sunstroke, heatstroke is a response to heat characterized by an extremely high body temperature and, often, a disturbance of the body's cooling mechanism—the ability to sweat. Heatstroke is a very serious medical problem, and can be fatal if not properly and *immediately* treated.

The immediate cause of heatstroke is a rise in body temperature brought about by inadequate body heat loss. It may be preceded by headaches, a feeling of malaise or excessive warmth, or bizarre or unusual behavior. The victim can lose consciousness suddenly, go into a coma, and/or develop convulsions. The skin is often hot to the touch, red, and noticeably dry, and the pulse is rapid. Shock can develop. *Both* the intensity and the duration of the fever determine the severity of the heatstroke. The key to survival is "Quick Recognition and Speedy Treatment."

Your aim in treatment is to reduce the rate of heat gain and lower the

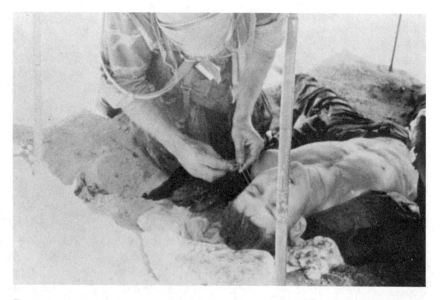

Figure 6-3. Cooling a victim of heatstroke. The victim should be in shade and insulated from hot surfaces. (Courtesy of Dr. Roger Hubbard, U.S. Army Research Institute at Natick, Mass.)

body temperature. To stop the heating-up process, the victim should immediately cease exercising, working, or even moving. He should rest in the shade, and, if necessary, insulate his body from hot surfaces. To lower the body temperature, immerse the victim in cool water, wipe with damp cloth, or fan him with whatever is available. Remember, quick action is critical. Be prepared to give CPR, as respiratory and cardiac problems may develop. Watch the victim closely for several days after his body temperature has been reduced to treat a possible relapse.

Prevention is always better than treatment, and crucial to prevention is understanding how heatstroke can develop. The rise in body temperature to a level of heatstroke risk is often caused by, for example, running, climbing, carrying heavy loads, or walking long distances without getting enough rest and water.

Exercising in hot weather causes you to sweat. In dry climates, the sweat evaporates quickly, but in wet climates the humidity limits the amount of sweat the air can absorb and thus reduces the cooling capacity of the person. Hot, humid conditions are the most likely to produce heat problems.

Possibly two or three hours of intense activity or four to six hours of moderate activity in a hot, humid setting, with inadequate fluid intake can result in progressive dehydration, steadily rising body temperature, declining sweat rate, and eventually heatstroke. You cannot depend on thirst alone to key you into your body's need for fluid. Make yourself drink, even when you don't feel thirsty. Better yet, drink up on a predetermined schedule.

A less obvious and therefore more insidious form of dehydration usually takes three to five days to occur. Its basic cause is loss of salt, which is necessary to hold water within the body. Thirst is not a symptom of this disorder, because although you may drink, the water is not retained by the kidneys. Loss of appetite, common to newcomers to hot climates, aggravates the condition by further reducing salt intake. Symptoms are usually heavy extreme fatigue, muscle cramps, nausea, vomiting, and progressive weakness. To prevent, reduce the amount of work in order to reduce sweating.

Heat Exhaustion. In the tropics, don't travel in direct sunlight without head protection. A head covering of leaves or cloth will be better than nothing. Don't overexert during the hottest hours of the day, especially if you are in poor physical condition. Heat exhaustion can result from physical work alone, even if you're not dehydrated or lacking in salt.

If the humidity is not too high, you can cool off after exertion in the heat by soaking your clothes with water. The resulting evaporation will keep you more comfortable.

Heat exhaustion is the result of intense activity of short duration in the heat or long exposure to intense heat with little or no activity. It may occur without exposure to the sun, and it can come about even in the absence of humidity.

A prominent feature of heat exhaustion is the pooling of blood in the extremities and the skin. Symptoms are different from heatstroke. The skin is clammy rather than dry, and the temperature may be normal. Treatment consists of various measures to promote the return of the blood to the heart. Have the victim lie down immediately and elevate the legs. Cooling the person will help alleviate the strain on the cardiovascular system. If the underlying cause is water or salt deprivation, drink salted water.

In addition to salt, ascorbic acid (vitamin C) is also lost through sweating. Replace it by eating citrus fruits, if available.

Effects of Cold

Regulating Heat Loss. Survival in low temperatures is a matter of balancing heat loss with the body's production of heat. You can limit heat loss to some extent by food intake and exercise, but for the most part you must rely on proper insulation (clothing) to regulate heat loss and keep you warm and alive.

Clothing should consist of a number of light garments that can be taken off or put on as needed to regulate heating and cooling. None should be tight enough to reduce blood circulation. See the chapter on survival in mountains and cold regions for more information on clothing and the effects of cold.

Outer garments should be windproof, but not so airtight as to cause excessive heat production and sweating. (Overheating is in itself deleterious, because energy and water are expended in coping with it, thus reducing overall efficiency.) Inner garments should act as insulators. They should be form-fitting, light, soft, and allowing of escape of perspiration. Shoes should be big enough to allow at least two pairs of heavy socks to be worn without compromising circulation.

Clothing is the "thermostate" by which survivors can balance heat production with heat loss. If you are overdressed and the day is calm and sunny, you may have to take off some clothes to prevent overheating. When walking or exercising lightly, removal of several layers may be necessary to prevent sweating. Control of sweating is essential, for wet clothing conducts heat from the body and increases the chance of freezing.

When keeping warm is a problem, never expose any more of the body than is absolutely necessary, since enough heat can be lost from uncovered hands, face, head, and poorly insulated feet to chill the entire body.

Frostbite. Frostbite is the freezing of tissue, complete with formation of ice crystals under the skin. Local freezing of face, feet, and hands is an ever-present danger at low temperatures.

Frozen flesh is white and stiff, while milder frostbite is dark red. Wrinkle

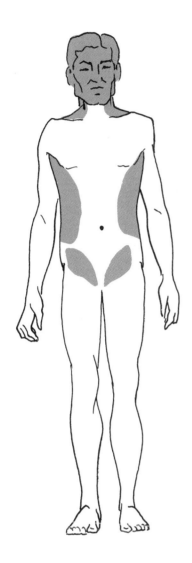

Figure 6-4. High heat loss areas of the body—the head, sides of the chest, the neck, and the groin.

the face continually to determine whether any part is frozen. Your ears are especially susceptible to frostbite. Press warm hands against them. When fingers become cold or frostbitten, warm them against the bare skin of the body. Place frozen toes against the warm flesh of a companion or cup your warm hands around them. Dry grass, moss, or feathers placed inside shoes or between socks provides insulation against frostbite. A cloth tied over your face below your eyes and allowed to hang loosely at the bottom will protect your face and allow moist breath to escape. Frostbite is espe-

Figure 6-5. A wool muffler tied around your head and allowed to hang loose at the bottom will conserve heat while allowing moist breath to escape. (Courtesy of the U.S. Coast Guard)

cially apt to occur when traveling into a wind. A 60-mile wind at 0°F feels colder and does more damage than a 15-mile wind at −30° or a calm wind at −50°F. Wind blows body heat away. Wild animals seek shelter in a cold wind, and you should do the same.

If you do develop frostbite, don't rub frozen parts or expose them to dry heat. Rubbing will break the skin and lead to infection. Thaw frozen parts rapidly in warm water. Remember that:

(1) Temperatures are often warmer below the snow than above it and any windbreak will help conserve body heat.

(2) Generally, hollows and valleys will be colder than protected slopes and ridges.

(3) Lowest temperatures occur during clear, still weather. Temperatures usually rise during a blizzard or snowstorm.

(4) Plenty of rest and food are most important in cold regions. Never travel when exhausted. Take frequent rests, and sleep when you feel the need. Unless you are sick, wounded, or exhausted, the cold will awaken you before you freeze. Food is required for exercise.

(5) For temporary rest and protection, dig a pocket in the snow and sit in it with your back to the wind and your arms pulled out of your sleeves and wrapped against your body for warmth. Do not sit directly on the snow if you can place something under yourself.

(6) If you get wet in extremely cold weather, make a fire immediately in

the most sheltered spot available to dry out. If you cannot make a fire, you should keep moving until your body heat has warmed and dried the inner garments.

(7)   Breathe only through the nose. This will warm the air before it reaches the lungs and reduce the danger of cooling the inner body.

(8)   Water is most important in preventing dehydration, improving circulation, and regulating temperature.

(9)   When the whole body has been exposed to cold, exercise and massage the limbs to increase circulation and consume something warm as soon as possible.

Hypothermia. The word *hypothermia* comes from the Greek *hypo* meaning low and *therme* meaning heat. Today it denotes a condition of lowered internal body core temperature caused by overexposure to a cold environment.

Cold has always been a killer of man. Most fatalities from hypothermia arise from water-related incidents, but hypothermia is an obvious danger in mountains and cold regions, too. Other conditions such as dehydration, physical exhaustion, injury, illness, and hunger can aggravate the situation and make the symptoms more pronounced. Elderly, small, or thin people, or those suffering emotional distress are more likely than others to suffer from hypothermia.

Figure 6-6. Construct a good shelter early and use it. Make use of natural windbreaks. (Courtesy of Dr. Murray Hamlet, U.S. Army Research Institute at Natick, Mass.)

Cooling Power of Wind Expressed as "Equivalent Chill Temperature"

Wind Speed (Knots)	MPH	\	Temperature (°F)																			
	Calm		Calm 40	35	30	25	20	15	10	5	0	-5	-10	-15	-20	-25	-30	-35	-40	-45	-50	-55	-60
			Equivalent Chill Temperature																				
3-6	5		35	30	25	20	15	10	5	0	-5	-10	-15	-20	-25	-30	-35	-40	-45	-50	-55	-65	-70
7-10	10		30	20	15	10	5	0	-10	-15	-20	-25	-35	-40	-45	-50	-60	-65	-70	-75	-80	-90	-95
11-15	15		25	15	10	0	-5	-10	-20	-25	-30	-40	-45	-50	-60	-65	-70	-80	-85	-90	-100	-105	-110
16-19	20		20	10	5	0	-10	-15	-25	-30	-35	-45	-50	-60	-65	-75	-80	-85	-95	-100	-110	-115	-120
20-23	25		15	10	0	-5	-15	-20	-30	-35	-45	-50	-60	-65	-75	-80	-90	-95	-105	-110	-120	-125	-135
24-28	30		10	5	0	-10	-20	-25	-30	-40	-50	-55	-65	-70	-80	-85	-95	-100	-110	-115	-125	-130	-140
29-32	35		10	5	-5	-10	-20	-30	-35	-40	-50	-60	-65	-75	-80	-90	-100	-105	-115	-120	-130	-135	-145
33-36	40		10	0	-5	-15	-20	-30	-35	-45	-55	-60	-70	-75	-85	-95	-100	-110	-115	-125	-130	-140	-150

Winds Above 40 Have Little Additional Effect

Little Danger
(for properly clothed person)

Increasing Danger
(Flesh may freeze within 1 min.)

Great Danger
(Flesh may freeze within 30 seconds)

Danger of Freezing Exposed Flesh for Properly Clothed Persons

Figure 6-7. The cooling power of the wind expressed as "Equivalent Chill Temperature," and the danger of freezing exposed flesh. Source: USAF Air Weather Service (MAC)

The key to prevention of hypothermia is good protective clothing; there is no substitute for preparation. A windbreaker with wool lining or down-filled clothing will provide good protection. Wool retains most of its insulating properties even when wet, and wool headgear is highly recommended, as most of the body heat is lost through the head. Avoid alcohol and other depressant drugs, because they lower the body's metabolic rate and core temperature. Avoid coffee and tea because they are diuretics. Drink a large volume of warm to hot liquid and eat hot food. Avoid exercising unnecessarily. Construct a good shelter early and use it. If you're forced to survive in the cold, keep your clothing dry and cover all exposed skin. Avoid the additional chilling effect of wind by making use of natural windbreaks such as trees, hillsides, and large rocks. Cover your mouth and nose with several layers of clothing to prevent excessive loss of heat through respiration. With careful thought and advance planning, you can survive in cold areas and avoid hypothermia.

The onset of hypothermia in a companion may be hard to perceive. You must be on the lookout to detect the early symptoms, which include:
- dullness
- mild uncoordination
- passivity
- uncommunicativeness
- shivering
- lagging behind the group.

It is possible to see it coming in yourself; you will make simple mistakes, be uncoordinated, and shiver.

As the body core temperature continues to drop, the respiratory rate, which had speeded up, gradually diminishes, and shivering is replaced by muscular rigidity. The pulse slows and becomes irregular. The skin is pale and cold to the touch. There can be disruptions to one's perceptional abilities. Late in the illness, delusions can develop. Victims often fluctuate in their level of consciousness, although deep, prolonged unconsciousness is possible. It is difficult for scientists to document, but it seems that people can be unconscious eight to ten hours with no bad after-effects.

The field treatment of a hypothermic varies with the level of consciousness of the victim. If the victim is awake, insulate his or her body from further heat loss. Provide dry clothing, if possible. Give warm, sweet drinks, a good many of them, but not coffee, tea, or alcohol, which are diuretic. Shelter the victim from the cold and wind—with tree boughs or in a snow cave, for example. Gentle, moderate exercise is recommended. Buddy warming is good, as well, but warm sweet drinks are more effective. Warming in front of a camp fire helps, too.

The treatment of a comatose victim is different from that of an awake hypothermic—and much more subject to controversy. Everyone agrees that the unconscious person must be handled with great care and gentleness when moved, but the controversy centers on whether an unconscious hypothermic, with no detectable vital signs, should be given CPR. Some hypothermia advisors say that in a field setting, the need for CPR is too difficult to determine with any precision and the administration too difficult to carry out. However, the U.S. Navy, as well as the Coast Guard, the Air Force, the Red Cross, and many rescue agencies and medical authorities do recommend the administration of CPR to those with no pulse and respirations. As Commander Alan M. Steinman, medical officer for the Search and Rescue Division of the U.S. Coast Guard, writes:

> . . . the indications for the administration of CPR to victims of accidental hypothermia are precisely the same as for . . . normothermic patients. Whenever a patient is found who has no detectable pulse or respirations, it *must* be assumed that this patient is in cardiopulmonary arrest. In hypothermia, however, more time (up to a full minute) should be devoted to the assessment of these vital signs.

Treatment of a comatose victim can be summarized as follows:
(1)   Handle carefully.
(2)   Insulate the body, providing warmth (to stabilize, not to raise, the body core temperature) by means of buddy warming or hot rocks wrapped in cloth and applied to the head, neck, trunk, and groin.
(3)   Check long and carefully for pulse and respirations.
(4)   If no detectable vital signs, administer CPR if it does not put you at risk. It is extremely rare that CPR will cause a severe hypothermic to recover pulse or respiration on his own. In a survival situation, once you commit to CPR you must continue to administer it for as long as you are able to or until help arrives.

Effects of Water

Saltwater Sores. Long exposure to saltwater (as when adrift in a boat or a raft) may result in sores and swelling. Fats or greases—obtained by drying out fish and bird guts in the sun—will help prevent saltwater sores, as will frequent washing with fresh water. If boils have already developed, do not break them open but try to keep them dry and clean.

Immersion Foot. Continued immersion of the feet in cold or icewater (60°F or below) or by continued hiking in wet, cold footgear causes a condition known as immersion foot. Pain is followed by swelling and numbness, and blisters and sores may develop. The best preventive is to keep feet as dry as possible (dry out socks and shoes) and to exercise your feet regularly. Don't wear tight boots or socks that bind the legs. In treatment, don't rub or apply direct heat and avoid breaking the skin. Raise the legs above body level and apply cold compresses or packs, keeping a layer of dry material between the compress and the feet to avoid wetting them again.

BIOLOGICAL HAZARDS

Biology refers to the plant and animal life of a region, and biological dangers are those that arise because of the presence of certain harmful plants or animals.

Size is not a reliable indication of the degree of danger; a malaria-carrying mosquito can be as deadly as a maddened elephant—and much more likely to be encountered. For the smaller the organism, generally, the more plentiful its kind and the greater your chances of meeting it. In combatting biological hazards, discretion is the better part of valor. If you can avoid the disease-carrier or predator, you will escape the danger.

If you know you will be going to an area where insect-borne diseases exist, you will want to supplement the general information in this section with specific information from your physician. You don't need to know a great deal about the workings of the diseases themselves, but you will want to ask about the presence, transmission, and prevention of diseases endemic to the place you are traveling to. Your primary concern is to learn about the parasite-carriers that are responsible for getting the disease-causing organisms into the human body. You will also want to receive all inoculations against diseases common to areas you are likely to be traveling to or stranded in.

The Smaller Forms of Life

Arthropods are small animals with jointed appendages or legs. Insects, centipedes, spiders, ticks, and crustaceans are all arthropods. Like all life, these small animals require certain environmental conditions for their existence. Some forms are widely distributed and others are localized, and the habits of many make it easy to avoid them. They may not be able to live in bright sunlight, or they may come out only during the day or only at night. They may not range far from their breeding areas, or may be limited in altitude or in latitude by their inability to survive low temperatures. Lack of proper breeding places will limit their numbers. Because of all these factors, you will have to take precautions against a limited number of these disease carriers at any one time or place.

A carrier that may be dangerous under certain circumstances or in a particular area may be perfectly harmless at another time or place. Frequently the particular disease organisms which they transmit to humans by their bite must at some time in the course of their life pass through other animals or hosts. When these hosts are specific, nothing else will do. In such cases, if the hosts are absent, the disease organism cannot be transmitted, no matter how many potential carriers are present. Malaria is a good example of a disease requiring a specific carrier and a specific host.

Mosquitoes. Mosquitoes may be found in any area with standing fresh or brackish water, including Arctic and temperate regions. Most dangerous mosquitoes are found in the tropics, however, where they transmit malaria, yellow fever, dengue fever, and filariasis. But even in the temperate climate of most of the United States, mosquitoes can carry encephalitis. Bites from some species may be merely unpleasant, but if you are exposed to these in large numbers over a long period they can lead to delirium and even death.

To protect yourself, rig up a head net, as the face and neck are usually the most difficult parts of the body to protect. You can improvise head and neck protection by using, for example, an undershirt or T-shirt. Tie the arm and neck holes shut with a strip of cloth or string. Pad the top of your head with wide palm leaves, bark, or similar material to prevent the cloth from touching your skin. Pull the shirt over your head, cut small slits for your eyes, and stuff the bottom under your shirt collar.

Mosquitoes can bite through light clothing. Keep clothing loose, padded with vegetation, leaves, bark, and so forth. Button down or tie at the wrists and ankles.

Apply insect repellent. Campfire smoke may also help keep the pests at bay. Take advantage of any breezy spot or attempt to evade them by seeking higher ground or by climbing a tree.

Mud placed on exposed parts of the body will offer some protection. A paste made of sunscreen, insect repellent ointment, and ground-up aspirin will help control itching.

Mosquitoes and Malaria. Malaria is common in tropical climates where humans live and where fresh or brackish water accumulates. It can also be contracted during the summer in temperate regions, but is not found in the cool climates of the northern and southern hemispheres. Symptoms include chills and sweats, headache, bone pain, and enlargement of the liver and spleen. Although antimalarial vaccines are under development, they are not readily available and are effective only against one of the four sorts of human malarias. Drugs in tablet form, however, are readily available (by prescription only in the United States) and are effective.

Malaria is transmitted to humans by some species of infected *Anopheles* mosquitoes. The disease itself is caused by a microscopic protozoan (*Plasmodium*) which is injected into the bloodstream through the bite of an infected mosquito. You can identify an *Anopheles* mosquito by the fact that it rests with its tail end pointing upward at an angle. Its wings tend to be spotted. It is active only in the early evening and at night, but it is a good idea to take precautions in dark or shaded areas, particularly on cloudy days. Because the mosquito feeds at night, you should in malarial regions

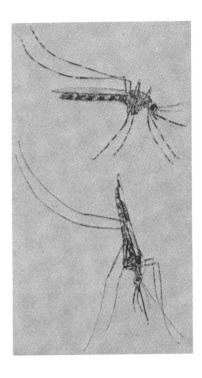

Figure 6-8. *Anopheles* mosquito

make camp and arrange your mosquito netting well before dark. Since malaria is most often contracted during sleep, you should always protect yourself with a net.

Mosquitoes and Filariasis. The term *filariasis* covers several infections caused by various species of nematode or roundworm. These are transmitted to humans by bloodsucking insects, such as mosquitoes, and also blackflies. Symptoms include swelling, pain, intense itching, destruction of the skin, and blindness.

Mosquitoes and Yellow and Dengue Fevers. The *Aedes aegypti* mosquito is largely responsible for transmission of yellow fever and dengue fever. Unlike the malaria-carrying *Anopheles*, yellow-fever-carrying *Aedes* are likely to bite during daylight hours.

A vaccination is available to protect against yellow fever, common in West Africa and in parts of Central and South America.

Dengue fever, which is weakening but seldom fatal, is widespread in the tropics and subtropics.

Aedes aegypti females which transmit the diseases seldom range more than a few hundred yards from the pools of water (discarded tires, tree hollows, and the like) where their larvae develop. They are especially abundant near human habitations.

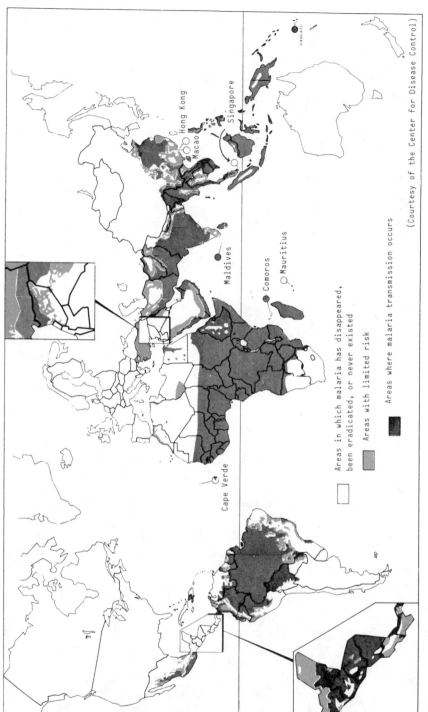

Figure 6-9. Epidemiological Assessment of the Status of Malaria, 1981

(Courtesy of the Center for Disease Control)

Areas in which malaria has disappeared,
been eradicated, or never existed

Areas with limited risk

Areas where malaria transmission occurs

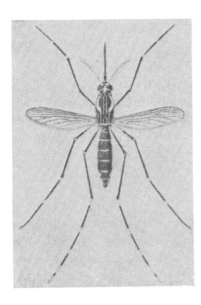

Figure 6-10. *Aedes* mosquito

Flies. Flies vary greatly in size, in breeding habits, and in the discomfort or danger they can cause humans. Some are vicious biters and the larvae of others infest wounds or even unbroken skin. Many contaminate food.

Like mosquitoes, some flies are active only at night, others only by day, and still others roam both day and night. In general, protective measures against mosquitoes will be effective against flies, although some fly pests, such as the sand fly and the no-see-ums or punkies, are so small that they will go through ordinary mosquito netting. Many such pests are limited in range to comparatively short distances from their breeding areas, so you can escape them by moving out of the vicinity.

Black flies or buffalo gnats can cause discomfort or danger, can transmit filarid worms, and are found throughout the world in wet forested areas, particularly in the vicinity of running water. Various biting deer flies and horse flies are abroad only in the day and may be numerous in regions where there are hoofed animals. They are stout-bodied and usually brightly colored. No-see-ums or punkies are tiny mottle-winged flies, which are found in fresh and salt wet areas throughout the world. They have an itching bite. Some species may carry filarid worms. If these gnats are abundant, move on; they are often local in distribution and are seldom encountered more than a half mile from their breeding areas.

Sand flies are tiny mothlike flies that bite at night. They breed in humid places out of the sun and wind, such as crevices in trees and rocks. They can pass through ordinary netting and are disease transmitters in such widely separated areas as Colombia and the Peruvian Andes, the Mediter-

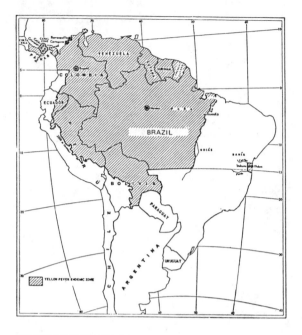

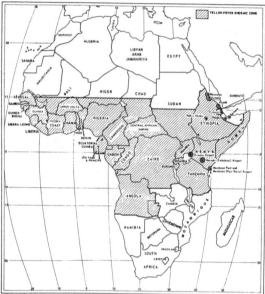

Figure 6-11. (*top*) Yellow Fever Endemic Zones in the Americas; (*bottom*) Yellow Fever Endemic Zones in Africa
NOTE: Although the "yellow fever endemic zones" are no longer included in the International Health Regulations, a number of countries (most of them being not bound by the regulations or bound with reservations) consider these zones as infected areas and require an International Certificate of Vaccination against yellow fever from travelers arriving from those areas. (Courtesy of the Center for Disease Control)

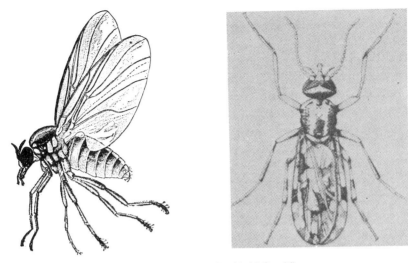

Figure 6-12. (*left*) Black fly; (*right*) Sand fly

Figure 6-13. (*left*) Tsetse fly; (*center*) Human bot fly; (*right*) Human bot larva

ranean, India, Sri Lanka, and China. They transmit verruga, pappataci, and kala-azar fever. These flies seldom fly more than ten feet above the ground and dislike air currents. Sleep off the ground or in a breeze.

Tsetse flies are found only in central and south tropical Africa. While some species transmit a sleeping sickness that may be fatal, the proportion of those infected is very small and so is the chance of contracting the disease. All require shade, usually bite only during the daytime, and prefer

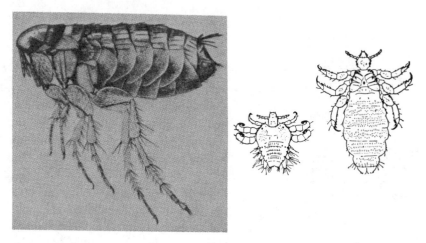

Figure 6-14. (*left*) Flea; (*right*) Lice

dark-skinned victims over those with light skin. Avoid the forested and brushy borders of bodies of water in areas of possible tsetse fly infection.

Screwworm flies are found in the Americas and southern Asia, especially the tropics, and are most likely to be abundant in the vicinity of unburied corpses and animal carcasses. They are active during the day and often deposit their eggs in wounds where the larvae feed on the living tissue. Danger is greatest when sleeping in the open as the flies deposit their eggs in the nostrils, particularly if these passages are irritated by colds or wounds. The larvae burrow into the nasal tissues causing severe pain and swelling. Stupefy the maggots with chloroform, then remove them with forceps. Where these flies are numerous, don't sleep during the day in the open without covering the face or using a net.

Blowflies with somewhat similar habits may be encountered in parts of Africa, India, Australia, and the East Indies.

Bot fly larvae bore into the skin producing painful swellings and boil-like lesions. Apply tobacco to the open boil to kill the larvae and squeeze them out without breaking them.

Fleas. Fleas are small wingless insects that move about by jumping and that live on warm-blooded animals.

In some areas their bites may transmit extremely dangerous diseases such as plague and endemic typhus. Fleas that live on rodents, particularly rats, can transmit plague to man after feeding on plague-ridden rodents. Plague, a fatal bacterial disease, is apt to be contracted only in regions where epidemics are flourishing. It persists among wild rodent populations in various parts of the world, and occasionally breaks out in epidemic proportions.

If you must make use of rodents as food in plague-suspect areas, hang the animals up as soon as they are killed and do not handle them until they get cold. Fleas will soon leave dead animals. But be careful. When normal rodent hosts are unavailable, rodent fleas will readily attack man.

The tiny chigoe, jigger or sand flea occurs in immense numbers in tropical and subtropical countries, particularly in dust near human habitations. The females burrow into the skin usually on the legs, feet, and under the toenails where they produce painful sores. The flea appears as a black speck under the skin, usually between the toes and the soles of the feet, and may be dug out with a sterilized needle or knife.

Precautions against fleas include use of derris or louse powder, and (in areas of sand flea infestation) wearing tight-fitting leggings or boots.

Lice. Lice or cooties are wingless insects that live and feed on birds and mammals. Head, body, and pubic lice infest humans living under unsanitary, crowded conditions. You need not worry about becoming infested with them in the wild. Their greatest danger lies in transmission of such diseases as typhus, trench fever, and relapsing fever. Disease does not come from the bite itself, but from scratching and thus rubbing the germs into tiny skin abrasions.

Both the lice and their eggs, which may be deposited on hair or clothing, must be killed. Control measures include use of louse powder, exposure of clothing to direct sunlight for a few hours, washing frequently in hot, soapy water, or leaving clothing near an anthill, since certain types of ants feed freely on lice and their eggs.

Bedbugs. Bedbugs are brown, wingless bugs with flattened bodies, which are found throughout the world but are most abundant in temperate regions. They feed at night, on human blood when available, and have a characteristic, disagreeable odor. They will leave bedding spread in bright sunlight.

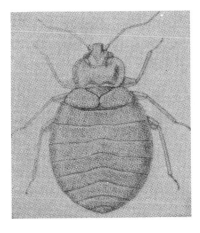

Figure 6-15. Bedbugs

Ticks. Ticks are distributed over much of the world and are especially numerous in the tropics and subtropics.

The hard or wood ticks are found chiefly in wooded or brushy areas; the soft or leathery ticks in caves, around rocky ledges, and in the nests and burrows of animals. Both types may transmit disease, but fortunately the percentage of infected ticks is in most areas extremely small.

Hard ticks, which may cause secondary infection or transmit Rocky Mountain spotted fever or tularemia, are reasonably easy to guard against. In temperate regions they are numerous only in late spring and summer and are found in the woods away from direct sunlight. They are most common along a path or trail. Since it takes several hours for most hard ticks to bite, a thorough check of your body and clothing two or three times a day will eliminate the danger of disease infection.

Soft ticks bite quickly and fill with blood in ten to sixty minutes. They may transmit relapsing fever, a weakening but usually not fatal disease.

In examining your body for ticks, look particularly at the base of the head, at hairy portions of the body such as under the arms or in the groin, and where clothing is tight. Don't crush them on the body, for you must be sure to get the head out or it may cause infection. A lighted cigarette or match held close to the tick's body will cause it to loosen its grip and it can then be removed intact. Kerosene or oil will have the same effect. In tick-infested areas, avoid sitting on fallen logs and wear trousers tucked into boots.

Rocky Mountain spotted fever is found in many areas of the United States but particularly in the Rocky Mountain regions. It has a high mor-

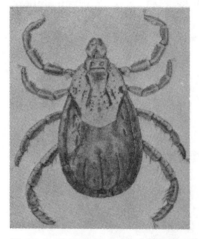
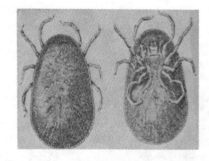

Figure 6-16. (*left*) Hard tick; (*right*) Soft ticks

tality rate but is comparatively rare. Closely related tick-borne diseases occur in the Mediterranean area, Brazil, and elsewhere. Tularemia, a bacterial disease of rodents which can be contracted either from insect bites or through contact with infected animals, is present in the United States, Europe, Japan, and Russia, but is nowhere very common. Don't handle, prepare, or eat rodents that were noticeably sick or very sluggish when killed.

Mites and Chiggers. Mites and chiggers are tiny arthropods, some almost invisible to the human eye, which cause annoyance and irritation through their bites or through diseases transmitted by them. They include the human itch mite which causes various skin diseases such as scabies, Norwegian itch, and barber's itch; and the harvest mites or chiggers, which cause irritating sores and may transmit Japanese river or Kedani fever in certain areas of the Far East, including the South Pacific Islands. Human itch mites infest the skin and live beneath the scabby crusts made by their burrowing and feeding.

Washing in strong soap followed by application of sulphur ointments will help eliminate mites and chiggers. To protect against chiggers before exposure, dust fine sulphur or louse powder on the skin and inside clothing, particularly around the ankles. Tucking trousers into boots will also help.

Human itch mites are particularly prevalent in areas where people live in crowded or unsanitary conditions.

Spiders. Spiders in general are not particularly dangerous. Even the much-advertised tarantula is not known to bite with fatal or even serious side effects. The black widow or hourglass spider of the southern half of the United States, together with tropical members of the same genus, should be avoided as their bites cause severe pain and swelling. All are of a dark color and marked with white, yellow, or red spots. A black widow spider bite is normally not felt immediately, but two tiny red spots usually occur with severe pain felt two or three minutes later.

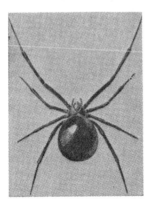

Figure 6-17. (*left*) Black widow spider; (*right*) Scorpion

Scorpions. Scorpions are usually small but some can be long as a human hand. They sting with their tail spine, but usually only when molested. Their stings are extremely painful, but seldom fatal. Since they hide in the daytime and are active at night, they may take refuge from light in shoes or clothing. In areas where they are found, shake out clothing well and knock shoes, bottom up, before putting them on.

Centipedes and Caterpillars. Many-legged centipedes, found under logs, stones, or leaves, are numerous in the tropics. Their bites are poisonous but rarely serious.

Numerous hairy or spiny caterpillars will cause severe itching and inflammation if brushed against the skin.

Bees, Wasps, and Hornets. They usually sting only in defense of themselves or their nests. The stings of an aroused swarm may be dangerous and even fatal. Varieties in the tropics range from small, stingless bees to large, militant varieties whose hives should be avoided even when in desperate need of food. In most cases, use of a smoke smudge to stupefy the bees, together with a head and hand covering, will permit you to take honey safely.

Some tropical ants sting severely and attack in numbers, but they can be easily avoided by moving.

Some people are much more susceptible than others to poisoning from stings. To susceptible individuals even a single sting may be serious. Applications of wet mud, ammonia, or soda will relieve the irritation. Juice from the leaves of climbing hemp weed—found near streams, swamps and seashores in parts of the Americas, Africa, and the South Pacific—is a good antidote for stings.

Leeches. Blood-sucking land leeches are common in very wet areas, particularly during the rainy season in Borneo, Sumatra, India, Sri Lanka, the Philippines, the South Pacific Islands, Thailand, Malaysia, Australia,

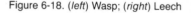
Figure 6-18. (*left*) Wasp; (*right*) Leech

and various parts of South America. Leeches found in mud and shallow water in other areas of the world are not apt to be numerous.

Leeches cling to blades of grass, leaves, and twigs and fasten themselves onto any passing individual. Leeches may be picked up through your shoe eyelets or over the tops of your shoes. Protect yourself by wearing socks and by tucking trousers inside tightly laced boots.

Bites may cause intense discomfort and loss of blood and may be followed by infection. If embedded in your skin, smother it with mud, a ground salt tablet, or tobacco juice or apply direct heat (such as a lighted match or cigarette). As a last resort, you can pull it off. Leeches can cause severe trouble if swallowed in drinking water.

Flukes or Flatworms. Blood flukes or flatworms, human parasites, are found in sluggish fresh water in Africa, parts of tropical America, Asia, Japan, Formosa, the Philippines and other Pacific islands. There is little danger in areas remote from human habitation or in saltwater. The flukes pass through part of their lifecycle in mollusks, usually snails, and the forms which emerge from the snails penetrate the skins of people who drink or bathe in infested water. They live in the blood vessels, feed on blood cells, and escape painfully through the bladder or the feces.

Hookworm. Hookworm is common in the tropics and subtropics. The larvae are usually acquired by going barefooted in areas where human excrement is found. There is no danger from hookworm in wilderness areas, away from human habitation.

Fungus Infections. Parasitic skin diseases (athlete's foot is one) are common in the tropics. They occur most frequently in the armpits, in the groin, and on the feet. The best protection is to wash and change your clothes, particularly shoes and socks, frequently and to bathe often with plenty of soap. To treat an infection, wash with strong soap, soak the affected part in saltwater, and use approved disinfectants as available. Such infections are incapacitating and difficult to cure.

Snakes

Fear of snakes is out of all proportion to the facts. Common sense dictates a healthy respect for the poisonous varieties, but no more than to cause survivors to take normal precautions. Cases of bites by poisonous snakes are relatively rare. In fact harmless species are more prone to attack than are poisonous ones, and although their bites do not carry venom, they can lead to infection.

Nowhere are poisonous snakes common or numerous over wide areas. Most of them are seclusive and timid, disappearing at the slightest disturbance. The majority of bites are by snakes which are suddenly surprised, stepped on, or grasped.

While the tropics contain the greatest variety of snakes, the danger in tropical jungles is actually less than in rattlesnake- and moccasin-infested areas of the United States. If you know a few facts about the habits of snakes, and the general and specific areas where they may be found, you can take normal precautions, give warning of your coming, and forget about fear of snakes.

General precautionary rules are:

(1)   Keep alert, particularly when climbing steep, rocky slopes.

(2)   Never tease or pick up a strange snake in a strange country. (This warning may seem unnecessary, but violation of it is the cause of many snakebites.)

(3)   Protect vulnerable portions of the body, particularly feet and legs. Even light clothing is an excellent protection against many poisonous snakes.

(4)   Many snakes roam at night, so cut down on night travel in snake country.

(5)   Learn the types, distributions, and habits of poisonous snakes, especially those indigenous to any area you may be traveling through.

(6)   Know the symptoms and emergency treatment of snakebite.

Snakes are cold-blooded meat eaters and live only in the temperate and tropic regions. Only two hundred of the twenty-four hundred different kinds of snakes are dangerous to people, and most of these will avoid humans if given a chance. Only in Australia do the poisonous species outnumber the harmless ones.

Some areas of the world are entirely free of poisonous land snakes, including Madagascar, New Zealand, the Polynesian Islands, Cuba, Jamaica, Haiti, Puerto Rico, the Azores, the Canary and Cape Verde Islands, and Hawaii. While most sea snakes (distinguishable by their paddlelike tails) are poisonous, they do not attack humans unless forcibly restrained, and they do not exist in the Atlantic area.

Most poisonous snakes are confined to particular habitats. In such places take every precaution and move out of the area if possible. At the very least, avoid places where snakes would be hard to see. Snakes cannot stand extremes of either heat or cold. In temperate regions they are active day and night during the warmer months, but hibernate or become inactive in cold weather. In desert and semi-desert regions, snakes are most active during early morning and evening. During the heat of the day, they lie in the shade. Give warning of your approach when you seek shade, scan the ground before you stop to rest, and travel in the open as much as possible. Many poisonous snakes are active only at night. When traveling in the dark, use a light, move slowly, and avoid brushy areas.

Snakes with few exceptions travel slowly, though many can strike very rapidly. They cannot outrun a person, and only a few can leap entirely off

Figure 6-19. (*top*) Rattlesnake; (*bottom*) Copperhead. (Courtesy of the National Zoo)

the ground or strike as far as their own length. A sharp blow with a stick will break the vertebral column of average-sized snakes. All snakes can swim and some can remain underwater a long time without drowning. The danger of being bitten by a poisonous snake is extremely small, almost nonexistent except in certain types of country and under certain conditions. Limited distribution, variations in habits and habitats, small numbers, and the mechanism of venom-transfer combine to mean that you are very unlikely to encounter and be bitten by a poisonous snake. Even if you do come across one, the seclusive and timid nature of snakes will most of the time lead it to slither off silently, out of your way.

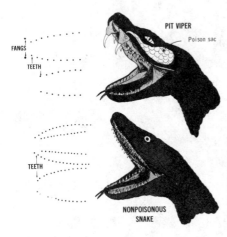

Figure 6-20. Different characteristics of pit viper family and nonpoisonous species. With the exception of the coral snake, all poisonous snakes native to the United States are pit vipers with fangs, triangular-shaped heads, slit eyes, three rows of overlapping scales beneath the eyes, and a "pit" or depression between each eye and nostril.

There are no characteristics common to all poisonous snakes, and considerable training is necessary to be able to distinguish with certainty poisonous from harmless species. Generally speaking, most poisonous snakes have fangs and two rows of teeth; nonpoisonous snakes typically have four to six rows of teeth without fangs—although who wants to get close enough to check? It is much easier simply to learn which poisonous snakes are likely in a particular area.

Colubridae. Represented by such familiar snakes as blacksnakes and gartersnakes, the Colubridae family contains nearly two-thirds of the known species of snakes. None are poisonous except some of the rear-fanged snakes of Africa and southern Asia.

Poisonous Long-Fanged Snakes. The true vipers and the pit vipers are long-fanged venomous snakes. Most of them are thick-bodied with a distinctly flattened head. Many have keeled scales that give them a dull appearance as compared with the polished or satiny appearance of smooth-scaled snakes.

The pit vipers include all the dangerous poisonous snakes of North America except the coral snake. They inhabit both the Eastern and Western Hemispheres, but the most numerous and the largest species are in the Americas. All have a deep pit between the eyes and nostril which is *not* easily seen, even at close range.

This family includes the various species of rattlesnakes, all dangerous and all confined to the Western Hemisphere, with the majority of species found in the United States and Mexico. The water moccasin is semiaquatic, inhabiting sluggish waters in the southern United States. Other pit vipers include the bushmaster of central and tropical South America; the fer-de-lance, a night prowler of southern Mexico and tropical South America; the arboreal palm vipers of Mexico, Central and South America (which frequently inhabit low trees or bushes and palm or banana trees); and the bamboo snakes of Asia.

True vipers are thick-bodied poisonous snakes found only in the Eastern Hemisphere: in Europe, India, and particularly in Africa. Well-known species include the Russell's viper of India, the cape viper of southern Africa, the puff adder of dry areas of Africa and Arabia, and the gaboon viper of tropical Africa.

Poisonous Short-Fanged Snakes. The elapine snakes (including the cobras, kraits, and American coral snakes) are among the most deadly of poisonous snakes, but even light clothing is a fairly good protection against them because of their short fangs. They comprise the majority of snakes in Australia, and many species are found in India, Malaya, Africa, and New Guinea.

There are ten or more species of cobras, all confined to the Eastern Hemisphere and all more or less able to spread the neck to form a "hood." The king cobra is the largest of all poisonous snakes. The Australian blacksnake, the tiger snake, and the death adder are among the most deadly and abundant Australian elapine snakes.

Coral snakes are small, brilliantly colored snakes confined to the Western Hemisphere. Many have a pattern of rich red, yellow, and black bands and few are more than a yard long.

Sea Snakes. Although sea snakes are poisonous, they do not disturb swimmers and do not bite unless forcibly restrained. Oriental fishermen throw them from their nets with bare hands. Sea snakes usually are found close to shore or in tidal rivers, but they may be seen a hundred miles from the coast. They can be distinguished from river snakes by their flat, vertically compressed, paddlelike tails. Venomous sea snakes are not found in the Atlantic, but may occur in large numbers off the shores of the Indian Ocean and the southern and western Pacific.

River Snakes. Frequenting the rivers and bays of the East Indies and found from Bengal through Malaya to northern Australia, river snakes are poisonous. But because they must bite and hold in order to inject poison, they are not especially dangerous.

Boas and Pythons. The slow-moving boas and pythons rarely attack humans unless molested. They are not poisonous, but they are vicious and dangerous if disturbed because of their sharp teeth and power of constriction. The large species live only in the dense jungle country of Burma, Indochina, the Malay Archipelago, the Philippines, southern India, China,

Figure 6-21. (*top*) Gila monster; (*bottom*) Mexican beaded lizard. (Courtesy of the National Zoo)

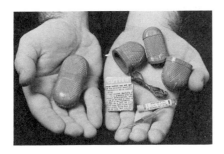

Figure 6-22. An example of a snakebite kit. (Courtesy of Cutter)

South America, and central and southern Africa. Species such as the regal python and anaconda average between seventeen and twenty-two feet in length.

Lizards. No lizards are poisonous except the gila monster of the American Southwest and the beaded lizard of Mexico and Central America, both found only in desert areas. These two poisonous lizards are so sluggish, and their mechanism for injection of poison so poor, that cases of their causing injury to human beings are extremely rare. No poisonous lizards are found outside the Western Hemisphere. Some lizards are excellent sources of food.

Symptoms and Treatment of Snakebite. Danger from snakebites is in proportion to the size of the snake, the type and quantity of venom injected, and the part of the body bitten. While venom may contain several toxins, the most important (the hemorrhagins and the neurotoxins) affect the blood and nervous systems, respectively.

Nausea, desire to defecate, thirst, severe headache, and bleeding from the wound, gums, and nose are frequent symptoms of snakebites.

Pain from the bite of the elapine snakes (cobra, krait, and coral snakes) is comparatively mild, but the poison is absorbed rapidly and directly by the blood, spreads to all parts of the body, and acts quickly by paralyzing the nervous system and respiratory centers. Within an hour the numb feeling progressively worsens and partial paralysis of the bitten area results.

Venom of the viperine snakes will cause severe local pain followed by swelling, which may continue for hours. The venom does most of its damage in the blood by liberating hemoglobin or producing internal hemorrhage or clotting. This venom is absorbed slowly through the lymphatic system.

Death-dealing bacteria such as the gas-gangrene bacillus (*Bacillus welchii*) and *Streptococcus hemolyticus* occur normally in the mouths and venom sacs of snakes and cause secondary infections which greatly increase the seriousness of snakebite.

For snakebite treatment, see the First Aid chapter.

FOLLOW THIS PROCEDURE IF YOU ARE BITTEN:

1. Avoid undue exertion. Lie down and remain quiet. A snug tourniquet (tight enough to impede the venous return of blood to the trunk, yet loose enough to allow arterial supply to the extremities) will further delay systemic absorption of the poison. Place the tourniquet between the bite and the heart, about two inches above the bite.

2. Daub the knife or razor blade and fang marks with antiseptic, if you have it.

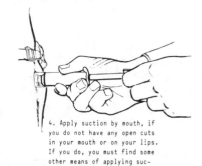

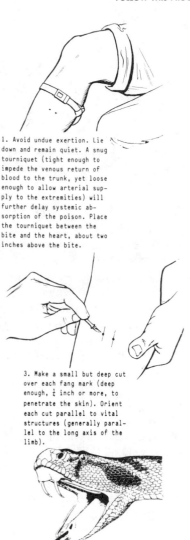

3. Make a small but deep cut over each fang mark (deep enough, ¼ inch or more, to penetrate the skin). Orient each cut parallel to vital structures (generally parallel to the long axis of the limb).

4. Apply suction by mouth, if you do not have any open cuts in your mouth or on your lips. If you do, you must find some other means of applying suction. Generally, though, mouth suction is much more effective than devices contained in snakebite kits.

5. Immobilize and splint the injured limb. This step is important in limiting the spread of toxin. Local application of cold wet packs will help relieve pain and reduce the spread of toxin.

6. A possible exception to steps 2 and 3 is if snakebites are sustained in the warm, moist tropics where any skin wound bears a high risk of infection. In this case, make no cut. Apply mouth suction, aided by deep massage with the teeth.

7. Use the antibiotics from the medical kit if you have one.

Figure 6-23. Follow this procedure if you are bitten by a snake.

Dangerous Aquatic Life

Rivers, lakes, swamps, and seashores harbor living creatures that may be hazardous to your health. For information on dangerous marine life that may be encountered in a deep water survival situation, see the second part of this book.

Scorpion, Stone, and Toad Fishes. The stone and scorpion fishes of the Pacific Ocean and some of the toad fishes of tropical America are the most dangerous of poisonous fishes. Their venomous spines may produce a sting that causes severe pain and swelling, followed by prostration. Treat a sting as you would snakebite. These fish are most apt to be encountered among coral head, where the unwary may accidentally step on them or touch them while turning over coral rocks in search of food. The flesh of these fish is edible, but don't pick up these fish or take them off a hook with bare hands.

Sea Anemones and Sea Urchins. Some of the sea anemones, small, plantlike creatures that cling to rocks on reefs and in tidal pools, may produce an annoying sting. Some species of sea urchins found in the southwest Pacific have long, poisonous, needlelike spines.

The Morays and Conger Eel. Snakelike fish inhabiting coral reefs, morays and conger eels normally bite only when touched or disturbed.

Shells. The sharp shells of oysters and other mollusks, coral and starfish, cause wounds that heal slowly. If you wade or swim through surf on coral shores without shoes, you will almost surely be cut.

Crocodilians. The crocodilians are confined to marshy lowlands, sloughs, rivers, and coastlines in the tropics and semi-tropics. The group includes crocodiles, alligators, gavials, and caimans. All species are potentially dangerous, some more than others. A blow from the powerful tail of one that is surprised could be more harmful or likely than being bitten.

All crocodilians prefer sluggish water and will rarely be encountered in swift water. Most of them are timid; if out on the banks, they will rush for water at the sight of humans. They will seldom attack unless you come on them suddenly or get between them and the water, blocking their natural path of escape. Mangrove swamps, bays, and tidal pools are common habitats. Circumvent these areas if you are traveling, especially avoiding them at night. Either on land or in the water, keep a sharp lookout.

The saltwater and African crocodiles are the most dangerous of the species. The former is found in coastal swamps, inlets, and tidal rivers of the South Pacific Ocean. The latter, abundant in some areas of Africa and Madagascar, has a reputation as a maneater. The American crocodile, found along coastal regions of Mexico, the West Indies, Central America, Colombia, and Venezuela, usually will avoid humans.

Largest of all the crocodiles is the Indian gavial, which lives largely on

Figure 6-24. Alligator

fish and is a timid creature confined to northern India. Natives swim in water where gavials are numerous.

Alligators are found only in the southeastern portion of the United States and along the Yangtze River in China. They are less active in the water and are more vicious and treacherous than crocodiles. They are often seen basking in the sun by day but become active and noisy at night.

Caimans, resembling alligators, are found in the rivers of Central America and in tropical South America, east of the Andes.

Fish. Only four freshwater fish are at all dangerous to man and all four are found in South America. They are the caribe, the electric eel, the candiru, and the stingray.

The caribes (also known as piranhas or pirayas) are far the most feared of this group. They inhabit the Paraguay, Amazon, and Orinoco river systems, are generally found in schools, and "go wild" if they encounter blood in the water. They are about the size of a large sunfish and have deep, blunt heads and powerful jaws armed with cutting teeth. They may attack any animal entering the water. People wading or swimming have been severely bitten and even killed by schools of these little fish. They live in smooth water, never in rapids. Clothing (including shoes) will protect very well against them.

The electric eel of the Orinoco and Amazon river systems delivers the most powerful shock of any fish, but the eel seldom comes in contact with humans.

Freshwater stingrays are abundant in the muddy and sandy areas of South American streams, ranging thousands of miles up the river systems. Take the same precautions as against marine stingrays.

The candiru is a tiny fish found in the Amazon and Orinoco river systems and apparently is attracted by water currents. Cases have been reported of this small fish swimming into the urethra of an individual urinating in the water. Small, hooklike head spines prevent it from getting out again.

Harmful Mammals

Generally, mammals, large and small, flesheating or herbivorous, are not of great danger to humans. You may travel in jungles, grasslands, deserts, or the Arctic without having to worry about danger from this source. All wild mammals avoid people. Most are timid and wary. You will have more difficulty locating lions, bears, and wolves than you will avoiding them. In fact, if you get to see some of the supposedly dangerous carnivores, consider yourself lucky. Mammals may be dangerous under certain conditions, usually if they are threatened or attacked by humans.

Large animals such as elephants, bears, tigers, moose, wild boars, and water buffalo will charge when wounded, especially if cornered. If it becomes necessary to shoot an animal that may become dangerous when wounded, use a large caliber gun if available; try to kill with the first shot.

Many mammals, which would otherwise run away, may fight if they think their young will be harmed. Avoid coming between a mother and her young, and do not approach them.

Mammals that live in herds can be dangerous if suddenly frightened into stampeding. Wild hogs or boars have been known to attack people.

Exiled elephants, boar, or buffalo, for example, that have been cast off by a herd are often cantankerous and may charge if disturbed or irritated. They will be alone or straggling in the vicinity of a herd. Almost all maneating lions, tigers, or leopards are old beasts that can no longer successfully hunt wild animals and have resorted to killing man. Such animals are rare. Take reasonable precautions when sleeping if such an animal is known to be in the area. A hammock or platform in the trees will eliminate danger from tigers or lions, although leopards are excellent climbers. Tigers roam primarily in the jungles of southeastern Asia, including India, Burma, and Malaya, Sumatra, Borneo, and Bali. Lions are confined to Africa and a very small region of western India and Persia. They are found in open lands of grass and scrubby trees. Both lions and tigers are shy and seldom seen, but may prove dangerous if suddenly disturbed or if game is scarce.

Bites from all canines (dogs, jackals, foxes) as well as some other meat-eaters may cause rabies. There is no need to worry unless this disease is known to be prevalent or the animal was particularly vicious or noticeably sick or paralyzed.

The Pasteur vaccine for prevention of rabies is highly effective. The treatment may safely be delayed for several days after you have been bitten unless the bite is in the region of the head or neck. In any doubtful case consult a doctor as soon as possible.

Blood-sucking vampire bats, found only in South America, are not dangerous unless their bite becomes infected. Mosquito netting will keep them away, and should be used at night in areas where these bats are found.

Poisonous Plants

Plants may be poisonous to eat or poisonous to touch. Some that are poisonous to eat are discussed in the chapter on wild plant food. We recom-

Figure 6-25. Poison ivy (*Rhus toxicodendron*)
• Grows as a small plant, a vine, and a shrub.
• Grows everywhere in the United States except California and parts of adjacent states. Eastern oak leaf poison ivy is one of its varieties.
• Leaves always consist of three glossy leaflets.
• Also known as three-leaf ivy, poison creeper, climbing sumac, poison oak, markweed, picry, and mercury.

mend that you learn the plants that are edible, and if you must try strange plants, perform the edibility test described in that chapter.

Plants may be poisonous to touch because of toxic juices or oils or stinging hairs. Only under certain conditions are poisonous-to-the-touch plants a serious hazard.

The dangers from poisonous contact plants in other parts of the world are no greater than those posed in the United States from poison ivy, poison oak, and poison sumac. Contact poisons may cause severe eruptions, swelling, and inflammation and are particularly dangerous near the eyes. Avoid contact with the milky juices of all unfamiliar trees and take particular precautions against getting such juices in your eyes.

Some people are immune or only slightly affected by contact poisons, while others are extremely susceptible. This is something each person

Figure 6-26. (*left*) Poison oak (*Rhus diversiloba*)
• Grows in shrub and sometimes vine form.
• Grows in California and parts of adjacent states.
• Sometimes called poison ivy, or yeara.
• Leaves always consist of three leaflets.

(*right*) Poison sumac (*Rhus vernix*)
• Grows as a woody shrub or small tree from five to twenty-five feet tall.
• Grows only in wet swampy areas.
• Grows in most of eastern third of the United States.
• Also known as swamp sumac, poison elder, poison ash, poison dogwood, and thunderwood.

should know about himself. There is a great danger of being affected when you are overheated and sweating. The plants themselves may vary in toxicity at different times of the year. Don't use the wood of any contact poisoning plants for firewood. It will be helpful to learn the appearance and effects of the contact-poisoning plants found in the United States and to use this background of experience in other parts of the world. The method of poisoning, the symptoms, and to some extent the appearance of the plants will be similar.

Most of these plants, both tropical and temperate, belong to two families—the sumach and the spurge.

Poisonous Contact Plants of the United States. The three most important contact poisonous plants in the United States are poison ivy, poison oak, and poison sumac. Their toxic principle is a resinous alkaloid that occurs in all parts of the plant.

It may take from a few hours to several days for the symptoms of reddening, itching, and swelling to appear. Blisters will follow. The infection may be localized or may spread over the body.

All of these plants have compound leaves and a small round grayish green or white fruit. You can easily avoid them if you know where they grow and what they look like. The best treatment after contact with these plants is to wash thoroughly with a strong soap.

Poisonous Contact Plants in Other Parts of the World. Most plants in other parts of the world that produce skin eruptions similar to poison ivy and poison sumac belong to the same sumac family:

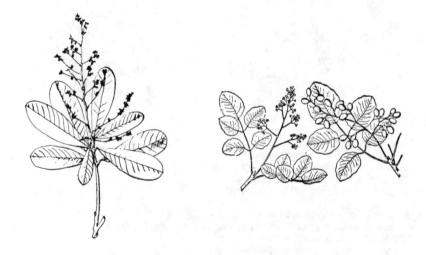

Figure 6-27. (*left*) Liga (*Semecarpus*); (*right*) Black poison wood (*Metopium*)

Figure 6-28. (*left*) Beach apple (*Hippomane mancinella*); (*right*) White mangrove (*Excoecaria*)

(1) The sap of the Rengas trees of India, Malaya, and the South Pacific islands causes severe skin eruptions. Liga, a small shrub of this group found in the Philippine Islands can be identified by the black sap along the trunk. Many of these plants are large forest trees and there is little likelihood of trouble unless you climb or cut them.
(2) Several species of *Mangifera*, to which the edible mango belongs, are found in tropical Asia.
(3) Black poison wood grows in Central America and the West Indies.
(4) Carrasco are common shrubs in the West Indies.
(5) The Chinese lacquer tree is found in China and Japan.
Among the spurges, the following should be avoided:
(1) The beach apple or manzanillo of Central America and tropical South America, the West Indies, and Mexico causes skin inflammation and may also cause blindness if the sap gets in the eyes. It is a small tree with smooth, pale-brown bark and "crabapplelike" fruits. It is found in thickets along the coast. Immediate bathing in seawater will counteract the effects of the sap. The fruits are poisonous to eat.
(2) The "blind eye," white mangrove found in Australia, the South Pacific Islands, and India grows in mangrove swamps, in salt marshes, and along the seashore. It is a shrub or small tree whose white sap causes severe skin irritation and may cause blindness.

Figure 6-29. (*left*) Sandbox tree (*Hura crepitans*); (*right*) Sapium jamaicense

Figure 6-30 (*left*) Stinging nettle (*Urtica Dioica*); (*right*) *Jatropha urens* of tropical America

(3) The monkey pistol or sandbox tree of tropical America, Panama, and the West Indies is a large tree with a spiny trunk whose sap is irritating and may cause temporary blindness. The small, pumpkinlike fruit is also poisonous.

(4) The milky juice of a number of species of the genus *Sapium* found in the tropics of both hemispheres causes serious skin inflammations.

(5) The castor oil plant contains poisonous and purgative qualities. A remedy that many natives use for juices in the eyes is to wash the eyes immediately with warm milk.

Also, the upas or ipoh tree is notorious for its poisonous properties. Natives of the South Seas and Indian archipelago use the sap of this tree to poison their arrows, but there is no danger from contact with the tree itself.

In addition, strychnine trees furnish curare, the poison which South American natives apply to their spears and arrows. Treat poison arrow wounds as you would snakebites.

Plants with Stinging Hairs. Plants of this group contain fine hairs that produce a burning sensation when touched, followed by the appearance of small red welts. This sting, due to formic acid, is usually not dangerous. Contact with the stinging nettle found in wastelands of the United States and Europe will give you an idea of what to expect from tree nettles and this group of stinging plants in other parts of the world.

CHAPTER 7

Tropical Rain Forest Survival

The Tropical Zone, lying between the Tropic of Cancer to the north and the Tropic of Capricorn to the south, receives the rays of the sun more directly than any other part of the earth. Its seasons are marked more by changes in wind and rain (called *monsoons* in India and southeast Asia) than by changes in temperature.

The mid-section of the earth contains the world's largest expanses of tropical rain forest—the Amazon and Congo basins. The word *jungle* is used colloquially to refer to such heavily vegetative areas. Proceeding north and south from the equator, the tropical rain forests generally give way to more open vegetation: savannahs (grasslands), steppes (sparsely vegetative open spaces), and even desert. But latitude is just one factor affecting tropical landscapes. Distance from the ocean, prevailing winds, and elevation are others. The high mountain ranges that lie in the zone, such as the Andes in South America, have climates more temperate than tropical.

There are two basic kinds of tropical rain forest, and the distinction is more in their history than in their appearance. Primary rain forests, characterized by great trees and a network of vines (*lianas*) are virgin tracts of jungle never tamed by humans. Secondary rain forests are composed of "second-time-around" vegetation that has reclaimed once cultivated or settled land. Both types look alike for the most part and contain similar plants and animals, but secondary rain forests may be somewhat closer to civilization, have a greater supply of such fruit trees as banana, papaya, and mango, and be more tangled and dense than the interiors of primary rain forests.

Whether you find yourself in a tropical rain forest in South America, Africa, Asia, or the Pacific Islands, the principles of jungle survival will hold true. Surviving in a tropical rain forest is comparable in challenge to surviving at sea or in the polar regions. It requires physical stamina, survival know-how, high morale, and some equipment. The priorities of survival take on a distinctive cast in a jungle environment. Tropical rain forests

Figure 7-1. Negrito aborigine instructors at the Jungle Environmental Survival Training in the Philippines draw water from jungle trees and plants. (Courtesy of the Defense Audio-Visual Agency)

present certain health dangers stemming from the prolific insect life and the primitive sanitary and health facilities of jungle villages. The slightest scratch can lead to infection if not promptly treated. Water may be available, but its safety questionable. Shelter has to protect you from the insects below and the rain above. Plants play a greater role in diet than they would in polar or temperate regions, because vegetative growth is so prolific. Travel will be most difficult at the periphery of the tropical rain forest rather than in the interior, because the margins are dense thickets of trees and vines while the interior forest floor is often relatively open. The forest canopy may be 200 feet above the ground and so dense that little direct sunlight strikes the earth and, thus, the growth of underbrush is limited.

You can survive in the rain forest if you keep your wits about you and if you have prepared yourself with the right information and equipment. This chapter will address the general principles of surviving in such an environment, but for more detailed information on first aid or environmental hazards, for example, see those chapters.

PREPARATION

Jungle survival training is best learned through overnight field trips. You should be able to perform the following tasks:
(1) Demonstrate knowledge of biological hazards by taking the proper precautions against insects and insect-transmitted diseases. Identify jungle noises. Surmount whatever physical hazards you encounter.
(2) Demonstrate your mastery of both improvised signaling methods and standard signaling devices.
(3) Obtain water from vines, bamboo, bromeliads, and other water-catching plants. Purify surface water.
(4) Select a campsite and improvise a shelter and bed.
(5) Collect and prepare bamboo shoots, hearts of rattan vines, and any other plant food available in quantity.
(6) Practice freshwater fishing techniques. Put out setlines at night. Try one or two trapping methods, and make sets during the night.
(7) Practice stalking and any other hunting techniques that would be useful in the area.
(8) Build a fire under wet jungle conditions; practice fire making with bamboo fire saw, fire thong, and fire plow. Use various jungle tinders. Cook food in green bamboo utensils, and in a rock or earth oven. Demonstrate various broiling methods.
(9) Travel in the jungle, laying a course so as to intersect varied topography and vegetation conditions (an excellent exercise is to hike landward through mangrove swamps into the primary tropical forest and return by way of river or stream).

FIRST AID

Diseases common in tropical regions include, among others, malaria, dengue fever, and yellow fever—all caused by mosquitoes. Symptoms are severe chills and high fever; treatment consists of rest and plenty of water while your body fights the illness; prevention, of course, consists of not getting bitten in the first place. Dysentery, caused by drinking polluted water or eating contaminated food, is also common. Boiling all drinking water (or using water purification tablets) and thoroughly cooking all foods will reduce or eliminate this problem. Inoculations to prevent typhus are very important to individuals traveling through tropical regions.

SIGNALING

The best method of signaling is radio communication using the stranded vehicle's radio or a separate, battery-powered emergency radio. The dense jungle canopy makes signaling rescue parties with fires, flares, and mirrors virtually impossible. Even when a search plane is directly overhead, you may not be able to see it and the pilot certainly won't see you. Find a clearing as soon as possible, and prepare signal fires, flares, and smoke signals for use.

WATER PROCUREMENT

Water is a basic necessity, and even in a tropical rain forest, where rainfall might average 100 inches a year, getting it can be a problem if you don't know how. Primary rain forests are well supplied with streams and rivers, and rainwater is generally available. Rainwater collected as it falls or

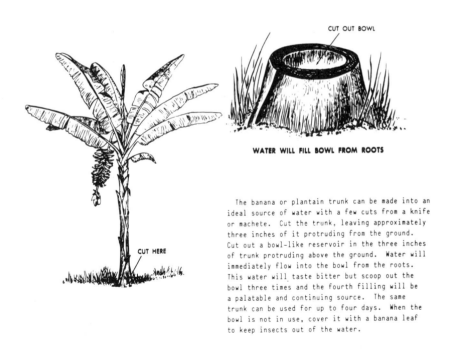

CUT OUT BOWL

WATER WILL FILL BOWL FROM ROOTS

CUT HERE

The banana or plantain trunk can be made into an ideal source of water with a few cuts from a knife or machete. Cut the trunk, leaving approximately three inches of it protruding from the ground. Cut out a bowl-like reservoir in the three inches of trunk protruding above the ground. Water will immediately flow into the bowl from the roots. This water will taste bitter but scoop out the bowl three times and the fourth filling will be a palatable and continuing source. The same trunk can be used for up to four days. When the bowl is not in use, cover it with a banana leaf to keep insects out of the water.

Figure 7-2. Getting water from a banana tree stump

trapped in pockets on the jungle floor is safe to drink, but many serious diseases can be contracted by drinking from streams or rivers near villages. Do not consider such water safe, even if clear and inviting, until boiled or treated with halazone.

Securing water will be a problem during the dry season in a primary jungle and all year round at the further edges of the Tropical Zone. Yet, in all tropical rain forests there are water-yielding plants that will provide pure, potable water, often in unlimited quantities. The large jungle vines or lianas are widely available and offer the best drinking water. It is safe to assume that any of the innumerable jungle vines that does not yield a bitter or colored sap will furnish water safe to drink. Never drink from a vine that has a milky, sticky, or bitter-tasting sap. The best vines contain clear water with a slight acid or mineral flavor. In general, large-diameter vines yield more water than small ones, and because this water is being pulled up the vine to be transpired through the leaves, more water is present during the heat of the day than at any other time, and it will be many degrees cooler than the air temperature.

To tap a vine, merely sever it as high as possible. Or cut a deep notch high on the vine and then cut off the vine at knee level, this gives you a tube six or seven feet long. Water will start flowing from the lower end. A single section of a large, rough-barked vine will provide from a pint to a quart of water.

The slender, smooth rattan vines are a particularly good source of water in some areas. To obtain a large quantity of water, cut several vines into six-foot lengths and then hold them horizontally until you have a bundle. Turn them all vertical at once, having arranged for the liquid to flow into a container. When the flow ceases, cut a foot off the top of the vines and more water will drain. Continue cutting down the vine until no more water flows.

In getting water from a vine, it is important to make the top cut first, otherwise the water will ascend and much or all of it will be lost.

Some species of bamboo contain water in the green stalks, which although in some cases is quite bitter, is usually good to drink. Old stalks that have dried and split often catch and hold rainwater between the nodes. Water trapped in this manner during the wet season is available during the dry season. Most of the climbing bamboos contain good water. To get a drink, cut a section for a container and than cut and drain the contents of each succeeding section separated by joints (node and internode) into the container.

Bromeliads are pineapplelike plants whose up-curved leaves form natural cups that catch rainwater. These air plants affix themselves to jungle trees or they may grow out of the ground. They are found throughout the Tropical Zone. In the tropical rain forest, they catch the dew and the small

Figure 7-3. Bromeliad

amount of rain that falls, holding it deep in the heavy leaf bases where it does not evaporate. During the driest periods, an apparently empty bromeliad will yield some water if you cut it and hold it upside down to drain. In the primary jungle, the water of these air plants is frequently laden with decayed vegetable matter and small insects. It is pure, however, and can be siphoned off with a hollow reed so as to leave the sediment undisturbed.

Keep in mind that water from plants is pure. Tapping this source will save time and maintain health. In some areas, plants may be the only readily available source of water.

Waterborne diseases are major hazards of tropical and subtropical regions. The presence of human beings in an area greatly increases the dangers. Amoebic and bacillary dysentaries are common, are highly debilitating, and can be fatal. Cholera, typhoid, blood flukes that transmit schistosomiases and other diseases, worms, and leeches—all can be picked up by drinking impure water. A good rule is to boil or chlorinate all surface water except in unpopulated areas.

SHELTER CONSTRUCTION

Constructing a shelter and a bed will help ensure a better night's sleep and will protect you from cold and rain, thus increasing your chances of surviving. Night in the jungle comes very fast, so bed down early.

Evaluate the factors most likely to prevent a good night's rest and then prepare against them. Often a bed off the ground—to protect against in-

A less elaborate jungle bed--good if you are on the move.

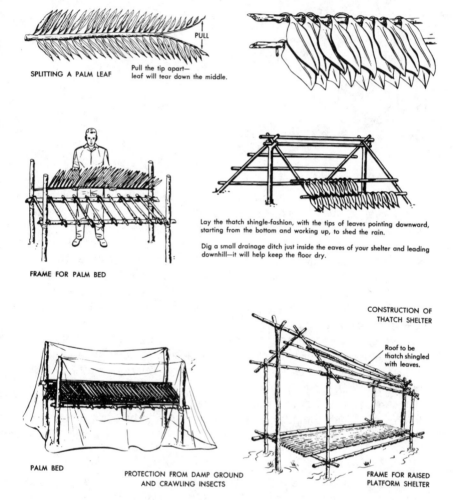

SPLITTING A PALM LEAF

Pull the tip apart—
leaf will tear down the middle.

FRAME FOR PALM BED

Lay the thatch shingle-fashion, with the tips of leaves pointing downward, starting from the bottom and working up, to shed the rain.

Dig a small drainage ditch just inside the eaves of your shelter and leading downhill—it will help keep the floor dry.

PALM BED

PROTECTION FROM DAMP GROUND
AND CRAWLING INSECTS

CONSTRUCTION OF
THATCH SHELTER

Roof to be
thatch shingled
with leaves.

FRAME FOR RAISED
PLATFORM SHELTER

Figure 7-4. Shelters for the tropics

sects and chills—is all that is needed. At other times, a waterproof shelter is essential. Mosquitoes, leeches, fire ants, or other jungle insects may necessitate special precautions.

In choosing a campsite consider the availability of water, bedding and shelter material, firewood, and food. Is protection offered from storms, falling trees, floods, and so forth? Can you catch a breeze, but not too strongly? Is your sleeping place level?

A key to surviving is conserving energy whenever possible. If you find a natural shelter, such as a large fallen tree trunk or a convenient juxtaposition of rocks, use it.

Because rain comes straight down in a heavy jungle, a waterproof roof directly over a hammock or platform makes an ideal shelter. To fend off rain, split and shingle palm fronds and lash them together with rattan vines. Alternatively, you can "rubberize" the broad leaves of young banana trees by building a fire on a large flat stone, raking off the coals, and placing one leaf at a time on the hot stone for a minute or two until it turns dark and glossy. Rig up a hammock from parachute silk or any other suitable material at hand. Under more benign conditions, a teepee or lean-to made from a blanket or large cloth or cut fronds offers adequate protection.

Sleeping platforms should be constructed one to three feet off the ground and then blanketed with palm fronds or other vegetation. The types of beds and shelters that can be constructed from jungle vegetation are limited only by your ingenuity. Remember, a bed off the ground, some type of roofing over it, and a mosquito net or head net will meet most requirements.

PLANT FOODS

Vegetation makes the tropical rain forest what it is. You have, in fact, a feast around you—even if you can't identify many of the edible plants—as long as you observe some general principles.

The type of fruits and nuts that monkeys consume are usually safe for humans. Just to be cautious, though, sample only a small quantity at first and wait.

Palms, as a group, are conspicuous, readily recognized, and usually an excellent source of food, for a great many species yield edible fruits, flowers, terminal buds, sugary sap, or starch from the trunk. Some fruits of Eastern Hemisphere palms are not edible, however, because they contain irritating crystals. Most Western Hemisphere palms are edible or at least can be safely tested.

Some groups of edible plants found in the United States are widespread throughout the world. Those you recognize abroad as similar can usually be used in the same way as those at home.

Plant food in the rain forest is generally easier to secure than animal

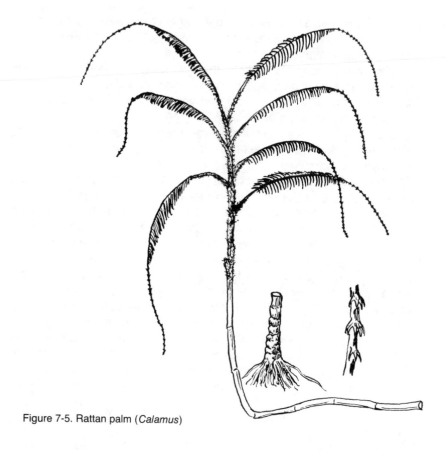

Figure 7-5. Rattan palm (*Calamus*)

food, but to make full use of the many edible plants, you have to be able to identify them. Although it may not be practical to learn the many different kinds, there are a few common jungle plants that you should know. Jungle fruits are frequently borne at the tops of high trees and can only be harvested on the ground. The most useful plants in the primary rain forest are rattan palms, bamboo shoots, ferns, and the fruits, nuts, and leaves of various jungle trees.

Rattan Palms (Calamus). Rattans are vinelike palms that look like climbing bamboos. These plants are common throughout the Pacific forests. Their growing tips are edible just as is the coconut heart and are obtained in the same manner. To obtain the edible portion, cut the vine and gradually pull it down through the jungle canopy. The thorny sheath about the stem of some species can be removed to ease pulling. The six-to-eight-foot growing tip should be cut off and the spiny outer sheath removed. This section of rattan can then be cut in short lengths and placed on a bed of coals to cook. When the outer covering is well charred, the tender inner heart will be cooked. Some species taste as good as the "coconut heart" and others are slightly bitter, especially when cooked in the sheath. Most are edible raw, but are more palatable and nourishing when cooked.

Bamboos. There are many species of bamboo, some of them climbing vines like the rattans. Their stems are hollow and divided into nodes. The new shoots of these bamboos, or the buds often found along the stems, can be cooked and eaten in the same manner as rattan.

Ferns. Almost every description of fern is found in the tropical rain forest. The young fronds of all of them can be boiled as greens. Some may be too bitter for your taste, but often a change of water will eliminate this. The better ones can be sorted out by trial and error.

Bago (Gnetum gnemon). The seeds and young leaves of the bago, a small forest tree, may be eaten—the seeds either raw or cooked, the leaves cooked as greens.

Pili Nut (Canarium). There are numerous species of pili nut, a large nut tree, in the rain forests. The single, more or less triangular seeds of the fruit are edible raw or roasted.

Breadfruit (Artocarpus). Various species of *Artocarpus* are found in the primary and secondary rain forests. The pulp of the round, spiny fruit of the *Artocarpus rotunda* is very tasty raw. The seeds should be boiled or roasted.

Other sources. In cut-over jungle and abandoned garden areas, bananas, papayas, mangoes, custard apples, soursops, jackfruit, limes, plantains, guavas and cashews will be found.

Yams are plentiful in both the primary and secondary rain forests, but

Figure 7-6. (*left*) Bamboo; (*right*) Bananas and plantains (*Musa*)

Figure 7-7. Negrito aborigine instructors at the Jungle Environmental Survival Training school in the Philippines show various uses of the banana tree—bed, poncho, hat, and plate. (Courtesy of the Defense Audio-Visual Agency)

some of them, such as the wild yam (*Dioscorea hispida*) are poisonous unless properly prepared. Natives do not use the wild yam except in time of famine.

There are few jungle trees whose fruits are edible. Some furnish young leaves that make excellent greens. Most of these edible and useful plants are known to the natives. A few hours spent learning edible plants from the people of a region will pay large dividends in an emergency.

ANIMAL FOODS

Streams and rivers are the best sources of animal food, for terrestrial animals come to their banks to drink and to bathe and aquatic animals live in their shallows and pools. If you are traveling, aim to strike a stream, and then camp and make arrangements to obtain a supply of food.

A gill net (12 by 3 feet, with 1½ inch mesh) will come in very useful. Stretch it across a small stream and weigh the lower side of it so that it rests on the bottom. Drive fish into it by throwing stones into the water or by wading toward the net, herding the fish ahead. Several dozen fish can be netted at one time. Take care not to tear the delicate net.

The hook and line is a good standby when baited with crushed snails, wood grubs, or insects. Trotlines, a short fishing line to which several

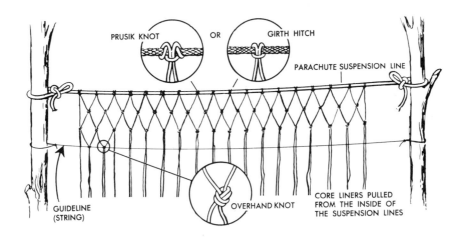

Figure 7-8. Making a gill net

Figure 7-9. Setting a gill net or fish trap in a stream

hooks are attached in a series, are always good for turtles, eels, and fish. You can improvise hooks from rattan thorns. The chapter on wild animal food discusses how to catch fish with your hands; how to noose, spear, or knife them; and how to improvise nets and seines, which are effective where minnows and small fish abound. In addition, you can gig—or, spear with several points—fish. You don't need to worry about eating poisonous fish, but be sure to cook thoroughly all freshwater fish.

Obtaining bait can be a greater problem than catching fish. Crustaceans, mollusks, and aquatic insects and larvae are present in jungle streams (and in temperate waters, also).

If you have no fishing equipment, you can make lines from the bark and fiber of plants. Toggle or gorge hooks can be improvised from bamboo or other hardwoods, or rattan thorns can be utilized as snell hooks. The idea is to rig a stick so that when the fish swallows the bait, it also swallows part of the stick, which lodges in its throat.

Firearms cannot be improvised, but if you happen to have a rifle the birds and mammals of the jungle are more available to you than they would ever be if you were solely dependent on traps and snares. No primitive method of catching or killing game, especially when used by the inexperienced, can compare with the modern rifle.

Unlike plants, you do not need to know how to recognize the many species of birds and mammals, because all of them are edible. It does help greatly, however, to know the habits of specific species, but such knowledge is gained only by long experience and you can make do without this advantage.

A few jungle foods are worthy of specific attention. Monkey meat is excellent, tasting somewhat like veal, and monkeys can be shot relatively easily. Wild pigs are common in many areas, their tracks and rootings being conspicuous in moist places. Because they are difficult to stalk, it is best to shoot them at a feeding place in early morning or late evening. Natives kill them by means of the spear trap. The large monitors, iguanas, and lizards found throughout the tropics are all excellent eating, once skinned and gutted. The long cylindrical tail muscle is best baked or roasted. Do not overlook snakes, for they too are far better eating than their appearance would indicate. The crocodile is also a good bet. Large ones should be left alone, but small ones can be shot on the bank or in shallow water where they can be retrieved. They can also be caught with large steel hooks or improvised toggle or gorge hooks, baited and suspended from bushes overhanging the water. A dead or wounded crocodile will sink to the bottom, so don't shoot one in deep water.

If things get really tough, you can always resort to termite larvae and beetle grubs, which are abundant in rotten stumps. Large termite nests in open grassland or along the jungle fringes are easily spotted. Cook these things if possible, but they can be eaten raw.

Sound hunting principles apply in jungle country as well as in more temperate regions.

(1)   As you move, take care not to be heard, seen, or scented.

(2)   Look for animal signs such as tracks, feces beds, runways, trails, and

feeding marks, and hunt where such indicators of game are conspicuous and fresh.

(3) You will see more animal life by stillhunting at a trail, waterhole, or feeding area than by hours of walking. Select a spot downwind from the most likely approach, and remain silent.

(4) Hunt when animal life is most active—during early morning and late evening.

(5) In general, it is a waste of time and effort to hunt during showers or stormy days.

(6) Look out for trees bearing fruit, as these attract many species of birds and the noise they make in feeding can be heard for a long distance in the jungle.

(7) Expect to find more birds at jungle edges and openings than in the unbroken interior of the tropical rain forest.

FIRE MAKING AND COOKING

In the tropical rain forest, the challenge is to secure enough dry tinder and wood to get a fire going. The fibrous leaf sheaths and dried fruit stalks of palm trees, the dead leaves of pandanas, and the fine-fuzz covering on the growing tip of tree ferns make good tinder. Generally, the inside of dead bamboo stalks is dry, and the fine, membranelike skin adhering to the inner wall will ignite when most other tinders will fail. Gather wood that is not on the ground and cut away the wet exterior to reach the dry wood inside. Wet wood will burn, once you get a good fire going. Keep dry tinder on hand at the camp and carry some when on the move.

The fire saw and fire thong are emergency fire-making methods that are particularly adapted to tropical rain forests. (See the section on each in "Fire Making and Cooking.") They are effective, but should be mastered before an emergency.

Wild game can be simply broiled over hot coals or roasted on a spit or in an earth oven. Fish can be similarly prepared, but is best roasted on hot stones. Food can be boiled in bamboo or leaf containers. Extra meat, fish, and fruit should be sun- or smoked-dried to preserve them for future use (see the section on preserving food in "Fire Making and Cooking").

TRAVELING

Traveling in the tropical rain forest is almost always difficult. The aggressive heat and thick vegetation are major obstacles and attempts to overcome them can lead to exhaustion and panic. Yet, there is usually a greater need to travel in this environment than in others because of the increased improbability of being found by rescuers. Before starting out, take time to relax and take stock of your equipment and survival requirements.

In general, maintaining a course is more important than ease of travel.

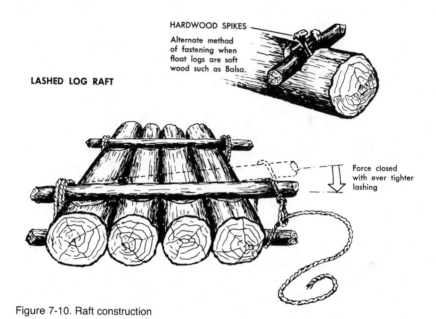

Figure 7-10. Raft construction

Direct your efforts to following a compass sight rather than selecting an easy route of travel. This is true not only in the tropical rain forest but in any unfamiliar country where vision is strictly limited.

Always wear a compass when you know you are leaving civilization. Without a compass in a rain forest it is possible to get completely turned around in a matter of minutes after leaving a known landmark. Rain squalls are numerous, and the jungle canopy is so dense that even on a sunny day it is often impossible to get your bearings from the sun. A map is a big help in traveling, but once you are oriented, you must use your compass to continually keep track of your whereabouts and must concentrate on memorizing landmarks and terrain. Whenever possible, it is wise to establish a baseline just in case you get lost.

In tropical rain forests, it is generally best to follow rivers and streams. You will eventually hit upon native or game trails, which usually follow the banks of large rivers. Many extra miles on a trail are preferable to a single mile cross-country. In the absence of trails, follow small stream beds until you reach larger streams and rivers and then build a raft. Bamboo, being hollow, is ideal for raft construction and can be used green.

Mountain jungle streams are fast running and flood quickly. It may be necessary to cross such streams frequently in a day's travel. A knowledge of swimming in rapids, selecting fording sites, and wading swift currents is of great practical value.

Although in most types of country it is easier to travel the ridges and divides than the valleys, in a tropical rain forest you should avoid ridges as they are often crammed with dense thickets of rattan bamboo and scrub growth. At high altitudes they may be matted with coarse ferns. The outlook is usually no better than along stream beds, and a stream offers a more definite course to follow. Even with the aid of a compass, branching spur ridges can completely confuse a traveler in dense vegetation.

Hurrying accentuates the discomfort of heat and humidity and brings on fatigue more quickly. A steady pace comfortable to your physical condition will take you farthest with the least effort.

The greatest annoyance to travel in the Pacific rain forests are thorny rattans and small pests such as mosquitoes, ants, and leeches. Rattans are trailing, climbing palms with recurved thorny stems and tendrils that rip skin and clothing. The smooth rattans form unyielding networks of vines that hinder a traveler at every turn. It is next to impossible to work through some thickets of rattan without becoming entangled in the thorns. A machete is useful only if it is sharp. You cannot tear yourself free by force, as this will only set the thorns deeper. It is far wiser to stop and carefully unfasten each thorn, or, if caught by one tendril, to make a slow spin away from it.

The best defense against mosquitoes and leeches is proper clothing. Trousers should be long, lightweight, and tucked into boot tops; your shirt should be mosquito-proof; and your hat, water repellent. Nylon top boots, eight to ten inches high, with instep vents to allow water to run out, are a light, cool, quick-drying footgear. Wool socks are preferable to cotton.

Where leeches or ticks are abundant, you will have to strip frequently to examine your body. A lighted cigarette or match held close to the body of an embedded tick or leech will cause it to loosen its grip and it can then be removed.

CHAPTER 8

Seashore Survival

When stranded near the coastline, you should head for the seashore whenever possible. Surviving near the beach is almost always easier than surviving inland and certainly much easier than in the open ocean.

Reaching the beach from the sea can be tricky. Along-shore currents (those that run parallel to the shore), rip currents (those that flow away from the shore), and large waves crashing over reefs are especially dangerous. Whether swimming or riding a raft, you should approach slowly, look the waves and beach contour over carefully, and pick the calmest time and place to travel through the surf. If caught in an outgoing rip current, swim or paddle the raft parallel to the beach until free of the current and then aim toward shore. Additional information on travel and navigation at sea is available in the Sea Survival section of this book.

Seashore survival techniques vary according to climate. While latitude is a key factor in making broad distinctions—tropical, temperate, or polar— it gives way to other factors in making finer distinctions. Prevailing winds, coastal mountains, and ocean currents are some of the other influences on seashore climate.

In the tropics, windward coasts are well-supplied with rainfall, and you should have no trouble finding fresh drinking water. On leeward coasts, however, deserts often run to the sea, such as on the western coasts of South America, Africa, and Australia. Mountainous islands, for example, the Hawaiian Islands, Borneo, Sri Lanka, and Madagascar, and the eastern coasts of Central and South America and Australia are well-watered on the windward side while remaining dry in the interior. On the beaches of the Temperate Zone, you may enjoy mild temperatures, but you'll have to contend with rain and fog, particularly in the U.S. Northwest. In the Polar regions, summer at the seashore may be pleasantly warm, but it is also usually very cloudy. Winter is the reverse: clear, but cold.

In discussing the various subjects in this chapter, we will note the climactic regions if the information is not universally applicable. But the seashores of the world can be categorized other than climatically. The *sandy* seashore is the more comfortable to live on; the *rocky* seashore provides more food. An ideal area will have both characteristics.

Foremost in your mind should be the priorities of every survival situation. Because seashores are the most amenable of environments, the traditional order of tasks generally holds true: first aid, signaling, water, shelter, food, and travel.

FIRST AID

Health hazards along the seashore may have either a physical or biological source. Many of the dangers—sunburn, heat exhaustion, saltwater sores, immersion foot, frostbite, hypothermia, insect bites, alligators, and poisonous snails and snakes—are discussed in the chapters on first aid and environmental hazards. A few words are warranted on poisonous coral and fish, however.

Puncture Wounds and Stings. To avoid puncture wounds or stings from venomous marine life, always wear footgear. Foot and leg protection can be improvised from material from the raft, parachute, or plants growing in the area. To treat puncture wounds:

(1)   Remove any material left in the wound.
(2)   Wash the wound with sterile water.
(3)   Soak the affected area in hot water (120°F or as hot as you can stand) or apply hot compresses on the area for at least thirty minutes. This will break down the toxin and also reduce the pain.
(4)   Treat for shock.

Poisonous Fish. In the tropics, some fish may be inherently toxic, while others, such as red snapper and trigger fish, may be poisonous only when their diets include poisonous coral or other poisonous fish. The visceral organs, liver, intestines, gonads, and brains of unfamiliar fish should never be eaten. Cooking will not remove the poison. Most inherently poisonous fish can be readily recognized by their odd shape. They generally are box- or ball-shaped with hard, bony skin and perhaps spines. Unless you are sure that a particular fish is edible, you should use the edibility test described in the chapter on plant food. If you become sick, induce vomiting. Remain quiet and drink large amounts of fresh water.

SIGNALING

On the reasonable assumption that survivors of disasters at sea or of accidents inland will head for the beach, search and rescue efforts are often concentrated along the seashore. For the survivor who has attained the beach, an open shoreline provides an ideal setting for easily observed signaling devices.

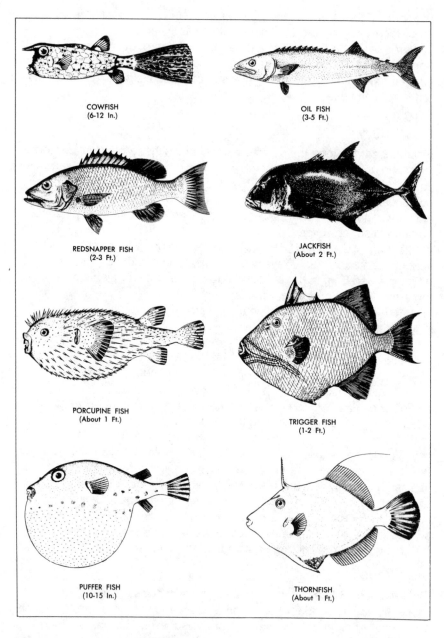

COWFISH
(6-12 In.)

OIL FISH
(3-5 Ft.)

REDSNAPPER FISH
(2-3 Ft.)

JACKFISH
(About 2 Ft.)

PORCUPINE FISH
(About 1 Ft.)

TRIGGER FISH
(1-2 Ft.)

PUFFER FISH
(10-15 In.)

THORNFISH
(About 1 Ft.)

Figure 8-1. Fish with poisonous flesh. (Some fish, such as red snapper and trigger fish, are poisonous only if they have been feeding on poisonous coral.)

Signal Fires

Prepare signal fires early and protect them from rain by placing large bamboo leaves or other material over the dry tinder. Remember, a good signal fire should light fast and burn well. Green plants on top of a good fire produce lots of smoke—an easily seen distress signal. Gasoline or oil from the disabled vehicle can be stored in a handy place, ready for use. When a search craft is either seen or heard, start your signal fires immediately.

Contrasting Colors

Brightly colored material from a parachute or raft may also be stretched out along the beach as a distress signal. To be seen from the air, the material must contrast in color with the background.

Signal Mirrors

Because the flash of a signal mirror may be seen by rescuers before survivors are able to detect a rescue aircraft, you should scan the horizon regularly with a signal mirror. Rescue might just come literally "out of the blue."

WATER PROCUREMENT

Potable water is a limiting factor in tropical seashore survival, fairly easy to find in temperate zones, and quite possible in polar regions. You must find a way to acquire it because without it, food is of little importance and a castaway's days are numbered.

Fresh or brackish water is usually under the soil back of the debris thrown up by high tides. Select a depression where drainage collects and dig a three-to-four foot beach well, preferably in the sand, which should reach water. The water may be discolored or brackish, but it is safe and potable.

In the tropics, where coconut palms line the shore, the green coconut will be the safest and most reliable source of water. The laxative property of ripe coconuts, which also contain drinkable water and are readily picked off the ground, has been generally exaggerated. Use ripe nuts if necessary. To get green nuts, however, select a low tree with a good nut crop and walk up the trunk, native style, using old leaf scars as toeholds. Pressure-grip the side of the pole with your hands. Don't lock your arms or hands around the trunk. Sever the nut by raising and then snapping it downward. Nuts can also be twisted off with a quick spin. Body water and energy can be saved if a good supply of nuts is obtained at each climb. With a sharp machete or by means specified on page 193, slice the rounded end of the nut until a small opening can be cut, from which to drink. To carry a water supply, husk the green coconuts to reduce weight, and string five or six of them together by running a dry leaflet through the fibrous

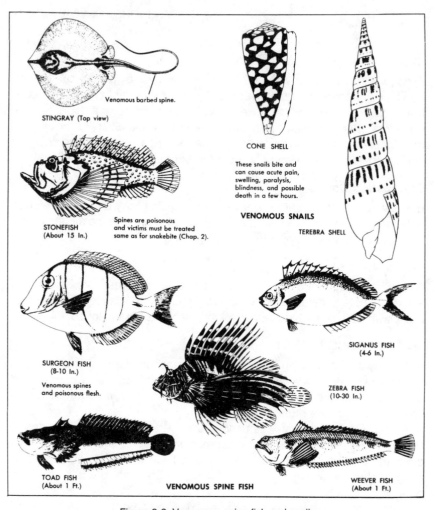

STINGRAY (Top view)

Venomous barbed spine.

STONEFISH
(About 15 In.)

Spines are poisonous
and victims must be treated
same as for snakebite (Chap. 2).

CONE SHELL

These snails bite and
can cause acute pain,
swelling, paralysis,
blindness, and possible
death in a few hours.

VENOMOUS SNAILS

TEREBRA SHELL

SURGEON FISH
(8-10 In.)

Venomous spines
and poisonous flesh.

SIGANUS FISH
(4-6 In.)

ZEBRA FISH
(10-30 In.)

TOAD FISH
(About 1 Ft.)

VENOMOUS SPINE FISH

WEEVER FISH
(About 1 Ft.)

Figure 8-2. Venomous spine fish and snails

Figure 8-3. (*left*) Climbing coconut palm; (*right*) Shinnying

covering at the tip of the nuts. It is not an easy task to climb a coconut tree, nor is it always self-evident how to make use of the food and water it supplies. Practice is necessary.

The fresh leaves of seaside purslane (*Sesuvium portulacastrum*) or common purslane (*Portulaca oleracoa*) can be chewed and swallowed to relieve thirst. Both may be found growing on the beach or strand. To improvise a vegetation still from these plants, place them inside a plastic bag and leave them in the sun. Wait for the water to collect.

In temperate regions, merely travel up or down the coastline until you run into a stream or river emptying into the ocean. Wildlife will lead you to fresh water. Further ideas on finding water can be found in the desert survival chapter and adapted to your situation.

As for the polar seacoast, consult the chapter on mountains and cold regions survival. Take care not to drink melted ice that was formed from sea water. Old sea ice, which is blue, is acceptable.

To be on the safe side, all drinking water, except that from vines or coconuts, should be boiled or chemically treated.

SHELTER CONSTRUCTION

The construction of shelters and beds is not as necessary in warm climates as in cold ones. Nevertheless shelter is essential for comfort in any prolonged situation. Shelter should give protection from rain, and beds should encourage sleep. If you have sufficient energy, make a bed the first night and later construct a shelter. In cold climates, of course, shelter increases in importance. See the chapter on mountains and cold regions.

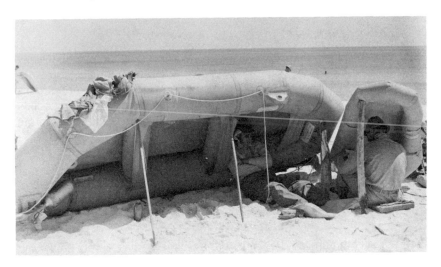

Figure 8-4. Life raft used to provide shelter

In the tropics, a comfortable bed can be made by laying down two parallel rows of split coconut fronds. The leaflets should slightly overlap in the center of the bed. To divide a frond, break or cut at the very tip and pull each side of the leaf so that it splits down the center of the midrib from top to bottom. If a layer of springy leaves such as *Scaevola* or *Tournefortia* are used as a base, the bed will be more comfortable. A final topping with a thatch sheet is ideal. The importance of a good night's rest cannot be overemphasized.

When tarps or parachute cloth are not available, a lean-to frame constructed from coconut midribs and shingled with thatch sheets will provide a water-repellent shelter. Face the shelter away from the prevailing winds, and place it in the shade, near sources of food and water.

Plaiting a coconut frond into a thatch sheet is simple. Start at the butt end of a half frond and bend the third leaflet back over the second and under the first. Next, bend the fifth leaflet back over the fourth and under the first. Next, bend the fifth leaflet back over the fourth and under the first. Continue this check-type weaving until the sheet is completed. The weaving of baskets, eye shades, and other articles can be quickly mastered with this basic technique.

Lashing for tying together shelters or beds can be stripped from the leaves, bark, and roots of numerous plants. A few examples: fibers from pandanus prop roots and the fibers within the midrib of a coconut frond; hibiscus or hau bark; the dried leaflets of the coconut and nipa palm; and pandanus leaves.

In temperate and cold areas, construct lean-tos or snow caves. Instructions are in the cold regions chapter.

FOOD PROCUREMENT

Food sources are plentiful around the seashore. Vegetation will most likely provide more food than you require, but shellfish and other animals are also plentiful. In virtually all climates, mollusks can be found among rocks and fish around the reefs. The chapter on wild plant food lists many edible plants common throughout the world, but with an emphasis on temperate climates. In this chapter, we'll concentrate on tropical plants.

Tropical Plant Foods

The vegetation of the tropics is lush, but you can't expect to fill your stomach and supply your body's nutritional needs by reaching out at random and plucking food from trees. You may have washed up on a beautiful tropical island, but you haven't died and gone to heaven. Below we discuss a few common varieties of edible plants. Learning to recognize and use these plants is like having a portable, well-stocked pantry with you at all times.

Palms, found throughout the tropical world and most numerous near the equator, vary from tall trees to shrubs and vines. The leaves are generally pinnate (arranged along a common axis) or palmate (radiating from a common point), and many palms have the well-known leafy crown. Palms are one of the best sources of plant food for inexperienced individuals. Widespread and conspicuous, many palms contain drinkable sap, edible fruits, and buds or starchy cores within the trunks. Palms also furnish sugar, fibers, shelter, and clothing material.

The terminal bud or growing point of most palms is edible either cooked or raw. Located on the tip of the trunk, it is enclosed by a crown of leaves or sheathing bases of the leaf stem. Eat any that are not too bitter.

The fruits of palm trees are generally produced in clusters below the leafy crown. The fruits of the coconut, nipa, and date palm are excellent food, but the fruits of many other Old World species are not edible. Some contain minute crystals that cause intense pain. Eat Eastern Hemisphere palm fruits with caution. Most of the Western Hemisphere palm fruits are edible or at least not poisonous or irritating.

Enormous quantities of starch are stored in the trunks of some of the palms. It is edible in all species in which it is found, but is not worth trying to get unless an axe or machete is available.

Thus, if you lack specific knowledge concerning edible palm species, you can obtain and eat the fruit, sap, starch, or buds of most palms with reasonable safety and success. A little specific knowledge, however, will greatly facilitate the use of palms for food.

The Nipa Palm. The nipa palm grows only in brackish tidal marshes and

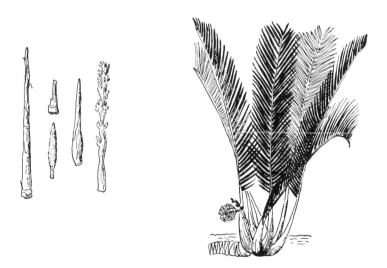

Figure 8-5. (*left*) Palm buds; (*right*) Nipa palm (*Nipa fruticans*)

mangrove swamps of the islands and coasts of the Indian Ocean. It looks like a stemless coconut palm with long leaves rising in tufts from the root-stock to a height of about 15 feet. The short, erect flower stem produces a cluster of seeds that are edible when young and resemble coconuts in taste. Old ones are very hard and rather indigestible. The flower stems give off large quantities of an edible sugary sap commonly collected in jointed bamboo funnels. The cabbage is edible and the leaves are one of the best thatching materials.

Coconut Palm. Coconuts and coconut sap are available year round. The nuts can be prepared in many ways. The soft white meat of green or "spoon nuts" is the best and can be withdrawn from a split nut by making a "spoon" out of a sharp shoulder slashed off the outside husk. It is more nourishing and digestible than the harder meat of ripe nuts. The meat of ripe nuts can be eaten fresh, grated, or dried to copra. Alternatively, the milk can be squeezed out of it for food or drink. Oil separates from the milk on standing. Good eating nuts are green and so completely filled with water that they do not rattle when shaken.

Old nuts sprouting beneath trees contain a spongy center that can be eaten raw, but is more tasty and nourishing when cooked. These sprouted nuts should be husked and then baked for two hours in a rock oven (see "Cooking" in this chapter). When done, the yellow potatolike core tastes somewhat like a boiled yam. To open the husked nuts, strike the three lon-gitudinal ribs successively with a knife handle or rock. The nut casing will split cleanly into equal halves. A large number of such nuts can be cooked

Figure 8-6. Coconut palm (*Cocos nucifera*)

at one time and they will keep, unopened, for three to four days. They are not only very nourishing but easy to get. Don't pass up sprouted coconuts.

The hearts or growing points of both young and full-grown coconut trees can be cut out with a machete and eaten raw or cooked. Peel off the outside layers until the tender growth is reached.

Coconut sap is high in sugar. To get it, tightly bind with twine all but the last few inches of a young flowering spike. Slice off the unbound tip and hang a container beneath it. (A bamboo joint or half a coconut shell will serve.) Collect the sap once a day (preferably in the morning) and cut a fresh cross-section sliver from the spike to ensure continued sap flow.

You must be able to open a coconut without a machete. Lacking the "know-how," this is not an easy task. The husk will eventually split off if you repeatedly strike the pointed end of the nut against a hard object such as a

Figure 8-7. Sago palm (*Metroxylon*)

rock, but it is much easier to use a hard, sharpened "husking stick" firmly anchored in the ground. A hardwood stick 3 feet long and 1 inch in diameter will suffice. The nut should be held by both ends and thrust down on the pointed stick, taking care not to puncture the inside shell. A backward twist of the wrist will pry off a section of the husk. Repeat this action until the nut within comes free of the husk.

The Sago Palm. The sago palm grows on the islands of the Indian Archipelago and the Malay Peninsula in damp lowlands, in freshwater swamps, and along streams, lakes, and rivers. The hard trunk contains an accumulation of starch which is at a maximum when the tree is between the ages of ten and fifteen years, just before the flowers are produced. Lesser amounts exist in immature or flowering trees. To obtain the edible starch, cut down the tree, using a wire saw, machete, or axe, split and remove the hard outer shell, and slice the core into small fragments. Boil these or wrap them in leaves and bake. Chew the starch out of the pith. A

Figure 8-8. (*left*) Sugar palm (*Arenga*); (*right*) Buri palm (*Corypha*)

flour can be obtained by crushing the pith and washing and straining it through a cloth or netting to remove the fiber. The terminal bud may be cooked and eaten.

Sugar Palm. The sugar palm is common throughout the open lands of the Indian Archipelago, but more abundant in the hilly interior than on the seacoast. The mature tree is 30 to 40 feet tall with a dense crown of leaves. The terminal bud is considered edible but should be eaten with caution. Starch can be obtained from the trunk. A sugary sap can be collected by cutting the flower spikes. The black fibrous material at the base of the leaf stalk makes excellent cord.

The Buri Palm. The buri palm is a very large, fan-leaved palm found only in tropical Asia. The leaves may be as large as 9 feet in diameter. The pithy portion of the trunk contains starch, difficult to obtain because of the thick, hard outer shell. The sap is sugary and the buds are edible. The leaf and leaf-stem fibers are used for making cord and rope.

Piva or Peach Palm. The piva palm is confined to the tropical Americas. Its slender trunk, 20 to 40 feet tall, is easily recognized by its alternating light and dark bands of spines. The mature fruits, red or yellow and growing in large clusters, may be eaten boiled or roasted. They taste like sweet potatoes or chestnuts.

Figure 8-9. Piva or peach palm (*Guilielma utilis*)

Figure 8-10. Bacaba and patawa palms (*Jessenia, Oenocarpus*)

Bacaba and Patawa Palms. Bacaba and patawa palms are found in the moist forested regions of the Guianas and Brazil. The pulp of the fruit can be chewed and eaten. The oily kernel within the pulp is also edible. The fruit is smooth, dark purplish in color, and about three-quarters of an inch long.

Assai Palm. The Assai palm and related species are native to the forests of tropical South America where they generally grow together in large masses. The Assai palm likes swampy places, particularly the banks of rivers within the tidal limits. It attains a height of 30 or 40 feet with a stem

Figure 8-11. Assai palm (*Euterpe oleracea*)

about as thick as a man's arm. When the fruit is mature, the soft purple pulp is edible.

Rattan Palms. There are many species of rattan or climbing palms with smooth reedlike stems, seldom more than an inch or two in diameter, which usually grow to a great length. Nearly all are native to Asia, being particularly abundant in the virgin forests of Malaya and the Southwest Pacific Islands. The leaf stalks are spiny and in many species prolonged through the divided blade into whiplike tails at the end. It is safe to try eating the terminal bud of all species. The swollen base of the vine in some species contains edible starch that can be obtained and utilized as described for sago. Drinking water can be drained from lengths of the stem, and the stems themselves serve as cord or rope.

Bamboo. There are many different kinds of bamboo distributed throughout the warmer regions of the world. They are found in open or jungle country, in either lowlands or mountains. The young shoots of all may be cooked and eaten, although some species are better than others.

Sugar Cane. The cultivated sugar cane and similar appearing wild species grow throughout the tropical regions, usually in open country along the banks of rivers and streams. Cultivated varieties are commonly found around abandoned plantations. The sugar content is high and can be obtained by removing the hard outer stem layer with a knife or the teeth and chewing the soft inner pith.

Bananas and Plantains. Bananas and plantains are found in the tropical and subtropical regions of both hemispheres. They are herbaceous plants in which the leaf sheaths encase the stem. Bananas and plantains look much alike and it is not necessary to distinguish between them. The fruit of both is eaten raw or cooked, although most plantains must be cooked to be edible. The fruits of the different species vary in shape and size. The slender terminal flower bud of some species is excellent when cooked, and the rootstock and leafsheaths of many of them can be cooked and eaten in emergencies.

Taro. Taro is related to our jack-in-the-pulpit, calla lily, and skunk cab-

Figure 8-12. (*left*) Sugar cane (*Saccharum officinalis*); (*right*) Taro (*Colocasia antiquorum*)

Figure 8-13. Buck yam (*Dioscorea penta-phylla*)

bage. There are numerous species in the Pacific regions, many of which are used by the local people as food. Taro is especially abundant in the Pacific Islands and also occurs in India, Sri Lanka, the West Indies, and Eastern Asia. It is found inland in low, wet areas of rich soil. The roots are rich in starch, though they are pungent and irritating unless thoroughly baked or boiled. The tubers may weigh from one to twelve pounds, and have a mottled bluish-gray appearance. The young leaves are edible if boiled thoroughly in several changes of water.

Yams. Yams are sweet-potatolike vines of the tropical forests. The large tuberous roots of cultivated and wild species are dug up by the natives and either boiled or roasted. Some species are poisonous unless properly prepared. The buck yam is common in tropical Asia, including the South Pacific Islands.

Manioc, Cassava, Tapioca. The fleshy and starchy root of bitter and sweet manioc, a shrubby plant about 6 to 8 feet high, yields the greatest portion of the daily food for many people of the tropical Americas. There are about fifty species and they are most abundant in the wet areas of Peru, the Guianas, Brazil, the Antilles and southern Mexico. It is also cultivated widely in the Eastern Hemisphere. Sweet and bitter manioc cannot be distinguished between except by taste. Sweet manioc can be eaten cooked or raw, but bitter manioc must be cooked (as described in the wild plant food chapter) to rid it of poisonous hydrocyanic acid. If in doubt as to the specific variety, it is best to cook it.

Seaside Purslane. One or the other of the seaside purslanes are found on the shores of most tropical countries near brackish or salt water. They

Figure 8-14. Manioc (*Manihot*)

Figure 8-15. (*left*) Seaside purslane (*Sesuvium portulacastrum*); (*right*) Wild and hog plums
(*Spondias dulcis*)

Figure 8-16. (*left*) Figs (*Ficus pretoria*); (*center*) Sour sop (*Annona muricata*); (*right*) Sweet sop (*Annona squamosa*)

are smooth, succulent plants with fleshy stems and leaves and a salty taste. The entire plant can be eaten raw or cooked.

Wild and Hog Plums. Native to the tropics of both hemispheres, wild and hog plums have fruits, some of which are edible. The Polynesian wild plum yields a yellowish fruit which tastes something like a pineapple.

Figs. Numerous species of edible figs are widely distributed throughout the tropics of both hemispheres. Wild figs resemble cultivated figs and are easily recognizable. The wild figs are usually small and all have a milky juice. Insects are often found in them, but the fruit may still be eaten unless definitely decayed.

Custard Apple, Sour Sop, and Sweet Sop. This genus of small fruit trees is largely represented in Central and South America, but various species are widely cultivated throughout the tropics. A wild custard apple is found in tropical Africa and is large, well-flavored and juicy. A similar cultivated species with pale green fruit is found in settled areas of the Pacific Islands. The sour sop is cultivated throughout tropical America and is found both wild and planted in the South Pacific Islands. The leaves are strongly scented when crushed. The spiny green-colored fruit is sometimes as large as a human head. It can be used to prepare a thirst-quenching beverage.

Stamvrugte and Star Apple. Members of this genus are found in the tropics of both hemispheres. The star apple is found in the West Indies and Central America, while the stamvrugte is found in tropical Africa on rocky outcrops and mountains. The fruit is red when ripe, about an inch in length, and has a tart flavor.

Sour Plum. The sour plum is a large, often thorny scrub or small tree

Figure 8-17. (*left*) Stamvrugte (*Chrysophyllum magaliesmonlonum*); (*right*) Sour plum (*Ximenia caffra*)

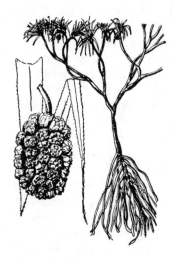

Figure 8-18. (*left*) Breadfruit (*Artocarpus*); (*right*) Screwpines (*Pandanus tectorius*)

bearing yellow fruits resembling plums. It is found throughout the tropics of America, Asia, Africa, and the Pacific Islands, often near the seashore. The genus contains numerous edible species. The pulp of the fruit, but not the seed, is edible.

Breadfruit. There are many species of breadfruit native to the Southwest Pacific Islands. They are closely allied to the North American mulberry and osage orange, and all have a milky sap. The fruits of some species are excellent boiled or baked, and the seeds of all are edible when cooked. Some species are seedless, but these must be propagated by shoots and are therefore not available in uninhabited areas. The pulp of some can be eaten raw. The fruiting season of the different species varies, supplying a year-round supply of the fruit. The common breadfruit tree is moderate in size with dark, green-lobed leaves, and bears a roundish, rough-surfaced green or brownish fruit. It forms one of the most important food staples in the South Pacific Islands. It may be eaten boiled, baked, roasted, or fried. Roasting is the best and easiest method of preparation. The milky juice of the tree can be used as glue for caulking canoes or prepared as bird lime.

Screw Pines. The screw pines are confined to the Eastern Hemisphere and a large number of them are limited to the islands of the Indian Archipelago. They are found principally in close proximity to the sea, sometimes covering large areas with an almost impenetrable mass of vegetation. Most of them are large bushes with long, narrow, leathery leaves, thick and often twisted stems, and many prop roots. The red fruits and the seeds are available the year-round and are edible either cooked or raw. The fruit itself consists of rounded grains or sections enclosed in a hard rind. The terminal leaf bud may also be eaten cooked or raw.

Mango. Mangos are tropical Asiatic trees, cultivated or wild. The common mango, one of the most delicious of tropical fruits, is cultivated in nearly all tropical countries. The fruits of the wild species are edible, but some have a strong turpentine flavor. The ripe fruits are generally yellow.

Sapodilla. The sapodilla is a medium-sized evergreen tree bearing

Figure 8-19. (*left*) Mango (*Mangifera*); (*right*) Sapodilla (*Achras sapota*)

brown fruits within which are large smooth black seeds. It grows wild in central and tropical South America, and is both wild and cultivated in other parts of the tropics. The fruit should be eaten raw, not cooked.

Baobab. The baobab tree occurs in Africa, Madagascar, and Australia. It is easily recognized by its stout, bottle-shaped trunk which is sometimes 30 feet in diameter. The large, oblong or globular, fruit, 4 to 8 inches long, has a woody shell which encloses numerous seeds embedded in a soft bready substance. The seeds are nutritious, the flesh tart, and the white gum which exudes from the tree makes an agreeable drink when diluted with hot water. Fibers of the wood can be used to make rope or twine.

Papaya. Native to Central and South America, the papaya grows cultivated and wild in all tropical countries. It is a straight, green- or brown-stemmed plant 6 to 20 feet high with large, melonlike fruits. The tree has a milky sap. The fruits of the wild plants are small. They can be eaten raw, and unripened fruits may be boiled as a vegetable. The milky sap contains the enzyme papain which will tenderize meat if put on it before cooking.

Cashew. The cashew is a spreading, moderate-sized evergreen tree found semi-wild in fields and on the sides of dry bushy hills in tropical regions of Central and South America and is cultivated throughout the tropics. A grayish, kidney-shaped nut hangs from the red and yellow fruit. The fruit can be eaten raw, but the nut is poisonous unless roasted until all the oil is removed.

Pandanus. Fruits of the pandanus tree ripen throughout the year. On all but the more poorly vegetated islands, some ripe fruits should be available when you need them. The fibrous succulent tips of the keys or fruit sections contain sugar and starch which can be chewed and sucked out. Edible seeds also lie within the keys. The amount of food obtainable is small in comparison to the other food plants, but is sufficient to keep you going. The pandanus is important because of its wide distribution and general availability. Some fruits may slightly irritate the mouth for a minute or so after eating. This possible stinging is not enough to cause discomfort and does no harm.

Arrowroot. Arrowroot thrives on both the inhabited and uninhabited tropical Pacific islands. It is found inland on the richer sandy soil and grows best in clearings or beneath trees where the undergrowth is not too heavy. The plant is quite abundant in the Marshall Islands, and the numerous rounded tubers are available throughout the year. They are shallow and easily excavated. The carrotlike and potatolike tubers are rich in starch, but must be crushed and washed before being cooked. This leaching process limits the usefulness of this plant to the survivor, but it should not be eaten raw.

Indian Almond. The Indian almond is most common along island shores,

Figure 8-20. Baobab tree and fruit (*Adansonia*)

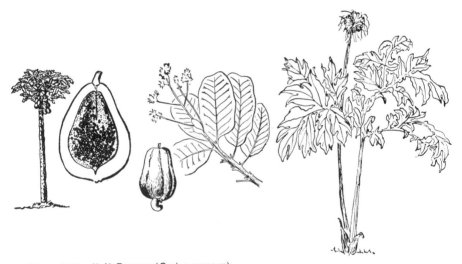

Figure 8-21. (*left*) Papaya (*Carica papaya*);
(*center*) Cashew (*Ana cardium occidentale*);
(*right*) Arrowroot (*Tacca leontopetaloides*)

but it also ranges inland. Chew the yellow or red fibrous covering of the nut for its sugar content, and eat the long, cylindrical almond-tasting kernel. The nuts can be split open with a knife or pounded open with rocks.

Turtle Grass. This plant grows in patches in lagoons back of the reef on muddy or mixed sandy bottoms. The seed pods contain pealike seeds that may be eaten raw. They are crisp, tasty, and slightly salty.

Passion Fruit. These orange fruits are quite common on vines along the shore and in open areas. The small fruits will furnish some food value and vitamins.

Thespesia Populnea. This plant grows along the shoreline and looks very much like hau or *Hibiscus tiliaceus.* The young leaves, flowers, and buds may be eaten raw or cooked.

Morinda Citrifolia. The ripe fruits are available the year round, scattered throughout the tropical Pacific islands. The soft, grayish fruits smell like limburger cheese. They are an acquired taste. The young fruits and leaves may be cooked as greens.

Pigweed. Despite its name, pigweed is a succulent plant that grows best along the seashore, in clearings, or on abandoned land. The leaves and stems may be eaten raw or cooked as greens.

Pemphis Acidula. A common tree along the shores of many islands, its leaves may be eaten raw.

Food from the Reef

The reef ranks a close second to coconuts as a source of emergency food. You must arrange your schedule around the daily tides. Low tides are the time to hunt lobsters, to spear fish, and to pick up shellfish on the reefs. Fish are active and can be caught on a hook and line on incoming tides. It is dangerous, however, to get caught far out on strange reefs by rising tides; these usually sweep over a reef, forming strong lateral currents.

Many types of shellfish can be gathered with ease, but obtaining other foods such as fish, lobsters, and crabs requires both equipment and skill. To tap the best food sources of the reef, you should be a fairly good swimmer in surf. A face mask, fishing spear, gloves, and a waterproof flashlight make reef foraging more efficient. A gill net can be used to advantage. A hard pointed wooden stick will do for a spear, but a metal rod from a plane fitted with a bungee cord (the kind of elastic rope often used to hold items onto a bike) at the rear and barbed at the point makes a better one, and it is elastic-propelled. To barb the point, burn it then rub it against rock.

Shellfish. Shellfish are the easiest source of food for the inexperienced survivor. One type or another may be found attached to mangrove roots, buried in sand, fastened to the reef, or concealed under rocks.

By looking for breathing holes in the wet sand at low tide it is possible to locate various species of small burrowing clams and to unearth them by digging.

Huge clams such as *Tridacna* embed themselves in living coral reefs. A swimmer can readily spot their brilliantly colored mantles, which are exposed when the shells are open. A muscle at the hinge of the shell attaches the *Tridacna* to the rock. Sometimes this muscle can be reached with a knife and the clam freed. The clam will open if a hole is cut between

Figure 8-22. Low tide is a prime time to do a little oyster hunting. (Courtesy of the Defense Audio-Visual Agency)

the hinged halves of the shells. More often *Tridacna* cannot be thus removed and the technique is then to thrust the knife blade to the bottom of the opened valves and cut the large adductor muscle which holds the shell shut. The contents can then be removed without freeing the shell. The large valve muscle and a fatty sack, the size of a tennis ball, are excellent raw.

The giant clam or *Hippopus* is not embedded in coral but prefers rocky bottoms or open sandy spots. To open giant clams, bash them in the shell where the valves close and insert a knife to cut the adductor muscle, but be sure to keep fingers out of the valves of live clams; the shells close slowly but with great force. You can cook large clams in the shell by placing them on a bed of coals. Heating will open them.

Shellfish such as cowries (*Cypraea*), cat-eyes (*Turbo*), and snails can be found under rocks. Sea urchins likewise lurk in such places. Their spines can inflict painful wounds, and though sea urchins have some food value, they are not worth fooling with. Many sea cucumbers are edible, but some contain sticky fluids and others contain poisons sufficiently powerful to kill fish. They should be considered only as a starvation food.

Lobsters and Crabs. Some crabs are active in the daytime, for example, the fiddler crabs (*Grapsus*) typical of muddy shores, which scoot over rocks at the water edge, and the landcrabs (*Cardisoma*). None of these contain enough meat to be considered really good foods. Hermit crabs, which make their homes in old seashells on the shore, may be removed from their shells by grasping their legs and claws and turning them with the spiral of the shell. Applied heat in the form of a match or a hot coal will make the shell open. Their best use is for baiting fishlines, but they can be roasted in the shell and eaten.

The best crabbing is at night on the reef. In the light of a coconut frond torch or a flashlight, crabs may be seen and speared or pinned down and grabbed by their big biting claws. The best results are obtained by crabbing under water, using a face mask and a waterproof flashlight. (A coconut frond torch is made by bundling together two or three dried fronds. These are wrapped at intervals with lashings. A longer lasting and brighter torch can be improvised by filling a section of bamboo with coconut cloth soaked in coconut oil.)

Spiny lobsters or "languster" are usually abundant on reefs where there are caves and crevices in the coral. They are most active at night during the early hours of the incoming tide, and can be grabbed in shallow water when located by torchlight. The survivor will be much more successful if he uses a face mask, waterproof flashlight, and gloves. He should swim over rocky bottoms in water from 1 to 5 feet deep and peer into all nooks and crevices under rocks. When caught in the beam of a light, the lobster will remain motionless for a long enough period to be grabbed or speared.

Lobsters swim backwards, so when grabbing them by hand, hold the light in front and reach them from behind. Once you have grasped the lobster, move him in against your leg and he will grab your trousers and stop struggling. The spines on the lobster can gash your hand, so wear gloves. Swim fully clothed, including shoes, as protection against getting cut by coral. Lobstering, even under emergency conditions, is sport and one good-sized lobster makes both an ample and a delicious meal.

Another delicacy that comes in a large package is the coconut crab or "robber" crab. It is a land crab with tremendous biting claws and a sacklike abdomen. It is active at night and cuts holes into coconuts to get to the meat. Old nuts so cut are a sign of the crabs' presence. In daytime the crabs hole up under rocks, and when located by their wellworn burrow entrances, can be dug up. At night they can be spotted with a light and picked up. Hold them down with a stick and grab hold of the big pinching claws. Be careful; they can crush a finger.

The quickest way to cook lobsters and crabs is to broil them on a bed of coals. The meat will remain more moist, however, if they are cooked in a steam pit. Most of the spiny lobster meat is in the tail, while in crabs it is in the large claws. The sacklike abdomen of the coconut crab contains a

Figure 8-23. (*left*) Hermit crab; (*right*) Blue crab

Figure 8-24. (*left*) Spiny lobster; (*right*) Common lobster

saucelike fat into which the meat can be dipped. Eat all seafoods while hot. They soon spoil in warm climates.

Octopus. Reef octopuses are small and haunt holes and crevices in the reef. They wedge their bodies into such openings until only their eyes may show. They can be speared and then finished off by turning the body sack inside out through the gill cleft. They will discolor the water with sepia when disturbed. If they grab your arm with their tentacles, run your hand down your arm to break the hold of the suction disks. Don't waste effort trying to pull off the tentacles. Octopus meat, though rubbery, has a delicate flavor similar to lobster. Prior to cooking, sprinkle the octopus lightly with sand and beat gently with a sprig of leaves. This relaxes the muscles and tenderizes the meat. An hour's cooking in a steam pit is sufficient. Before eating, slough off the red skin and disks to reveal the tasty white meat.

Fish. Coral reefs teem with fish, and spearfishing is well worthwhile if a survivor is equipped with goggles and can improvise a spear. Schools of small fish are abundant in shallow water, but are hard to spear. Spend your time looking under rocks and in coral crevices where such fish as sturgeon-fish, butterfly-fish, and rockfish can be easily located and cornered. Look for flounders and small stingrays on sandy bottoms. Small sharks can often be cornered in tidal pools and shallow water and are very good eat-

Figure 8-25. Small sharks, cornered in shallow tidal pools, make very good eating. (Courtesy of the Defense Audio-Visual Agency)

ing. Good-sized parrot-fish and sturgeon-fish are abundant just beyond the reef and in tidal channels. Coral heads rising up from sandy bottoms are good fishing spots since fish will seek sanctuary there when a swimmer approaches. When a fish is speared, do not move the spear until the fish has been pulled up on the shaft where it cannot wriggle loose. Spearfishing is more successful if conducted at night with an underwater flashlight. Fish "hold" to the light. Carry a line for stringing your catch. Under the right conditions "chop fishing" produces a big haul. Fish attracted to a light at low tide can be stunned or slashed in shallow water by hitting them with the back of a machete. Needle fish, goat fish, mullet, and other school-fish are easily obtained in this manner.

A gill net used where chop fishing is effective or in shallow channels at changing tide will be productive. Care must be exercised to keep big fish out of the net.

Reef fish such as puffer, trigger, and parrot-fish can be poisonous to eat. But many others are delicious. If you're doubtful, cook the fish, eat a few bites, and then wait a few hours. If no bad results are felt, you can eat more.

Hook-and-line fishing is usually not profitable on the reef. Practice this method instead in tidal channels, preferably at night, and use hermit crabs as bait. First crush a number of these crabs and throw them into the water to "chum" the fish. With a rubber raft, survivors can successfully bottom-fish in lagoons and bays, using hermit crabs or chopped-up shellfish for bait. In an hour's time, a long fishline can be made from plant fibers. Most palm leaves, as well as the inner bark of many palms, contain suitable fibers. Fibers from dried, immature coconut husks make both line and ropes.

FIRE MAKING AND COOKING

Without matches, the best method of making a fire is to use flint and steel or a magnifying glass. You can, without too much trouble, make fire using either the native fire saw, bow and drill, or the fire thong methods. All need to be practiced if you're going to be successful under emergency conditions.

Tinders are numerous. A very good and well-distributed one is the dry coconut husk. Husks make too slow a fire for cooking but are made to order for banking a fire. Coconut "cloth," found at the base of the leaf fronds, and dry coconut leaflets serve well as tinder. Soft woods make the best kindling, and hard woods furnish hot, lasting coals. Tropical Pacific island species such as *Scaevola* and *Ochrosia* are soft, while *Pemphis*, *Cassuarina*, *Tournefortia* and *Callophylum* are hard. See the chapter on Firemaking and Cooking for further information applicable to temperate and Arctic seacoasts.

Most seashore foods such as crabs, fish, lobsters, and even breadfruit

Figure 8-26. Rocks will hold heat and cook meat and fish slowly. (Courtesy of Steve Netherby, *Field & Stream*)

and coconut heart can be cooked on a rock broiler. Rocks first heated in a bed of coals should be arranged so that food can be broiled on their hot, flat surfaces. Broil fish, unscaled, to keep them moist. Peel off skin and scales before eating.

Cooking in a rock oven is another method well suited to the seashore where digging is easy. A fire is built in a pit about 2½ feet wide and a foot deep. After you've got a hot bed of hardwood coals, place a grate of hardwood over the fire and put rocks on top of it. By the time the grate burns through, the rocks are well heated. Rake out the burning brands and coals and use the rocks to pave the bottom and sides of the pit. Place a layer of green leaves on the rocks; next, lay food such as sprouted coconuts, lobsters, clams, or fish on the leaves. Then, shingle a top layer of leaves over the food. Pile sand over the leaves and leave the food to cook. If steaming is desired, place an upright stick on the hot rocks before the pit is filled. After the food is covered with sand, remove the stick and drop a little water in the hole before it is closed. Cooking time varies with the food. Let the food cook for at least an hour. If you build and use a pit correctly, you can forage all day and return to find a warm meal ready.

The young whole leaves found on sprouted coconuts are ready-made dishes and can also be used for wrapping food. Coconut flower spathes, empty coconut shells, and large clam shells are serviceable as either cups or plates.

Seafood may be preserved from one meal to another by wrapping it with leaves while still hot and placing it close to a fire or in the hot sun to discourage flies.

TRAVELING

Shore travel is generally easier than inland travel—cool breezes, little or no vegetation to push through, a greater range of vision. Night travel along the reefs is still cooler and less tiring. The best time to travel is at low tide. Travel, foraging, and heavy work should be done during early morning, evening, and at night. During the day it is advisable to immerse frequently in the water to prevent heat exhaustion and undue fatigue. Keep fully clothed to prevent sunburn.

Reefs of windward island shores are flat shelves, easy to travel over at low tide, but the beaches are usually higher and rougher than those of lee shores. Sturdy shoes are needed as protection against rock bruises and coral and shell cuts.

Mangrove swamps, or forests, line many tropical shores. When small, they can be circumnavigated by walking or wading around their seaward side at low tide, or they can be traversed by following the high-tide mark which divides the mangrove forest from the strand or interior jungle. This is usually a clearly defined belt where vegetation is sparse. In traveling either seaward or shoreward through a mangrove swamp, follow tidal channels. Avoid fighting your way through the tangle of roots. Swimming may be necessary and must be resorted to whenever muck or water makes wading impossible. Inflate your shirt first by wetting it and then blowing into the front opening while submerged. An air bubble will blossom above your shoulders. Trousers tied together at the ankles make a very good flotation device (see the Sea Survival section). When you encounter freshwater streams, cross them where they enter lagoons rather than farther out on the reef where they may be exceptionally deep.

If interisland travel within an atoll is deemed necessary, try to row or sail with the prevailing winds and follow the atoll contour, keeping to the lee side of the reef or bar. When rafting on the lee side of the atoll, keep within the lagoon to prevent being blown out to the open sea. On the windward side, keep to the lee side of the islands and reefs. Distances between atoll islands are short and water is shallow. You can often wade from one island to another at low tide.

CHAPTER 9

Desert Survival

A desert is any area that receives less than 10 inches of rain a year. By contrast, tropical rain forests average nearly 80 inches annually. Even the small amount of rain does not oblige the parched earth by falling at regular intervals. In parts of the Sahara, in fact, rain has not touched the earth's surface for decades, although the average annual rainfall is 4 inches. When it does rain, however, the downfall can be incredible. It is as though a gigantic sluice has opened in the sky, releasing not individual drops of rain but virtual walls of water. The water plummets to earth, gouging channels in the landscape and creating flash floods. Wadis (dry watercourses of North African and Southwest Asian deserts) and arroyos (water-carved gullies of the U.S. Southwest deserts) fill up in an instant with raging torrents. Although such cloudbursts are rare, one of the basic principles of desert survival is: Do not camp in a wadi or an arroyo.

Deserts cover 20 percent of the earth's surface but are home to only 4 percent of the world's population. At the word *desert*, most people conjure images of vast seas of sand, as exemplified by parts of the Sahara. Deserts, however, present many different faces—some of sand, others of salt, but most of stone. Terrain also varies, from monotonous flatlands to dramatic mountains.

The world's deserts lie generally in the subtropics. Northern Hemisphere deserts are the Sahara (the greatest of all), the Arabian, part of the desert of Iran, and regions of Mexico and the southern United States. In the Southern Hemisphere lie South Africa's Kalahari and the Australian Desert.

Deserts also occur on the western side of continents. They lie in the path of cool winds, which have been robbed of their moisture by cold ocean currents. The Namib Desert on the coast of Southwest Africa and the 1,200-mile-long Atacama Desert on the Pacific coast of South America are such deserts.

Other arid expanses result from the "rain shadow" effect of mountain ranges. The four great North American deserts—the Chihuahuan, Sonoran, Mohave, and Great Basin—owe their existence in part to the

Figure 9-1. Dry river beds, such as this one in Death Valley, are good places to look for water but never camp in one. (Courtesy of the National Park Service)

mountain ranges of the West Coast. In Asia, the Himalayas have helped create the formidable Gobi Desert, which covers large areas of northern China and Mongolia.

A desert is what it is because of a dearth of rain; temperature is not necessarily a defining characteristic. Much of Antarctica, for example, receives less than 10 inches of snowfall a year and is therefore considered a desert, albeit a cold one. Generally speaking, however, little rain and high temperatures go together. In this chapter we consider the problems of surviving in the hot deserts of the world.

During the day, the desert floor can reach temperatures of up to 185°F. The lack of cloud cover and the lack of moisture in the air leave the earth exposed to 95 percent of the sun's rays. Again by way of contrast, only 1 percent of the sun's radiation is able to penetrate the dense canopy of the tropical rain forest. At night, the same atmospheric conditions prevent the earth from retaining heat, and temperatures can drop 70° or 80°F within a few hours.

How does anything survive in this extreme environment? Plants and animals have managed to adapt biologically over generations, but humans must make use of their minds to prepare ahead of time for the possibility of an ordeal in the desert.

PREPARATION

If you were to be left without clothes, water, or food in a shadeless, waterless desert at the dawn of a hot summer's day, you would probably not live to see the sunset. By late afternoon, when the temperature could be hitting

120°F, you would have sweated away about 2 gallons of water. Your body would be drawing on water stored in the fat, tissues, and blood. Before the cool of the evening, you would be feverish and delirious. Eventually you would die, most likely from circulatory failure. Even if you drank eight or ten pints of water a day, within a few days the effects of sunburn on your unprotected body would kill you.

Humans can prevail in a desert, but they must be equipped with supplies and tools to increase their margin of safety. Water is the most crucial supply. An adult, whether traveling at night and resting during the day or just sitting tight, will need at least one gallon of water a day. Take extra water bottles with you. Getting water from the desert is tricky, but it can be done. The minimum tools you will need are a knife, a sheet of plastic, a plastic bag, and a sponge.

Four pieces of cloth

Making a burnoose

Improvised footgear

T-shirt used as face protection against sand

Facecloth

Neckcloth

Figure 9-2. Desert clothing

Water alone will not save you if you've failed to dress appropriately. Light-colored and free-flowing clothing—from head to foot—offers the best protection. An imitation Arab burnoose can be fashioned from a piece of cloth or a T-shirt. This will keep your head cool and protect the back of your neck from sunburn. In a dust or sand storm, wrap it around your head to keep particles out of your eyes, mouth, nose, and ears. At all times, good boots, and socks to prevent blisters, are a must. Sunscreen lotions should be included in your survival kit.

There are stories—some true—of people who just "disappeared" after setting off in a motor vehicle for an oasis "only" a few miles away. Be sure you have an adequate supply of gas, for the great natural petroleum reserves of the Middle Eastern deserts, for example, don't come equipped with handy pumps. Your vehicle's radiator may get thirsty for water, too. Desert sand and dust take a toll on ordinary motor vehicles. Attempt great distances over desert tracks only in vehicles that are specially prepared.

Since World War II, deserts have been more accurately mapped than ever before because of advances in aerial and satellite photography. Take the latest maps of an area with you and always carry a compass. A mirror will double as a signaling device and as a means of starting a fire.

Any list of priorities can be only hypothetical. You may find that in a certain environment or at different times in a survival episode, particular tasks assume significance over others. In a desert, heat and aridity are your major enemies, and water is the key to combating heat cramps, heat exhaustion, and heat stroke. Thus, securing water becomes part of your preventive first aid. Together, first aid and water procurement occupy the top place in our list of priorities.

Signaling, which in other circumstances would edge out water in the list of priorities, must drop down a place. Energy expended on signaling must be replenished by the intake of water. Unless rescue is imminently probable, you would most likely do better to attend to your sources of water first. Primitive methods of signaling, such as signal fires, contrasting messages, and so forth, require a great deal of effort and should not be undertaken in the heat of the day. If no other means of signaling is available, wait until night to construct your signal.

Shelter and food follow next in the priorities of survival. Shelter from wind and sun is a must if you're to prevent excessive loss of water. Eventually, if you decide to try to walk out of your predicament, the exigencies of travel will become pressing.

FIRST AID

Providing you have no traumatic injuries to deal with, your basic first aid goal is to prevent dehydration. To lessen the body's loss of perspiration to evaporation, keep yourself fully clothed. Do not ration water; small amounts may quench thirst but will not replenish your body. There is no substitute for water to prevent dehydration.

Remain as calm and inactive as possible. Sit in the shade cast by some vegetation or by your disabled vehicle. Physical exertion combined with exposure to the searing desert sun can lead to any of three ailments: heat cramps, heat exhaustion, or heat stroke (also discussed in the chapter on "Environmental Hazards").

Heat cramps, as well as heat exhaustion, can be prevented by upping your intake of water and—only if there is plenty of water—salt. Heat cramps, affecting arms, legs, and abdomen, usually precede heat exhaustion. Heat exhaustion is indicated by first flushed then pale skin, which is usually moist and cool. Pulse is strong and rapid, sweat is profuse. Treat heat cramps and heat exhaustion in the same way: rest and take two salt tablets per quart of water.

Heat stroke is the most serious of the three and may come on suddenly. Skin is red, hot, and usually dry. Sweating stops. Headaches are severe and unconsciousness and death may result. Place the victim in the shade and cool him by any means possible. Fanning will accentuate the cooling effects of shade and water.

The concentration of ultraviolet light in deserts may cause severe sunburn and sunblindness. Your best safeguard is adequate clothing and sunglasses. Wear long pants and a long-sleeved shirt, a cloth neckpiece to protect the back of your neck, and a brimmed hat or an Arab-style burnoose to shade your eyes. Reflected sunlight can also burn, so expose your skin only if well-shaded.

If you do not have sunglasses, you can make slit goggles. Charcoal or dirt smudged across the bridge of your nose and below your eyes will cut down on glare.

Sunblindness is indicated by burning, watery, and inflamed eyes. Vision deteriorates, and halos appear around lights. Your head aches. Your eyes must have immediate rest. Wrap them in a light-proof bandage or find a dark shelter. Take aspirin to relieve the pain and prepare to wait eighteen hours. A sunblinded person can be led by a companion, if travel is necessary. Once sunblinded, you are susceptible to recurrences.

Take care of your feet, especially if you've decided to travel.

WATER PROCUREMENT

Traces of running water are evident nearly everywhere in the desert, but it takes a knowledgeable eye and a bit of luck to find enough water in a form you can make use of. Whenever you travel through desert country, carry extra water with you. Remember you'll need a minimum of a gallon per day per person. Plastic bottles, filled with clear clean water and stored in your vehicle or plane, will do wonders for your sense of security.

CATCH POOLS
ROCKS
CONTAINER
PADDED STICK
CLEAR
PLASTIC
BAG

Figure 9-3. Vegetation still

Figure 9-4. Saguaro cacti, largest of all American cacti, grow as tall as fifty feet, draw up water by the ton, and may live for two hundred years. Saguaro cacti assume marvelous shapes: (*left*) a ten-gallon-hatted gun fighter; (*right*) a neck-craning dinosaur. (Courtesy of the National Geographic Society)

Failing your own supply, your second line of defense against the elements depends on being able to coax water from the earth or, usually more felicitous, collecting water in a clear plastic bag in which vegetative matter has been placed. This is known as a vegetation still.

Vegetation Still

A vegetation still is useful in a desert, especially where fleshy plants such as the saguaro cactus abound. (The saguaro, largest of all cacti, grows up soft and tall, weighs up to ten tons, and holds gallons of water. It is found in American deserts.) Wherever there are plants, a vegetation still will provide fresh water with very little effort on your part. All that is needed is a large plastic bag, preferably a clear one, although a dark one will do, and the vegetation itself. The pulpy interior of cacti, leaves of the mesquite tree, and fruits, flowers, stems, or roots of any vegetation can be used. Place the vegetation inside the bag, taking care not to puncture the bag. Inflate the bag, tie the top closed, and place it in the sun. Moisture drawn from the vegetation will collect in the bag. If you can't cut the vegetation, or if it is simply easier, you can place the bag over branches or bushes, blow it up, and tie it. Moisture will still collect.

Solar Still

A solar still will draw moisture directly from the earth, but is especially effective if vegetation is placed under the plastic. When no vegetation is

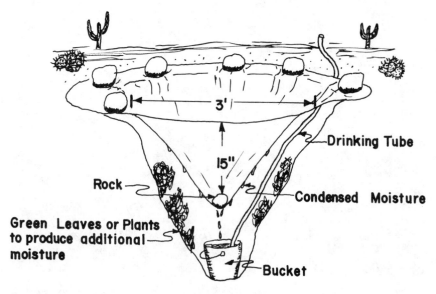

Figure 9-5. Desert solar still

available, the earth will still provide water. Figure 9-5 describes how to make a solar still. The drinking tube is not a necessity, but with it you can reach the water that collects without disturbing the plastic sheet. In a dire situation, the still can be used to purify polluted water such as body wastes.

To make a still, you need the following material:
- a piece of plastic, about 6 feet square
- a container for the water
- a piece of plastic tubing, about ¼ inch in diameter and 4 to 6 feet long (desirable but not necessary).

Some places are better than others for a still: a low point in a wadi or arroyo; clay soil rather than sand; and, obviously, damp or wet sand rather than dry. Direct sunlight is necessary for best results. Disturb the sheet as little as possible during the day, as it takes ½ to 1 hour for the still to begin collecting water again. If you must use polluted water, take care that none splashes on the rim of the still or comes in contact with the container.

Condensed Moisture

Dew can be collected from the surface of cool objects just before sunrise in deserts where the night air is moist. Sponge it up with a cloth and wring the water out into a container. Australian aboriginals sometimes mop up as much as a quart an hour this way.

The best dew condensers are exposed metal surfaces such as aircraft wings or tin cans, but leaves and flowers are also good. Stones gathered from beneath the desert floor and placed on a waterproof tarp may collect enough moisture for a refreshing drink.

Wells

For desert peoples, wells are the usual source of water. They may cover them with heaps of brush to stave off excessive evaporation. Look under brush piles or in sheltered nooks for wells in semi-arid brush country.

Look for intersecting game trails; they will generally lead to wells or to another source of water. Evidence of a campsite—ashes, stakes, litter— could indicate that a well is nearby. Follow paths out of the camp area; they may go to the well.

In the Old World deserts, particularly the Persian, Sahara, and Gobi, natives devised, where possible, systems of underground irrigation channels (*foggara*) to connect oases and wadis via water-bearing strata. Where these conduits occur, the shafts to the tunnels will occur more or less in a straight line, every 100 feet or so. In the Sahara, you will need a very long rope—allow 100 feet—to draw water from these canals. In the Gobi, a 30-foot rope will reach most wells. If water is too salty to drink, then you can catch the steam from boiled water or place containers under a solar still.

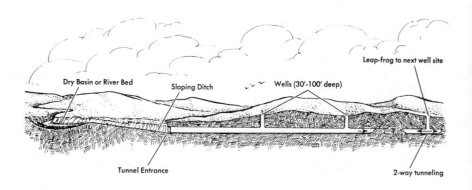

Figure 9-6. A desert well system

In the Sahara, watch for flocks of doves. Because they are seedeaters, doves must be close to a source of water. Their presence can lead you to a shaft, for they nest in the cool underground tunnels.

Sometimes water in a well can taste so revolting that you might think it is poisoned. The unappetizing taste is probably due to a high salt, alkali, or magnesium content. All water, except that drawn directly from plants, should be purified.

Springs and Pools

Following a rain, springs may be found at the foot of cliffs or rock piles and in gullies and side canyons. The vegetation that clusters around a spring will differ markedly from the drier surrounding countryside. Because spring water may have traveled for miles underground, filtered by sand and soil, it is clean and fresh-tasting.

Also potable is water captured in the deep hallows of rock formations after a brief but torrential downpour. Such pools may not evaporate for several days, but there is no way to predict where they may occur. If you know that it has rained recently in your area, keep a sharp eye out for natural depressions and cups in the landscape.

Plants

Plants are useful in two ways: certain plants indicate the presence of surface water or easily obtained groundwater; other plants provide liquid themselves. After a rain, eat flowers and fruit for moisture. Especially good is the fruit of the saguaro cactus.

Desert palms usually indicate surface water. Plants such as salt grass, rushes, sedges, cattails, greasewood, willows, and elderberry grow only where groundwater is close to the surface.

Water may be obtained from the roots of some desert plants that have their roots near the surface. The "water trees" of arid Australia are a part of the mallee scrub, one of the largest and most distinctive plant formations of Southern Australia. Roots of these "water trees" run out forty to eighty feet at a depth of two to nine inches under the surface. To get water from them, locate the root four or five feet from the tree trunk, pry it out of the ground, cut it into two- or three-foot lengths, and peel off the bark. Drain each section into a container, or suck out the water. One large mallee root usually will supply the water needs of two or three thirsty people.

Trees growing in hollows between ridges will have the most water, and roots one to two inches thick are ideal in size. Water can be carried in these roots by plugging one end with clay.

Water from the roots of all water-producing plants is obtained in a manner similar to that described above. These plants include the Australian needle bush, desert oak, bottle tree, bloodwood, and several varieties of Acacia. The "water tree" or vine of Africa and South America is utilized in the same way.

Signs of Water

Converging game trails, the direction of flight of some birds, the presence of certain plants or insects—such are some of the numerous indicators of water in the desert.

Pigeons are always within reach of water. They may feed in the desert, but they will fly to water in the late morning or late afternoon. Water can be found by following the direction of flight. This rule may be of use in places as widely separated as the American Southwest, the Australian Desert, or the deserts of Africa and Asia. The sand grouse of Eurasia and Africa are pigeon-like birds that fly many miles to congregate at water holes, for they must drink at least once a day. Crested larks and desert species of weaver birds and coursers may fly regularly to nearby water in the evening. Presence of diamond or zebra birds in the dry country of Australia is an almost infallible indication of the nearness of water. Many desert bats visit water regularly at the beginning of their evening flight.

Circular mounds of camel dung often surround wells in Old World deserts. Places where animals have scratched or where flies hover may show where water lay recently on the surface. By digging you may find some.

Not all vegetation is a tell-tale sign of water. The mesquite tree of the American deserts has a widespreading deep root system. To find water under a mesquite tree, you might have to dig 60 feet. Instead, use its leaves in a vegetation still.

Digging for Water

There are wiser places to dig for water than under the spreading roots of the mesquite tree. Along the shores of desert lakes, you would do best to dig a hole in the first depression behind the first dune, for rain often collects there. When you hit wet sand do not dig any deeper or you run the risk of drawing salt water. The first water that seeps into your hole will be fresh or nearly so. If you're among dunes far from surface water, the best place to dig is at the lowest point between dunes. Dig down three to six feet and, if the soil feels damp, keep digging until you hit water. If you hit dry rather than damp sand, look for a lower point and begin again.

At the edge of a sand dune expanse, dig beneath the hard valley floor rather than amid the dunes. It will be harder work, but a reward is more likely.

Springs

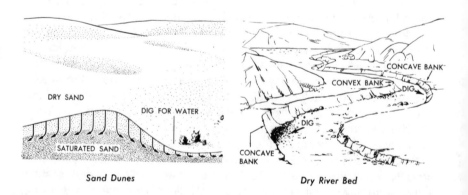

Sand Dunes   Dry River Bed

Figure 9-7. Possible sources of water

Figure 9-8. Mirror signaling is especially effective in the desert because of the strength of the sun and the open landscape.

In wadis and arroyos, delve into the soil on the outside bends of watercourses. You might just cadge a drink.

Some desert land is hard-packed and without tools you'll find it hard to excavate the earth. It's a good idea to include in your survival kit a small spade or shovel.

SIGNALING

Rescue parties usually look for disabled vehicles, so you will want to do all you can to make your vehicle more visible either from the air or from a distance over land. Set signal fires using fuel, oil, and other inflammables. Spell out "SOS" or "HELP" with rocks or vegetation or by scraping through the top layer of sand to the different color below. A signal mirror is especially effective in a desert because the sun and the open country allow the signal to be seen from just about all directions. Because the desert is harsh, do not overlook any potential signaling device and prepare signals as soon as possible.

SHELTER CONSTRUCTION

In the desert, finding shelter from the intense heat is of prime importance. Also of concern in some deserts are the cold temperatures at night. Protection from wind-blown sand and dust will also be required in most deserts. Take advantage of your stranded vehicle or of natural shelters, for you must be careful not to become exhausted or dehydrated in attempting to construct shelter. If construction is necessary, wait until the cool of the

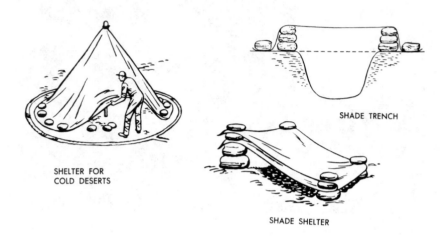

SHELTER FOR
COLD DESERTS

SHADE TRENCH

SHADE SHELTER

Figure 9-9. Desert shelters. Alternatively, you could seek shelter in the shadow of your vehicle.

night. Under a full moon, the desert is almost as bright as day. Also, keep these points in mind:

- Flash floods can result from sudden heavy rainfall, so reject dry river beds or gullies as potential camp sites.
- Try to arrange a bed that is off the ground, as temperatures are several degrees lower a foot above the desert floor.
- If caught out in the open during a sand storm, lie down with your back to the wind.

FOOD PROCUREMENT

Food is scarce in the desert and difficult to find. But unless you have to survive for a long time, you will probably not need it at all. Where food is not plentiful, ration it. Eat no food during the first twenty-four hours and never eat unless plenty of water is available to drink at mealtime. Hard candy, which should be part of the survival kit, can be consumed without water.

Rodents, lizards, prairie dogs, snakes, and birds may be found near water holes. In general, wherever there is water, there will also be edible plants. One of the most common types of desert plants is the prickly pear, which is found throughout North and South America, North Africa, the Near East, and Australia. When there is no food, conserve energy by resting as much as possible, especially during the heat of the day. More information is available in the chapters on wild plant and animal foods.

TRAVELING

Most desert areas are vast uninhabited wastelands, and civilization could be days away. Because of the distance involved and the extreme hostility of the environment, the decision to travel in the desert must be made only when there is virtually no chance of being rescued. If you decide to travel, leave a sign for possible rescue parties and proceed slowly and carefully, keeping the priorities of survival in mind. Carry all the water possible and travel in the early morning and late evening. Maintain the desired direction and don't travel when visibility is bad. Take shelter during sandstorms. You may get twenty miles per day on one gallon of water provided that your perspiration is controlled and you travel during the cooler hours.

CHAPTER 10

Mountains and Cold Regions Survival

At the height of the last Ice Age—about 18,000 years ago—the shallow Bering Strait lay exposed, a land bridge linking Asia with America. Thus, during one of the coldest periods in the history of the planet, humans entered the New World. Here the ancestors of North American Indians hunted at the edge of vast ice sheets, able to survive the rigorous climate because they had developed not only hunting and butchering tools but also the sewing awl. With the technology to fashion animal hides into clothes to trap body heat, shoes to protect against crippling frostbite, and tents and blankets to block wind, early peoples managed to cope with the extreme conditions in high latitudes. Today, earth's harshest frontiers continue to challenge. In no environment does sophisticated gear play a more crucial role in your chances for survival than in mountains and cold regions. Exploring polar lands, climbing lofty peaks, or merely combatting cold until help arrives requires warm footgear, protective clothing, a down sleeping bag, and knowledge of how to build a suitable shelter.

Altitude and latitude tend to mirror one another in their effects on temperature and vegetation. The higher one climbs on a mountain, the lower the temperature becomes (figure a three to five degree drop for every thousand feet gained), and, generally speaking, the further from the equator one travels, the colder it grows.

In the Northern Hemisphere, the lower slopes of mountains are covered with mixed forests, which may give way to pine, or coniferous, forests, then to upland meadows, and finally to low-lying, tundra-type vegetation. As one travels northward, one passes through a similar sequence of forests, eventually reaching the tundra of the Arctic.

High mountains and arctic regions have coldness in common. This makes many survival principles applicable to both. Yet each has distinct characteristics, and a survival experience in either is something to tell your grandchildren about.

Figure 10-1. Covering your head and layering your clothing is the key to cold weather survival. (Courtesy of Melanie Barocas)

Mountains

Although isolated mountains do occur, most mountains are part of a range. A group of ranges closely related in form and origin is called a mountain system, and elongated systems make up a chain. When ranges, systems, and chains combine together on a continental scale, the result is known as a cordillera, zone, or belt.

The world's greatest mountain masses are the North and South American cordillera (Andes, Rockies, Sierra Nevada, and the coastal ranges of the United States, including Alaska, and Canada) and the Eurasian belt (Pyrenees, Atlas Mountains, Alps, Balkans, Caucasus, Hindu Kush, and Himalayas).

Regardless of the location of your particular mountain, your major nemesis in a survival contest will be the weather, followed by problems of terrain (avalanches, crevasses, and so forth). Mountain weather is dictated by the triumvirate of altitude, slope exposure, and wind. As an illustration of the interaction of these three conditions, Mount Washington in New Hampshire's Presidential Range serves well.

The 6,288-foot peak is small compared with the earth's greatest mountains (Mount McKinley, highest summit in North America, is 20,320 feet; Mount Everest, loftiest of all, reaches more than 29,000 feet). Because the

Figure 10-2. The summit of Mount Washington in New Hampshire. Subject to fierce winter weather, the mountain has been the setting of many a survival ordeal through the years. (Courtesy of the National Geographic Society)

range of mountains of which it is a part has a north-south exposure and prevailing winds are west-northwest, and because it lies at the intersection of three storm tracks, Mount Washington hosts some of the world's most awesome weather. Winds register hurricane force about every third day; wind chill can reach −115°F; and the highest wind speed on earth was recorded here at 231 mph. It inflicts on those who would brave its furies unprepared frostbite, hypothermia, and death.

Mountains are places of contrasts. At their bases may be tropical rain forest; at their summits, arctic-like rock and tundra. On their windward slopes, lush vegetation; on the lee side, desert. In the course of a day's climb, you may have to unbutton your parka for ventilation because of warmth and then bundle up later against rain, hail, or snow. Despite the unpredictability of a mountain's weather, your life could very well depend on your ability to anticipate problems and to respond appropriately.

Cold Regions

The term *cold regions* refers specifically to the Arctic and subarctic zones but implies, of course, the climate of high mountains, regardless of their latitude. For example, 12,392-foot Mount Hagen in Papua New Guinea is just south of the equator and surrounded by tropical rain forest at sea level, yet glacier-clad year round.

For the moment, however, we will exclude mountains and consider only the distinctive characteristics of the Arctic and subarctic. We will not discuss Antarctica, because few people other than scientists and occasional tourists visit that most forbidding of continents. The Arctic, on the other hand, commands attention because native peoples have long made it their home, oil discoveries are stimulating much recent development, it is the scene of circumpolar aviation routes, and it bears an ecological relationship to high mountains farther south.

The Arctic Circle is an imaginary line at 66°-31′North, but this demarcation does not reflect the gradations of plant and animal life on the way north. A more realistic indication is the irregular and shifting 50°F July isotherm (another imaginary line joining points on the earth's surface having the same mean temperature at a given time), which closely relates to the northern limit of tree growth and may vary north or south of the Arctic Circle. Thus the places classified as Arctic include the Arctic Ocean, northern Canada, Alaska, the northern reaches of the USSR, Norway, part of the Atlantic Ocean, the Svalbard archipelago, most of Iceland, all of Greenland, and the Bering Sea.

Long, extreme winters and brief, cool summers are the rule. Arctic climate can be subdivided into tundra climate (the temperature of the warmest month averages between 32°F and 50°F) and ice cap climate (no month averages above 32°F). Although lands bordering the oceans are generally warmer and wetter, the interior is colder and drier, receiving less than 10 inches of precipitation a year and therefore qualifying as a desert.

Seasons in the Arctic are marked most strikingly not by changes in temperature but by changes in the lengths of days and nights. The twilight of the Arctic winter and the glare of the Arctic summer have implications for survivors in terms of first aid and travel.

The word *tundra* designates treeless Arctic (as well as mountainous) expanses. A few feet beneath the surface, the soil is permanently frozen, but during the short summer months, moss, lichens, and some flowering plants—as well as mosquitoes—appear in abundance.

South of the tundra are the great coniferous forests of North America and Eurasia, which comprise one-third of the world's woodlands. Here the winters are severe, but only six or seven months long. In high mountains, the timber line marks the division between the coniferous elevations and the tundralike summits. On lower slopes and farther south, the conifers merge with deciduous forest or grasslands.

The habitat you find yourself stranded in will dictate where and how you'll find water and food and, most important, what kind of shelter you'll provide for yourself. Surviving in cold regions is distinguished from survival in other environments by the immediate need for shelter. As with the earliest peoples, protection against wind and frigid temperatures starts with good clothing.

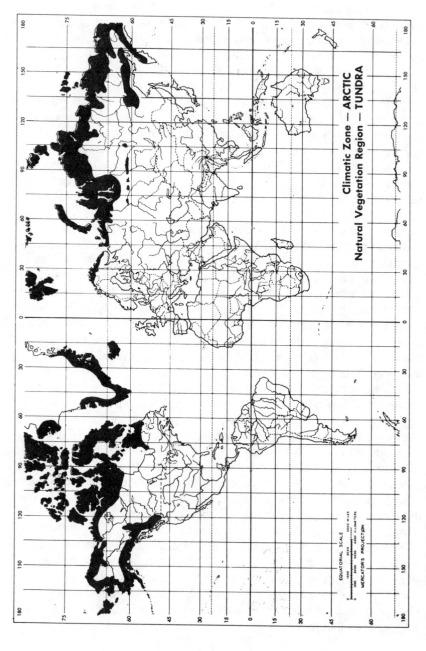

Climatic Zone — ARCTIC

Natural Vegetation Region — TUNDRA

EQUATORIAL SCALE

MERCATOR'S PROJECTION

Figure 10-3. Arctic Zone—tundra

PREPARATION

Controlling the temperature directly surrounding you is the key to surviving the cold. If your body temperature drops a mere seven degrees, you become incapable of making rational life-saving decisions. A naked person exposed to −40°F temperatures and 30 mph winds—conditions common in the Arctic—would have a life expectancy of about fifteen minutes. If you know that you will be flying over or driving through cold places, carry a sleeping bag and wear clothing and boots that would stand you in good stead should you be forced to land or your car break down. If you deliberately enter the wilderness in winter—to backpack, climb, ice fish, snowshoe, or whatever—be prepared. Animals when they are cold will curl up in a ball to minimize the surface area exposed to air. For humans, there are more effective ways to retain heat than to try to make yourself a pinpoint.

Clothing

Clothing insulates by providing air pockets that trap air, thus slowing the replacement of warm air by cold. The insulating effect is enhanced if you wear several layers of clothing rather than one heavy garment. Loose, porous clothing covered by a light windbreaker is warmer than a single heavy outercoat. The layers of insulating clothing hold warm air in while wind-resistant fabric keeps cold air out.

Insulation is reduced if clothes get wet, if they are worn too tightly, or if the windbreaker is not up to the job. You don't have to wade through a stream or fall into a pond for clothing to become wet enough to pose a danger; perspiration, which can be caused by as simple an exercise as walking if the day is warm and you're overdressed, can soak clothing too. The chilling effect of damp clothing, particularly wet cotton, which is a heat conductor not an insulator, can be dire. Shed layers as the need arises.

Tight clothing narrows the still-air zone around your body and also prevents free circulation of the blood. Always leave clothing loose and full-fitting.

Wind is as dangerous an enemy as wetness. A windy day always feels colder than a still day at the same temperature because the turbulent air carries off your body's warmed air and replaces it with cold. A windbreaker is crucial. When you find or build shelter for the night, in timbered regions, try to do so out of the wind.

In choosing your outdoor clothing, keep in mind the characteristics of different materials. You will want a fabric whose microscopic fibers have a relatively large amount of surface area, as these will trap more air.

Down has long been a favorite, but it is costly. Synthetics are gaining in popularity, not only because they are more affordable but because they

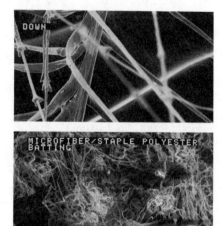

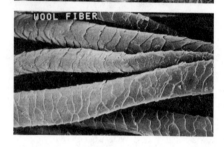

Figure 10-4. Microscopic fibers. (*top*) Down; (*middle*) Polyester; (*bottom*) Wool. (Courtesy of Dr. Murray Hamlet, U.S. Army Research Institute at Natick, Mass.)

have some advantages over down. If down becomes wet, it mats, the air spaces compress, and the clothing loses its warmth. Two different types of synthetic compounds used in outdoor clothing—polyester and polyolefin fibers—absorb almost no water but instead "wick" it away from the skin. Additionally, the synthetics—for example, DuPont's Hollofil and 3M's Thinsulate—are nonallergenic, odorless, and resistant to microorganisms. Synthetics have the advantage of retaining "loft"—trapped air—when wet, and they dry quickly, even in freezing temperatures.

Another natural fabric facing competition from the new synthetics is wool. Wool fibers present a large surface area and, because of their interlocking wavy structure, make for a strong, warm, fabric. Wool retains much of its insulating capability, even when wet. Cotton, on the other hand, absorbs water and is therefore generally unacceptable.

The technique in dressing warmly is to layer your clothing. Several thin layers are warmer than one thick one.

Underwear. Begin with wool or polyolefin, or fishnet long underwear. The open weave of fishnet traps warm air while allowing ventilation if clothes are opened because of warmth. If you prefer the feel of solid cloth against your skin, choose polyolefin first over a thin wool. Absorbent, solid cotton underwear is only asking for trouble, but fishnet cotton is marginally acceptable as the small amount of material actually touching the skin limits the chilling effect.

Pants. Wool pants are very good. The wool should be of hard or smooth finish, as opposed to fuzzy, so that snow can be brushed off easily. Polyester/wool blend pants are less acceptable and, again, cotton pants are not recommended. For ventilation, install zippers on the outside leg seams, if you plan an extended cold weather activity such as hiking or climbing.

Shirts and Vests. Knitted turtleneck shirts feel cozy, and shirts and sweaters slip over them comfortably. Wear a light wool shirt under a larger wool shirt or light pile jacket or vest. Layers can be added or subtracted as desired.

Windbreaker. You want something that will stop wind but allow perspiration to evaporate. A coated jacket is unsuitable as a windbreaker because it holds in your perspiration, soaking your undergarments. An uncoated, hooded jacket of nylon defends against frigid blasts. GoreTex, a fairly new synthetic, is wind-, freeze-, and water-resistant while still allowing body moisture to escape. It needs careful handling and is costly.

Insulated Parka. A parka insulated with down or with one of the new synthetic fillers envelopes the body in warmth. It should come down to your hips and overlap generously in the front.

Mittens. Woolen mittens, one or two pairs, or a nylon-shell pair should come well above your wrists.

Figure 10-5. Wear eye gear to protect against glare.

Hat. An uncovered head can release more than half of your body heat in temperatures below 40°F. A woolen hat—pulled down well over the ears—or a wool or orlon balaclava is indispensable.

Goggles. Eye gear should protect against glare, help you see better in flat light, and keep driven snow and ice out of your eyes. Sunglasses or tinted goggles will come in very handy. You should have fog-resistant goggles. If you must improvise, cut narrow eye slits in a piece of wood, leather, or cloth. Soot rubbed across nose and cheekbones cuts down on glare.

Footgear

Extra socks and dry boots are the ideal combination in fighting frostbite.

Socks. When you buy boots, allow for a couple of layers of thick wool socks. Silk socks make good liners for those with sensitive feet. You could place dry grass between layers of socks or between sock and boot. It makes a good insulator, but change it every day. If necessary, improvise warm linings by wrapping your feet in parachute cloth or other available fabric. Don't overdo it, though. If an extra sock cuts off blood circulation, you can get frostbite.

Boots. There are three basic types of boots for cold outdoor weather. Government surplus "Mickey Mouse" or Korean vapor boots have sealed insulation which will keep out water unless the boot is punctured, but they lack good traction on hard snow. Leather-topped, rubber-bottomed boots with removable liners are as warm as "Mickey Mouse" boots but the insulation is not sealed so water could pose a threat. A second set of liners would be useful. Probably the best of the three, certainly the most expensive, are technical winter climbing boots of leather or plastic. They come with an insulated, removable inner- or overboot and have good traction on hard snow.

Sleeping Equipment

If you have a good sleeping bag, many of your worries are over. Space blankets, developed as a result of space research, will also enhance your comfort and your chances if you have packed them aboard your plane or vehicle.

Sleeping Bag. Essential in cold and mountainous regions, a high loft sleeping bag—down, or down mixed with some polyester—will keep you from freezing, regardless of whether you have a fire or shelter, as long as you are out of the wind and insulated from the ground. The bag should be kept dry and loosely fluffed and have a water-repellent cover. Turn the bag inside-out each day to allow the sun and wind to dry the moisture that collects inside.

Extra protection is needed beneath the sleeping bag. Do not use it directly on the snow if insulating material, such as boughs, grass, or outer garments, is available. In general, it is best to remove your heavy outer clothes before getting into your sleeping bag.

Space Blankets. Light-weight, wind- and waterproof, and flexible even at −60°F, space blankets have many uses—as a ground cloth beneath your sleeping bag, as a windbreaker, even as a poncho against the rain.

Because of the danger to life posed by extreme cold, shelter is second only to first aid in a survival situation in mountains and cold regions. In fact, shelter can be considered preventive first aid. Signaling is third on the list of priorities. You must, obviously, decide where you will build your snow cave or snow house before you can arrange to signal its location. If, on the other hand, your downed plane or disabled vehicle is serving as your ready-made shelter, you will be able to turn your attention to signaling much sooner. Water, and then food, procurement are the next priorities. Travel, the lowest priority, is especially dangerous in mountainous and cold regions because of physical hazards such as soft ice, loose rock, and deep snow. Set out only after carefully weighing the alternatives.

FIRST AID

The main threats to health in very cold environments are hypothermia and frostbite. These are discussed in detail in the environmental hazards chapter and in the chart in the first aid chapter. Other dangers are snow blindness, carbon monoxide poisoning, mountain sickness, and traumatic injuries.

Snow Blindness. Snow blindness is a painful inflammation of the inner side of the eyelids caused by constant exposure to the reflection of the sun's rays from snow. Its effect may range from slight inflammation to temporary, painful blindness of several days duration. Preventive measures include traveling at night; using a shade to protect the eyes from *below*; blackening the eyelids, cheeks, and bridge of the nose; wearing a dark mask with small eye slits; or, best of all, wearing dark glasses. The first sign of inflammation is a feeling of sand in the eyes. Cold water may relieve the pain. If you or a companion become temporarily blinded, wear a dark bandage over the eyes. Be prepared to rest for about eighteen hours.

Carbon Monoxide Poisoning. Carbon monoxide poisoning is more easily prevented than detected and treated. Be careful to ensure adequate ventilation in any shelter. If you use combustible fuels to generate heat, the smoke should be vented to the outside through a hole in the top of the shelter. Check regularly that the vent has not frozen over. Never fall asleep for the night with a stove or lamp burning. Keep the exit path clear for a quick escape.

Carbon monoxide, a colorless odorless gas, gives little or no indication of its presence. A yellow flame, as opposed to a blue flame, generates carbon monoxide. If possible, leave three inches between the bottom of your cooking pot and the top of the burner. The flame should stay blue if the stove is working properly.

Carbon monoxide poisoning can occur in an unventilated shelter if a fire is left burning or in a ventilated shelter if combustion is incomplete. There may be no early symptoms, or the onset may be so subtle that unless you know enough to watch for pressure at the temples, headache, drowsiness, burning eyes, pounding pulse, or nausea, you may not flee to fresh air fast enough to escape unconsciousness and death. If you have the slightest suspicion of carbon monoxide poisoning, get out of the shelter at once into the fresh air. If a companion falls victim to carbon monoxide poisoning or smoke inhalation, take him or her into fresh air immediately. Keep the victim calm, quiet, and warm. If indicated, apply CPR. The damaged blood cells will be replaced by good ones in a few days to several weeks, depending on the severity of the poisoning.

Mountain Sickness. There are three types of mountain sickness: acute mountain sickness (AMS); high-altitude pulmonary edema (HAPE); and high-altitude cerebral edema (HACE). AMS, the most common, affects people who go to high elevations too quickly without waiting to become acclimatized. To prevent AMS, set a slow pace and make frequent overnight stops. Preventive medicine is available. Symptoms include headache, nausea, dizziness, disorientation, malaise. To treat, descend to lower elevations and rest.

The second most common form of mountain sickness is HAPE, which is fluid in the lungs. It usually affects some people who ascend to ten thousand feet quickly, although it has been known to occur at lower levels. It is life-threatening, and the victim must be brought to lower altitudes immediately. Sometimes a difference of only five hundred feet may result in a remarkable alleviation of symptoms. The symptoms consist of coughing, bubbling noises in the chest, difficulty in breathing, blue lips, and spitting up of foam or blood from the lungs. If you've had it once, you're likely to get it again.

The least common form of mountain sickness is that of cerebral edema. HACE may be foreshadowed by problems in vision, and it can develop into delirium and death. It occurs at very high altitudes and is therefore a danger only to the most adventurous of mountaineers. A stricken individual must be brought down the mountain immediately.

Traumatic Injuries. In mountainous terrain, the potential for falls is much greater than in other types of terrain. While most survival situations come about because of a violent accident, few environments present greater possibilities for further traumatic injuries than do mountains. Any injury will make survival more difficult, especially if it occurs in cold regions, so do not be careless. See the chapter on first aid for treatment of traumatic injuries.

SHELTER CONSTRUCTION

In cold environments, and especially if it is windy, an adequate shelter may be the most important element in survival. If shelter is essential to sustain life, it moves ahead of signaling and water procurement on the list of priorities, becoming part of preventive first aid.

The primary purpose of shelter is to slow the air movement around and retain the heat from your body and other heat sources. A shelter should be small, windproof, and adequately ventilated. Remember that it takes less energy to build and heat a small shelter than a large one.

In the open tundra, a camp or shelter should not be built in a lee, as it may get covered with drifting snow. In mountainous or forested country, however, do make a camp in a lee, as it is generally warmer and drifting snow does not usually pile up. If at all possible, make camp below timberline in mountainous country even though there may be a problem with deep, soft snow. Timber breaks the wind, and wind is a major factor in reducing temperatures. The contour and depth of the snow which lies on the ground is the best indicator of whether a lee will be safe from heavy drifting.

Figure 10-6. Take advantage of natural shelters. (Courtesy of Dr. Murray Hamlet, U.S. Army Research Institute at Natick, Mass.)

Figure 10-7. Small snow caves make better use of your body heat than larger ones. (Courtesy of Dr. Murray Hamlet, U.S. Army Research Institute at Natick, Mass.)

Mountainous regions abound in natural shelters: caves; cavelike formations of rocks and vegetation; tree hollows; and the natural pits around evergreen trees caused by branches that prevent snow from falling there. If you can't find appropriate natural shelter, though, you will have to provide your own. There are numerous types, suitable for various circumstances and locations.

Snow Caves. Building a snow cave requires a digging tool and about two or three hours of hard work. Into a packed snowdrift, dig a tunnel that slopes upward before leveling off just before the door to the cave itself. Keep the cave small, and a tiny fire or even a candle can raise the interior temperature many degrees above the outside air. About 18 inches above the floor of the cave, shape a bed platform. Place boughs on it to insulate your sleeping bag from beneath. The space allowed should be no more than required for you to remove heavy outer clothing for sleeping and to redress in your sleeping bag. A small wall bordering the sleeping platform would help conserve heat. If desired, a cooking shelf could be built about a foot above the sleeping space. Absolutely necessary is a ventilation hole in the roof and another in the block of snow used as a door. Keep an eye out to be sure they are clear, especially if you're using a stove or lamp. The dome and sides can be glazed with a candle or firebrand to keep snow from flaking down. It does not take too long, and it prevents condensation drip. It would be a good idea to take your digging tool inside with you at night, in case you have to dig your way out in the morning. A snow cave is cramped and uncomfortable, but, with a sleeping bag, it makes one of the best cold weather shelters with the least expenditure of energy.

Lean-to. In timbered areas where snow is not yet plentiful, a lean-to makes a quickly built, relatively protective shelter. The leaning side of the shelter should be in the path of the prevailing winds. A wall of branches or large stones placed on the opposite side of the camp fire from the lean-to helps reflect heat back into the lean-to.

Snow Trench. In areas where snow is not deep enough for a snow cave, you can dig a trench and cover it with a parachute, tarpaulin, or any other material close at hand.

Windbreaks. Windbreaks of snowblocks or boughs increase the comfort of a camp, protect a fire, and even serve as emergency sleeping shelters. A windbreak 2 or 3 feet high placed about 2 feet to windward of a shelter in exposed country is generally quite effective. Windbreaks at a distance of 5 to 10 feet will cause a snowdrift to form that will bury the camp.

Snow House. A snow house is generally worth the effort only if there are two or more survivors and they expect to be stranded for a while. Constructing a house of snow blocks requires patience and experience, as well as tools—a knife, saw, or axe. The placement of each block is critical, as is the downward slope of each row of blocks in the dome. The snow bonds together and the sum becomes stronger than the individual blocks. A snow house offers the most complete protection against Arctic cold, if the time and difficulty of its construction is warranted.

Figure 10-8. A lean-to. (Courtesy of Dr. Murray Hamlet, U.S. Army Research Institute at Natick, Mass.)

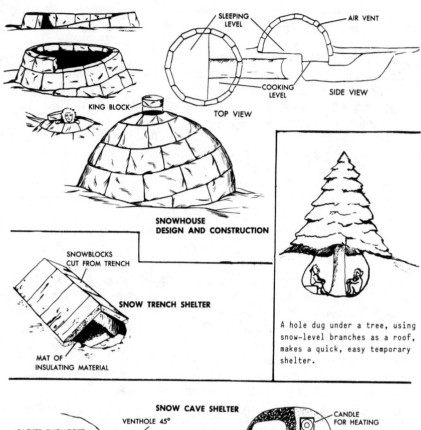

SLEEPING LEVEL

AIR VENT

KING BLOCK

COOKING LEVEL

SIDE VIEW

TOP VIEW

**SNOWHOUSE
DESIGN AND CONSTRUCTION**

SNOWBLOCKS
CUT FROM TRENCH

SNOW TRENCH SHELTER

MAT OF
INSULATING MATERIAL

A hole dug under a tree, using
snow-level branches as a roof,
makes a quick, easy temporary
shelter.

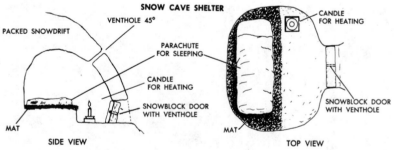

SNOW CAVE SHELTER

VENTHOLE 45°

CANDLE
FOR HEATING

PACKED SNOWDRIFT

PARACHUTE
FOR SLEEPING

CANDLE
FOR HEATING

SNOWBLOCK DOOR
WITH VENTHOLE

SNOWBLOCK DOOR
WITH VENTHOLE

MAT

MAT

SIDE VIEW

TOP VIEW

Figure 10-9. Shelters for mountains and cold regions

Figure 10-10. (*top*) Bough bed (laid); (*bottom*) Bough bed (inserted)

SIGNALING

Signaling in ice- and snow-covered areas is usually easier than in most other environments because of the uniformity of the background. Inclement weather, however, is more likely and will significantly reduce the possibilities of visual communication.

An effective visual signal for snow-covered regions can be made by arranging contrasting material, such as green foliage, vehicle debris, or survival equipment, into a sign (SOS or HELP) on a clear patch of ice or snow. You can also prepare signal fires and have them ready for lighting when you spot search aircraft. You must make arrangements to protect them from the weather in the meantime. A group of survivors should try to stay together and may need whistle signals during snowstorms.

WATER PROCUREMENT

Severe thirst and dehydration are major problems that affect survivors even in ice- and snow-covered areas. Body fluids may be lost rapidly because of heavy physical exertion expended in coping with the environment. Fluid is also lost merely in exhaling warm, moist air and inhaling cool, dry air. Melt snow or ice and let the sediments settle, or strain through several layers of cloth to get good water. Never eat ice or snow. This will lower your body temperature and actually increase the likelihood of dehydration. Old sea ice—which is blue in color—is relatively free of salt and can be melted into drinking water. Remember to treat all water, regardless of source, by boiling or by adding purification tablets. If treatment is impossible, try to use the purest water such as from high mountain streams in uninhabited regions or from fresh snow from a pollutant-free environment.

Figure 10-11. Signaling for help; (*top*) with X as a ground signal; (*bottom*) with smoke and mirrors. (Courtesy of the Defense Audio-Visual Agency)

FOOD PROCUREMENT

As one travels north or south from the equator, disease-transmitting insects, parasites, diseases, poisonous snakes, plants, and animals decrease. Physical hazards, however, such as snow and cold, increase. Food in the form of plant and animal life grows less abundant, even while the body requires more nourishment. Living off the land becomes increasingly difficult, but is possible with a gun, fire, equipment, and suitable clothing. It helps to have some food packed away in your survival kit.

In general, the plants and animals of the Arctic zone and of the subarctic forests are circumpolar in distribution, so living off the land will be basically the same throughout Alaska, Northern Canada, Labrador,

Greenland, Northern Europe, Iceland, and Siberia. Plant life above tree line in the high mountains of the temperate and even tropic zones is similar in many respects to that in the far north and the Arctic. If it is necessary to live off the land in such regions, proceed as if in the far north.

Although plant and animal food is present in the Arctic, it is not always easily available. Scattered vegetation is most plentiful along the banks of lakes and rivers. Game may be abundant over a large area, yet scarce in local areas at specific times.

Plant Food

When animal life fails and even such food as mice, fish, and grubs are not available, you can still find plant food that will stave off starvation. In summer there is no great problem finding plant food, and even in winter, berries and roots are available beneath the snow if you know where to look for them.

In Arctic and subarctic regions, only the water hemlock and buttercups should be avoided. The *Amanitas* (mushrooms) are present, but in many cases even these are not poisonous or at least not deadly poisonous in far northern regions. Although most plant varieties are safe to eat, it is important that you be able to recognize the relatively few nutritious plants from the far greater number that have no food value.

Berries. The *salmon-berry*, most important of the northern berries, is

Figure 10-12. (*left*) Salmon-berry (*Rubus chamaemorus*); (*right*) Crowberry (*Empetrum nigrum*)

circumpolar in distribution and always grows in a peaty soil. Its fruit is yellow and looks like a raspberry. The plant grows close to the ground, often covering many acres. These berries are available in summer and may be found frozen on the stalks in the winter and early spring. They can be eaten raw but are better cooked.

The *crowberry* is a small evergreen heathlike plant whose berries are brownish black, single-seeded, juicy, and sweet. Also circumpolar, it can often be found on bushes in winter.

Currants, cranberries, strawberries, raspberries, and blueberries are found where conditions are favorable for vegetative growth such as timbered regions, bogs, hillsides, and along streams. Remember the spots where they have been found, and look in the same types of places again.

Roots and Greens. Snakeweed is a low plant with white or pink flowers in dense solitary spikes and is common on dry tundra. The rootstock, slightly astringent when eaten raw, is starchy and potatolike when roasted. Circumpolar.

Wild rhubarb or alpine knotweed grows 3 to 6 feet high and has small flowers. It likes moist open or alluvial soil along river banks. The leaves and red stems are edible when cooked. After it becomes frosted it may be poisonous.

Woolly lousewort, a low plant with woolly spikes of rose-colored flowers, is found on dry tundra regions of North America. The yellow root is sweet like carrots and may be eaten raw or cooked.

Figure 10-13. (*left*) Cranberry (*Vaccinium macrocarpon*); (*right*) Mountain cranberry (*Vaccinium vitis-idaea*)

Figure 10-14. (*left*) Snakeweed (*Polygonum bistorta*); (*right*) Alpine knotweed (*Polygonum alpinum*)

Figure 10-15. (*left*) Woolly lousewort (*Pedicularis lanata*); (*right*) Licorice-root (*Hedysarum boreale*)

Licorice-root is a legume with pink flowers. Found throughout the north as far as the Arctic Ocean, its long tap roots taste like licorice when raw and like carrots when cooked. In summer the root becomes tough and woody but remains edible.

Bark and Buds. The bark and buds of certain northern trees that are

Figure 10-16. (*left*) Iceland moss (*Cetaria islandica*); (*middle*) Reindeer moss (*Cladonia rangiferina*); (*right*) Rock tripe (*Umbilicaria*)

eaten by animals can also be eaten by man. The bark and buds of aspen can be eaten raw or cooked but should preferably be boiled to a gelatinous mass. The buds of basswood, poplar, maple, the shoots of spruce and tamarack, and the inner bark of willow, alder, hemlock, basswood, and birch are all edible. The leaves of mountain sorrel, young willows, and fire-weed can be eaten when boiled.

Lichens. The most widespread and surest source of emergency food in the far north are the lichens, some of which resemble moss. Often these small plants cover large areas, growing on rocks, trees, and logs, in sand and gravel, even sometimes where there appears to be no soil. The lichens are gray, brown, or black in color and rich in carbohydrates, furnishing food for many northern mammals. Northland natives eat some lichens during famine periods. None are poisonous, but some contain a bitter acid that causes internal irritation unless they are cooked in water, dried until brittle, and then powdered and boiled.

Among the most useful edible species are the following:

- *Iceland moss* grows best on sandy soil and resembles a brown sea-weed. Boil for an hour or longer.
- *Reindeer moss* is gray-green in color and has a small globular "fruit" in a cuplike receptacle. Most abundant of the food lichens, it often covers extensive areas. Wash it to remove grit and then boil or roast it.
- *Rock tripe* or *famine food* are flat, leathery, crinkle-edged lichens that grow on acid rocks throughout the north. They are smoky-colored and brittle when dry, but dark-green on the upper surface when wet. Tasting bitter but not unpleasant, rock tripe should be dried before being boiled, or it will cause diarrhea. When properly prepared it is nutritious and easily assimilated.

Animal Food

Survivors can live on meat alone if they eat both lean and fat. One cannot remain healthy on a diet of lean meat only.

Within the Arctic Circle are such animals as musk oxen, wolves, polar bears, foxes, muskrats, lemmings, and seals and such birds as ptarmigans, gulls, owls, hawks, geese, brants, swans, dovekies, cranes, loons, ducks, snow buntings, and pipits.

Many of these animals migrate south during the long Arctic winter, but

Figure 10-17. Lemming

Figure 10-18. Uncovering birds' eggs. (Courtesy of the Defense Audio-Visual Agency)

others such as caribou and musk oxen do not. Some ptarmigan remain north of the circle and can be approached and shot, clubbed, or snared. Hares are found in the same local regions the year round and can be snared along their runs. Lemmings can also be trapped or clubbed along their runways. You may have to dig down in the snow for them. They are fun to hunt when you're not really hungry.

Farther south where trees occur, a greater diversity of birds, mammals, and plants are found. Many of the deer family are in this area. The porcupine is often encountered and can be easily clubbed on the ground or shaken from a tree. Porcupines feed on bark, so limbs stripped bare are good signs of their presence. To avoid their sharp needles, pick them up by the loose skin under the chin.

In summer, birds and bird eggs will abound in certain areas. Gulls, terns, murres, and dovekies nest in colonies along the coast, while ducks and geese can be found in the vegetation along the streams and lakes.

Seals are the staff of life for native peoples in the Arctic, but it requires exceptional skill and knowledge to spear them. Even with a gun they are not easily obtained. Other large aquatic mammals such as whales and walrus are even more difficult to get.

Seals concentrate in favored areas and are absent in other parts of the polar ocean. Even in those places where they are found in numbers they cannot always be hunted successfully. In winter they are hunted where there is an even layer of ice over water of fair depth. They can be expected in numbers where the ice is broken by current holes and tidewater cracks. Where the ice is thick and unbroken they will be scarce. Seals snort at their water holes and remain for some time taking air. Sneak up to the hole while the seal is taking a breath or is dozing. Flatten out on the ice and remain still when it looks around. Move slowly and silently. They can hear slight sounds, even through the ice. It will help to construct a white shield of parachute silk and use it as a blind to slip up on the seal. When ready to shoot, try for a brain shot; otherwise, it may escape wounded through the ice hole.

The walrus comes up to breathe, but does not scratch breathing holes and is thus harder to locate. It is one of the most dangerous animals of the Arctic region.

The polar bear, also a dangerous animal, is found in practically all Arctic coastal regions, seldom far from sea ice.

The caribou and reindeer are the most abundant of Arctic land mammals. Their presence can be located by tracks, but careful stalking is necessary for a shot.

All of the large animals may supply food, implements, fuel, and clothing. When hunting these animals with a gun, remember they are wary and stalking them takes tremendous skill and patience.

Fish are plentiful in small northern streams. Salmon can be found from early spring to fall in coastal streams and rivers from Oregon through Alaska and from the New England states northward. When they are traveling upstream to spawn, they can be picked up by hand or clubbed. Salmon die after spawning in the headwaters. Their flesh deteriorates the farther they get from saltwater. The flesh of these live but dying salmon may be poisonous. Watch for white salmon and let the pink ones pass. Trout can be caught in the larger lakes by fishing through the ice.

TRAVELING

Polar Travel

The polar and sub-polar regions are vast expanses of relatively unexplored territory. Distances alone make travel a major problem. In general the best bet is to stay with a downed plane or other disabled vehicle unless fully equipped for polar travel. You can live by hunting, and before you set out you should have equipped yourself with a hunting gun or knife.

The hazards and problems that a traveler will encounter in polar and sub-polar travel are so varied that they can only be treated briefly here. The problems on polar seas are different from those on polar land, and these in turn are quite different from those in the forested and mountain regions.

Generally speaking, spring is the worst season for traveling in polar regions, because the snow becomes soft, heavy, and wet. (Spring is also the season for insects—innumerable and voracious.) Ice melts, opening streams, bays, and seas. Circuitous routes of travel are necessary to avoid such hazards as flooded streams, quicksand, muskeg (bog), ice break-up, snow avalanches. Insects are a torment. For a properly equipped individual, winter is the time to cover distances in the polar regions.

Deep snow and cold present serious obstacles to winter travel anywhere, and specialized gear such as snowshoes, skis, and sleds are necessary. Do not attempt to travel any distance in deep snow without snowshoes or skis; it is exhausting work and your energy is better utilized in improvising a camp. Crude snowshoes can be made from willow and other woody vegetation, but in general this task should not be attempted until a camp has been established. Parachute cord or stripped clothing makes usable webbing for snowshoes. The use of snowshoes can be mastered much faster than skis, and it is not necessary to have specialized footgear to snowshoe. For these reasons snowshoes are better emergency traveling equipment than skis.

It is generally wiser to remain in camp than to travel into a cold wind. Wait for a shift in the wind or a rise in temperature before venturing forth. If

Figure 10-19. Flies and mosquitoes make spring in mountainous and far north regions a torment. Protective clothing is a must. (Courtesy of the Defense Audio-Visual Agency)

survivors must head into a cold wind, they should try to lay their course so that they hit the lee side of timber, hills, ridges, or escarpments. The protection afforded usually more than compensates for a longer trek.

In mountains, snow above timberline is generally hard-packed along the ridges, but in the timber it is deep and soft, making travel without skis or snowshoes frequently impossible. The best traveling is generally on the windswept ridges.

When traveling above the timberline, try to avoid cornices and steep southern exposures where the snow may avalanche. In such places a cracked, crumbled appearance indicates that the snow has already avalanched and that the slope can be negotiated with safety. On any slope, the avalanche hazard is greatest during the warmest part of the day, or on a day following several days of relatively high temperature or heavy snowfall, the greatest danger occurring in early spring.

When fording polar or high mountain streams, remember that the water is ice cold. Your ability to swim, wade, or hold on is greatly reduced in cold water, and cold, wet clothes are to be avoided at all cost; therefore proceed with utmost caution.

Crossing deep, snow-covered streams is particularly dangerous. Snow itself is an excellent insulator. If a heavy snowfall has occurred before safe ice has formed, the blanket of snow will frequently prevent further ice formation. Small streams wind-protected by high banks or heavy vegetation are more apt to have thin ice beneath deep snow than large windswept bays or rivers. A probing stick is vital in such cases.

If you are alone and you fall into water, you should make a fire before attempting to change to dry garments.

Mountain Travel

Mountainous or deeply eroded country offers special difficulties. What appears as a single ridge and valley from a distance may prove to be numer-

Figure 10-20. Body position. Weight should be poised over or slightly in front of the feet. Hands should be used for balance, never for the full support of the body.

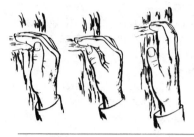

PULL HOLDS

PULL HOLDS are those with which you pull down; they are the easiest to use but also the most likely to break out.

PUSH HOLD

PUSH HOLDS are ones with which you push down; they help you to keep your arms low. They rarely break out, but are more difficult to maintain in case of a slip. A push hold is often used to advantage in combination with a pull hold.

JAM HOLDS

JAM HOLDS involve jamming any part of your body or an extremity into a crack. Put one hand into a crack and clench it into a fist or put one arm into a crack and twist the elbow against one side of the crack and the hand against the offset side.

PINCH HOLDS

PINCH HOLDS involve a protruding piece of rock being firmly held between your fingers and thumb, or clasped between your hands.

FRICTION HOLDS depend solely on the friction of your hands or feet against a smooth surface. They are difficult to use because they give you a feeling of insecurity, which most climbers try to correct by leaning close to the rock, thereby increasing their insecurity. Friction holds often serve well as intermediate holds, some of which give needed support while you move over them but which would not support you were you to stop on them.

FRICTION HOLDS

Figure 10-21. Basic Holds

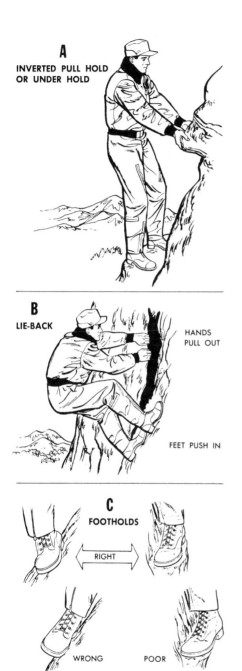

A
INVERTED PULL HOLD OR UNDER HOLD

A. The INVERTED PULL or PUSH HOLD is also called an UNDER HOLD. It permits cross pressure between your hands and feet.

B. LIE BACK. Lean to one side of an offset crack with your hands pulling and your feet pushing against the offset side.

C. The FOOTHOLD is a common hold. The service shoe with rubber sole will hold on rock slabs that slope as much as 45 degrees. On steep slopes, keep your body vertical and use small irregularities in the slope to aid foot friction.

D. In CHIMNEY CLIMBING, exert cross pressure between your back and feet, hands or knees.

D
CHIMNEY CLIMBING TECHNIQUE

B
LIE-BACK

HANDS PULL OUT

FEET PUSH IN

C
FOOTHOLDS

← RIGHT →

WRONG   POOR

Figure 10-22. Combination Holds

ous ridges and canyons, all of which must be crossed before reaching the main ridge. Snow fields which drop off in a sheer cliff may blend with those beyond to give the appearance of a continuous line of easy travel.

The best tactic in the mountains is to follow valleys or ridges; do not try to go at right angles to them. If you strike a blind canyon with near perpendicular walls, start over and try another route. Days of extra traveling may be worth the added safety. Game trails may indicate the best path.

If you absolutely cannot avoid climbing or descending a cliff, first choose a route that offers hand and footholds, cracks, and ledges in an unbroken path from top to bottom. *Chimneys* are vertical cracks or troughs in a wall, and offer a variety of holds.

In climbing cliffs:

1. Test every hold carefully before trusting full weight to it.
2. Distribute weight on three points (two hands and one foot) while moving. When standing, keep feet apart.
3. Be cautious of getting into tight spots where it is impossible to go in either direction without danger. It is easier to climb up than down, so this position is easy to get into.
4. Don't climb on loose or rotten rock. Remove loose stones while descending so they won't fall later from above.
5. Maintain balance and keep moving, as a continuous movement from one hold to the other conserves strength. Use legs as lifting power and hands mainly for balance.
6. Use a rope, if possible, for descending steep cliffs or slopes. (See rappelling below.)
7. Always face the cliff on a vertical descent.

Descending Cliffs. When two people are present, one of the safest methods of descent is for one person to lower the other in a seat formed from a Spanish bowline. Use two ropes if possible. Secure one rope firmly to a tree and drop it over the cliff. Secure one survivor to one end of the second rope via a Spanish bowline or other knot. Wrap this rope around a tree and have the second survivor pay out the line as the first survivor de-

Figure 10-23. Spanish bowline

Figure 10-24. Rappelling Training

scends, steadying himself or herself with the first rope. The last person will have to rappel down.

Rappelling is a way of descending a steep or vertical face by using the friction of a rope against the body. (It is good for abandoning ship, as well as for descending a cliff.) If you're too weak to climb down a rope, you can still rappel down, rest on the way, and save the rope for future use. Rappelling has its dangers, however, so be careful.

To rappel, pass the rope around a tree or rock where it will not bind. Tie the ends together in a large knot, and throw the rope down the cliff. Be sure it hits bottom or gets to a point with a good anchor so that you can rappel again. Sliding down a rope is easy compared with climbing back up, especially if you are hurt or cold or if it is snowing or raining.

Straddle both ropes, while looking at the anchor, and pass them around one thigh, across the chest, over the opposite shoulder, and down across the back to be grasped by one hand. Grasp the rope in front of the body with the other hand. The arm that reaches forward is on the opposite side of the body from the encircled thigh. Ease the grip of the hands and slowly and carefully "walk down" the cliff, keeping the legs perpendicular to the cliff. The feet should be apart and against the cliff. Slow or stop your drop by wrapping the rope more tightly around your body or by tightening your

Figure 10-25. Glissading, or sliding, down a steep snowfield. (Courtesy of the Defense Audio-Visual Agency)

grip. After descending, retrieve the rope by pulling on one end. Rappelling requires gloves, a heavy shirt and trousers to avoid rope burns.

Negotiating Talus Slopes. A talus is a steep slope composed of loose rock at the base of a cliff. If it is of fine material, turn slightly sideways, keep joints loose and go down on a diagonal course, taking long steps. If the talus is of coarse materials or large rocks, go more carefully, as a loose rock may roll under a person's weight.

Crossing Mountain Snowfields and Glaciers. The easiest and quickest method of getting down a steep snowfield may be to slide or glissade down—that is, stand or sit—and dig a short, tough stick into the snow to slow or stop your descent if you should fall. Beware of crevasses that are lightly covered with snow or invisible from a distance.

Crevasses are particularly apt to occur on glaciers at right angles to the glacier flow at an area where the angle of the glacier changes. They seldom go all the way across the glacier, and thus may be detoured. As you pick your way through, thrust a long pole into the snow a few feet ahead of you to test for a snow bridge across the glacier. Only in mid to late summer are crevasses visible. Most of the time they lurk beneath the snow cover and can swallow an unsuspecting traveler.

Kick and flatten steps in a steep snow slope if you must cross it. Be on the lookout for avalanches of snow or rock, especially during thaws or in cold weather after a fresh snow. Rock falls are frequent in rugged mountains. Avoid traveling at the base of slopes or cliffs where they are likely to fall.

In topping a snow-covered ridge from the windward side, you may pass the sound part of the ridge and walk out on a snow cornice that may break under your weight. From the leeward side, you can see such a cornice. Follow the ridge just below it.

PART 2

WATER SURVIVAL

CHAPTER 11

Preparedness and Priorities

There are tremendous differences between surviving on land and surviving on the open ocean. Humans feel much more at home on land. The aquatic environment is so foreign that good swimmers can exhaust themselves without knowing it; their controlled breathing may produce anoxia and they may drown. Even if you have a life raft or other flotation device, you face exposure, thirst, and hunger. You must also cope with depression, which seems to strike more quickly in an open-water, extended survival situation than it does on land.

Because the best protection against misfortune is preparedness, this chapter addresses the problems of preparing for and setting priorities in a deep water survival situation. Your second line of defense is the ability to swim well; a study of naval pilots downed at sea found that good swimmers fared better even though most never had to swim at all. Chapter 12 therefore focuses on those critical moments of abandoning ship and, just in case, survival swimming. The final chapter of the water survival section alerts you to some of the myriad hazards of this alien environment.

PREPARATION

A particular individual may be quite capable of proceeding rationally on terra firma but may tend to panic in a similar life-threatening situation on water. To short-circuit the panic button, accept and prepare to counter the unpredictability of the sea.

Preparation starts with the individual, your mental strength and physical skills, and is consolidated by the supplies and tools, kept ready at hand, that could prove invaluable in a life-or-death situation.

Personal Preparation

Avoid the "it can't happen to me" mentality. A skipper should rehearse the crew so that, in an emergency, each person would know his or her respon-

Figure 11-1. The pilot of a single-engine plane awaits rescue after ditching out 430 miles northeast of Honolulu. Fortunately, he was prepared with a life raft.

sibilities. Such a rehearsal could involve the actual use of some emergency equipment, for knowing that your equipment works can stave off panic at the last minute.

If the unexpected happens, the sooner you can make the transition to acceptance of the situation, the better your chances of ultimate success. Accepting the new reality helps you to react constructively. Fear and panic subside as you turn your attention to the work that must be done.

This work involves counteracting the effects of cold, fatigue, thirst, hunger, and pain. If any of these conditions gain the upperhand, it can weaken your will to prevail. You must fight to establish some measure of control, by means of your own will and your resourcefulness.

Perhaps even more so than on land, good physical condition can affect the outcome of a survival ordeal at sea. Swimming requires physical fitness and teaches you proper breathing control and conservation of energy. An extended experience aboard a life raft draws heavily on your emotional and physical reserves. Previously acquired skill in swimming, and in such life-prolonging skills as first aid treatment, water procurement, and food procurement can equip you personally and serve to fend off depression or panic.

However much you can accomplish with your body and powers of reason, you will be limited, perhaps dangerously so, without the right equipment. The final aspect of personal preparation is to educate yourself regarding your survival equipment.

Equipment Preparation

When you begin assembling a life raft survival kit, refer to the list of items below. They should be stored in the raft container and tied together with line. They are not to be used as substitutes for emergency equipment required by law. You must also consider the quantity you need, given the number of people your parent craft usually carries. Any special medical requirements of your frequent passengers should also be provided for. Finally, different areas of the seas require different equipment: an exposure suit for the North Atlantic in winter; covering, but cool, clothing in the South Pacific in summer.

- First aid
  - (1) Items one through ten on page 11
  - (2) sunglasses
  - (3) stainless steel tweezers
  - (4) stainless steel scissors
- Signaling
  - (1) radio (in addition to ELTs or EPIRBs carried on parent craft)
  - (2) mirror
  - (3) whistle
  - (4) flashlight (batteryless)
  - (5) flares
  - (6) smoke signals
  - (7) dye (sea marker)
  - (8) two foot by two foot sheet of bright colored material (international orange)
- Water
  - (1) canned water
  - (2) solar still
  - (3) plastic containers
- Shelter
  - (1) blankets (space blankets or wool blankets)
  - (2) thermo suits or exposure suits
- Food
  - (1) hard candy
  - (2) beef jerky
  - (3) fishing gear
  - (4) knife (floating type)
- Navigation (see page 289)
  - (1) chart or map of the area
  - (2) compass
  - (3) a chronometer-quality timepiece

PRIORITIES

The survival priorities that have been stressed throughout this book—first aid, water procurement, shelter construction, food procurement, and travel—retain that order, but in a survival episode at sea, flotation must head the list.

Figure 11-2. A family with appropriate PFDs. (Courtesy of the U.S. Coast Guard)

FLOTATION

Regardless of whatever else you do to stay afloat, you must first conquer the impulse to panic. The effort involved in providing yourself with auxiliary support in the water will replace a panicky reaction with a positive one.

Even good swimmers tire eventually, and survival swimming techniques will not support you indefinitely. A personal flotation device (PFD) is to open ocean survival what a warm sleeping bag is to cold regions survival: the pivotal piece of equipment. This doesn't mean that all is hopeless if you don't have one. It does mean that, if you're wearing a PFD when you fall overboard or abandon ship, your chances of living through the experience are greatly enhanced.

Once in the water, you will want to draw around you as much flotsam as possible. Holding on to or climbing aboard a floating piece of equipment will extend the time you are able to live in the water and will help rescuers spot you more easily. In addition, some of the pieces of "junk" will inevitably prove useful in meeting the various priorities of survival. People have used seat cushions and inverted ice chests as life-saving aids. Any object that floats may serve as a makeshift life raft, but the most common improvisation is some form of air bladder.

Some items of clothing can be inflated to provide flotation. A pair of trousers, if the material is not too porous, will make an excellent flotation device:

(1)   Remove the trousers, making sure that one leg is not inside out.
(2)   Tie the legs together with an overhand or square knot as close to the cuffs as possible.

Figure 11-3. Gather as much debris around you as possible; it will help you to float and will make you more visible in the water. (Courtesy of the U.S. Coast Guard)

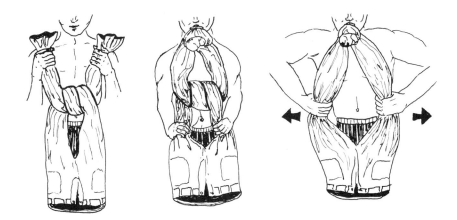

Figure 11-4. Tying the knot for inflation of trousers

Figure 11-5. Three methods for inflating trousers: (1) swinging over the head; (2) splashing; or (3) blowing.

Figure 11-6. Fully inflated trousers properly donned for flotation

(3) Inflate the trousers in one of several ways:
   (a) Splashing: Hold the rear of the waistband with one hand while pounding air into the trousers with the other. Take care that the waist band is not lifted out of the water and that the fly is down.
   (b) Blowing (probably the least strenuous): While holding the waistband on either side, duck under water with lungs full of air and blow one-half to two-thirds of it into the waist opening. With the trousers inverted, air is trapped in the legs. One or two breaths is generally enough to achieve buoyancy, but keep blowing until fully inflated.
   (c) Swinging over the head (fastest, but most difficult; not recommended for weak swimmers): As you give a strong leg kick, preferably the frog kick, pull the trousers—waistband first—out of the water, over the head, and then straight down into the water. Note that the movement is up and down, not a "flip."
(4) Hold the waistband flat and tight to your stomach. To free your hands, put a belt (rope or line, for example) through the belt loops of the trousers and around your waist. Another way to free your hands is to hold the waistband between your legs.
(5) Maintain buoyancy by keeping the trousers wet as the drier the material becomes the faster it leaks air. You can splash air into the trousers without removing them from their floating position, or you could "blow" air into the pant leg directly through the material.

If your trousers have a hole in them, position them so that the hole is sealed against your body or pinch it closed with a free hand. Auxiliary flotation devices can be improvised from, among other things, dresses, shirts, plastic bags, and canvas luggage.

FIRST AID

Although it may sound cold-hearted, it is in fact logical and necessary to attend to your own welfare first. Unless you can survive, you will be of no help to anybody. Once you have provided for your own flotation and first aid needs, you can lend a helping hand to your fellow survivors. Virtually all the first aid procedures you could apply on land you can also do in the water or life raft although some require modification.

External Bleeding

A prompt and thorough check for bleeding should be made following any accident. In the water, open wounds or cuts may go unnoticed until the victim has lost a lot of blood. To staunch the flow, use the same techniques in the water as you would have done on land (see the first aid chapter).

Mouth-to-Mouth Resuscitation

With the conventional method of mouth-to-mouth breathing, the rescuer assumes a position above the victim. In the water, however, the rescuer merely floats the victim in front of him on his back, interlocks his arm with the victim's (right with right or left with left) such that he is able to reach under the victim's back and support the victim's head. The rescuer's free hand is then used to tilt the victim's head and pinch the victim's nose, just as he would do on land. To administer air to the victim, the rescuer turns the victim's head slightly toward his own and turns it away for the victim to exhale.

Cardiopulmonary Resuscitation

External cardiac compression is hard to administer in a small raft and very difficult in the water, because the sternum (breastbone) of the victim, if he is an adult, must be depressed approximately one and one-half to two inches and the body must be horizontal or inclined with head lowered for adequate circulation. A firm support for the backbone is necessary for effective compression of the heart. Inflated tubes of the life raft may provide sufficient support, or another person may lie stretched out and rigid between the victim and the floor of the raft.

In the water, when PFD's are worn, the most effective method for cardiopulmonary resuscitation is for the rescuer to assume a position beneath and behind the victim. By reaching around the victim (underneath

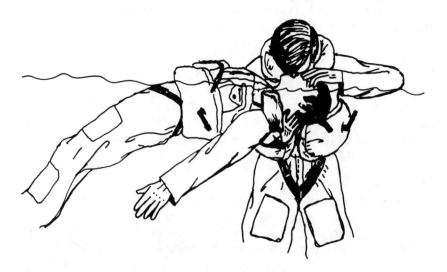

Figure 11-7. Mouth-to-mouth resuscitation in the water

Figure 11-8. One possible method, under evaluation by the U.S. Navy and the U.S. Coast Guard, for administering cardiac compression in the water

his PFD) and placing a fist (thumb down) on the lower one-third of the sternum with the other hand palm down on top of the first, the sternum can be compressed. The lower body must be floated or held on the surface by whatever means available. Cardiopulmonary resuscitation is very difficult to perform in the water. If there is no other choice, however, it should be attempted. For the mechanics of CPR, as opposed to the positions to adopt in the water or aboard a life raft, see the first aid chapter.

Immersion Hypothermia

Sudden entry into or an extended period in cold water (below 72°F) may lead to immersion hypothermia, a major cause of death in water-related accidents. Because water is a powerful conductor of heat, a body in water loses heat approximately 24 times faster than in air. Anyone traveling over or working around cold water should prepare himself by wearing protective clothing—hats, coats, mittens, and so forth. If immersion is likely, don a survival suit. Also known as exposure suits, these head-to-toe, one-size-fits-all, international-orange suits provide buoyancy in the water and insulation against the cold.

Prevention. Your behavior when accidently immersed in cold water may well spell the difference between life and death. If possible, climb out of the water quickly using floating objects that may be at hand. At least, get as much of your body out of the water as possible. Do not remove any clothing. If you must remain in the water, assume the Heat Escape Lessening Position (HELP), discussed in the next chapter. This position is designed to protect those areas of the body that lose heat most rapidly—the head, neck, sides, and groin.

Movement in the water should be kept to an absolute minimum, or heat will be lost even faster. If several survivors are in the water, they should huddle together so that they collectively present less surface area to the hostile environment. Even when out of the water, individuals should hug each other closely to minimize heat loss.

Symptoms. The first danger signal is uncontrolled shivering, followed by slurred speech, mental confusion, and the loss of the use of hands and feet. Eventually, unconsciousness may result, and cardiopulmonary arrest.

Treatment. Treatment of hypothermia victims under survival conditions will be very difficult. The first aider should follow these recommendations when treating a victim of cold water hypothermia:

(1)   Remove the victim from the water, taking care to handle him gently.
(2)   Put the victim in an enclosed space away from wind and cold air.
(3)   Remove wet clothing and wrap in warm blankets, if possible.
(4)   If the victim is conscious, give warm, sweet drinks. Under no circumstances give alcohol or diuretics such as coffee or tea.

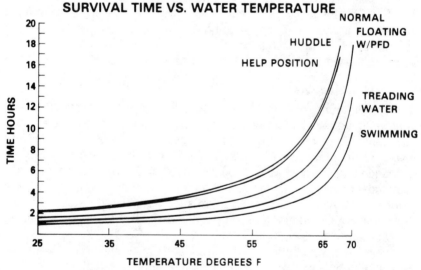

Figure 11-9. Hypothermia Median Lethal Exposure Survival Time vs. Water Temperature (Source: U.S. Coast Guard)

Figure 11-10. Contrary to general impressions, alcohol must never be given to a cold person. (Courtesy of the U.S. Coast Guard)

(5) If the victim is unconscious, check for an open airway, for respirations, and for a palpable pulse (carotid or femoral artery). You may have to check closely for two or three minutes to detect slowed vital signs. If any signs of life are detected, CPR is not indicated.

(6) If the unconscious victim has no detectable pulse or respirations, assume he is in cardiopulmonary arrest and administer CPR, if doing so does not put you at risk. Once begun, CPR must continue until the victim regains pulse and respirations on his own (exceedingly rare in severe cases), until you and your companions are too exhausted to continue, or until the victim is delivered to a hospital.

(7) Add heat, not to raise the body core temperature but to prevent any further heat loss. In a survival situation you could possibly apply external heat packs, made up of hot rocks, to the head, neck, trunk, and groin or you could engage in buddy warming. Do not attempt to warm the limbs.

SIGNALING

If you have time before you must abandon ship or ditch your airplane in the sea, radio the authorities of your dilemma. This will set rescue forces into action and may considerably shorten your ordeal. In signaling the U.S. Coast Guard or other authority, give the name of your vessel and the number of people aboard; your position; the nature of the emergency; and the type of assistance needed.

Once in the raft or water, you will need something that will signal your whereabouts to rescuers. Visual devices such as flares and rockets,

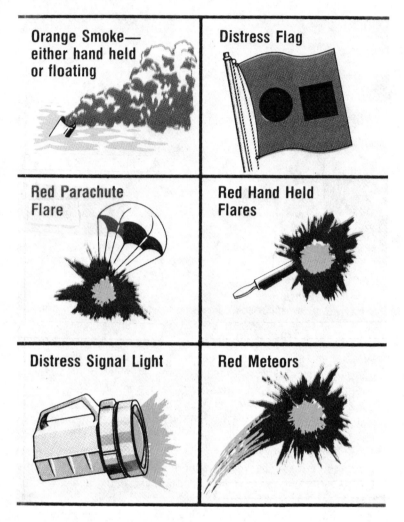

Figure 11-11. Various ways of signaling for help

strobe lights, sea dye markers, smoke signals, distress flags, or mirrors are the traditional methods by which castaways signal for help. In the modern world of autopilots, self-steering gears, radar scanners, and gyro-compasses, however, such signs may go unobserved. Many survivors live to tell of the first, second, third, even more ships that "got away." Rockets and hand-held flares are more visible at night, rockets up to a distance of twenty miles, flares up to five. Be careful to hold flares downwind and over the edge of the raft so that sparks do not fall onto the raft, giving you an even bigger emergency. During the day, smoke signals, sea dye markers, and sun-reflecting mirrors are especially useful for attracting the attention of pilots. Smoke and sea dye are best used when the day and sea are calm, to cut back on dissipation. On hazy days, pilots can spot the flash of a mirror before you can see the aircraft. If you know an air and sea search has been mounted for you, keep flashing.

The most effective means of signaling is by modern methods such as emergency locator transmitters (ELTs) or emergency position indicating

Figure 11-12. U.S. Navy airman holds signal flare over downwind side of raft.

Figure 11-13. An Emergency Position-Indicating Radio Beacon (EPIRB). (Courtesy of NASA)

radio beacons (EPIRBs). These small, lightweight, shock-resistant, self-energizing beacons are capable of at least forty-eight hours of continuous broadcasting. The signal, which is broadcast on emergency distress frequencies, may be received by either passing aircraft or ships or by a search and rescue satellite system. The signals received by satellite are relayed to a network of ground stations and then to the rescue control center. The satellite-aided search and rescue effort is a multinational cooperative project involving the United States, Canada, France, Norway, the Soviet Union, and other nations.

Whistles come in handy if you're trying to make contact with other survival craft that have become separated.

The potential for improvised signaling is limited because of the nature of the environment. If rescuers are nearby, the sea is calm, and the day clear, you can wave the proverbial tattered shirt or sail. If you're in the water, you might try splashing and calling. But anything that is really going to do you any good is going to have to be brought along when you abandon ship or stored regularly in the life raft.

WATER PROCUREMENT

Do not drink salt water, for the salt draws upon water stored in the body's cells, setting up a vicious cycle of increasing dehydration and increasing thirst that is broken only by death. A theory has been advanced that under certain conditions seawater can be drunk, but medical opinion and government recommendations strongly reject it. For the survivor, it is better to turn your attention to practical means of obtaining fresh water and conserving your body's natural fluids than to be tempted by false relief.

Taking in Water

If you have time before abandoning ship, drink your fill. Then, do not ration water aboard the life raft, but take it as you need it. Store water in the body. Cut down on body waste and do not eat unless you have plenty of water. People have died trying to save water. Your survival odds are better if you drink the water that your body requires.

There are two primary sources of potable water: bottled or canned water and rain water. In addition, there are supplemental sources.

Bottled or Canned Water. Aboard the parent craft, water containers— filled only to the three-quarters mark so they will float if necessary— should be stored in various locations. In a crowded life raft, buoyant water containers can be towed. Water should also be stored in the life raft, and survival kits should include desalting tablets, containers to collect and store water, and solar stills.

If it rains before you've gone through your bottled water, save it and drink the rain water instead. Bottled water will stay fresher longer.

Figure 11-14. Nimbostratus clouds (with fractostratus below). These almost certainly bring precipitation, either rain or snow depending on the temperature. Low, amorphous, dark, and usually uniform, they block out the sun. These clouds are often accompanied by low *scud* (fractostratus) clouds when the wind is strong. At hand are rough weather, high winds, and a hazardous sea.

Figure 11-15. Stratus clouds (with fractostratus present). These clouds give the sky a low, leaden, grey appearance. Other than perhaps a light drizzle, no precipitation should be expected except from higher clouds when stratus forms in front of a warm front.

Figure 11-16. Stratocumulus clouds. Grey or white irregular layers with rolling patches characterize these clouds. They do not, generally, produce much more than light precipitation.

Figure 11-17. Fair-weather cumulus clouds. When separate and lacking in vertical development, these clouds portend good weather.

Figure 11-18. Cumulus clouds (with vertical development). When cumulus clouds swell to great heights, heavy showers are likely, associated with gusty surface winds.

Figure 11-19. Cumulonimbus cloud (with classic anvil). These thunderheads bring rain but also very gusty surface winds, lightning, frequently hail, and high seas.

Rain Water. The water that you bring with you can only last for so long. As soon as you establish yourself in the life raft you should consider ways of collecting and storing rain water. One of the lookout's responsibilities is to watch for possible showers. Rain or snow may result when the following conditions occur:

- when a cold, warm, or occluded front approaches
- in about twenty to forty hours after you first note that cirrus-type clouds are beginning to thicken and lower
- in about fourteen to sixteen hours after you see cirrostratus clouds and a halo around the sun or moon
- within six to eight hours when the morning temperature is unusually high, the air is humid, and cumulus clouds are building
- within about an hour in the afternoon when you see swelling cumulus clouds (there will be static on a radio)
- when the sky is dark and threatening to the west
- when a southerly wind increases in speed and the clouds scud across the sky from the west
- when the wind—especially a north wind—shifts counterclockwise, from north to west to south.

Once a rainshower seems imminent, you must prepare receptacles to catch the life-giving rain. Much more is involved than simply tilting back your head, opening your mouth, and croaking, "Hallelujah!"

You want the largest collection surface possible: the roof of the raft, an upsidedown umbrella, oil skins, a sail. Some early rain is wasted because it has to wash off the salt that has impregnated these surfaces. You can get good water sooner if, before the rain falls, you have rinsed the article in seawater, which dissolves some of the accumulated salt. The first, still somewhat salty water can be used for auxiliary needs such as cleaning or moistening lips.

Fill every available container. Be imaginative in identifying receptacles: plastic bags, shoes and boots, knapsacks, even the intestines of turtles or large fish (turned inside-out and knotted at one end).

Algae may form in plastic containers. Chlorinating tablets or potassium permanganate, items likely to be included in a survival kit, would inhibit growth. As for water stored in receptacles improvised from nature, check every day to be sure it's not going bad.

If you have stored all you can and have drunk your fill, and the climate is warm, take a shower in the rain. It will improve your morale and any skin lesions will benefit from fresh water and gentle dapping. This is assuming a warm climate, of course.

Condensation. Layers of small drops of fresh water collect on surfaces exposed to air when days are warm but nights, especially just before dawn, are cold. If surfaces are coated in salt, the dew may not be much good, but if not, sponge the dew off with a cloth reserved for that purpose only. Wring out the cloth over a container and enjoy a drink. *Old Sea Ice.* Old sea ice, which is blue and rounded on the edges, will be devoid of salt and is safe to drink when melted. It splinters easily. New sea ice is grey and hard. It carries a lot of salt and is of no value. *Fluid in Marine Life.* The spinal fluid in fish is fresh. Break the backbone and suck it out of the vertebrae. Fish eyes also contain a high percentage of fluid. Turtle blood, if drunk very quickly after the killing, supplies necessary liquid to the body. Do not, however, use fish blood as a substitute for water. Treat it like food; do not consume it unless plenty of fresh water is available.

Do not mix animal fluid, salt water, and urine hoping to stretch your water supply. Urine contains waste products from the body and may be almost as concentrated as sea water. Drinking it will only increase thirst and draw water from the body tissues. You may in fact have difficulty passing urine, which will be thick and dark. Such a reaction to dehydration is natural.

Regulating Loss of Water

Coupled with efforts to take in water should be efforts to slow its outflow. Water evaporates through the skin. Some survivors have reported that by remaining in the sea for hours at a time they prevented evaporation and even absorbed enough to increase kidney activity. Care must be taken not to expend energy by too much activity and—very important—not to become lunch for a passing shark.

If there is little or no water, you should not eat as digestion and elimination use up water. In such a situation, do not expect a bowel movement and do not take any medicine for constipation. In fact, you should put off as long as possible any such fluid elimination.

Keep your body protected from the sun and wind, because heat and air movement increases evaporation. Heavy clothing in warm weather, strenuous exercise, and worry induce sweating with a subsequent loss of water. You can also reduce sweating by deflating the floor of the life raft, sprinkling the covers of the raft with sea water, soaking your clothes in the sea, and tying back the flaps to provide maximum ventilation.

Even an experienced seaman may have to acquire his sealegs anew after leaving the parent craft and getting used to the motion of the life raft. Take seasickness pills before vomiting starts. If you are sick, you should take extra water. Similarly, you should avoid foods that induce diarrhea. Your health goal is to take in as much water as possible, while letting out as little as possible.

SHELTER CONSTRUCTION

Protection from the elements is a major challenge in ocean survival. Shelter takes two forms: that which envelopes your body itself and that which your small craft offers against the vast and heedless sea.

Survival Clothing

Clothes will provide some protection from the threat of hypothermia in cold climates as well as the danger of sunburn in hot climates. In abandoning ship, try to wear and throw into the survival craft clothing that will protect you. Oilskins are a must in any climate. In the tropics, think in terms of long pants and long-sleeved shirts, white socks, and some kind of headgear and neck cloth. In cold climates (anywhere where water temperature is below 70 degrees) you couldn't do better than to have a survival suit.

Survival Craft

Upon leaving the parent craft, the life raft or life boat will be your shelter against a harsh nature. All affairs of living must be carried out within that cramped space. It may happen that your craft is overcrowded, being asked to support more people than the manufacturer recommends; it may be that you are alone in a twenty-person life raft. Whatever the circumstance, you must do the best you can within its bounds. Climate and type of craft indicate certain actions.

In Cold Oceans. Difficult as it may seem, your objective in a cold water survival situation is to be warm and dry. Erect a windscreen and, getting behind it, remove your wet clothing and replace it with dry, if you can. Don hats, mittens, and extra socks. Huddle with your companions in the bottom of the craft, allowing them to warm their hands and feet against your flesh (they should return the favor!). Extra clothing should be given to the watchstander.

To insulate the craft, put cloth or sails on the floor. Anything extra can go overhead. Although a life raft canopy is important in cold weather, more heat can be lost through the bottom of the raft than from above because water conducts heat away faster than air. Keep the floor of the raft inflated.

Regularly exercise your muscles to restore circulation: wiggle facial muscles to check on frostbite; stretch and bend fingers and toes; elevate feet for a minute or two every now and then. Shivering is the body's normal way of generating heat quickly, but extreme shivering can lead to muscle spasms—another reason for mild, regular exercise.

Digestion generates some heat. Therefore, eat slowly and often, provided water is available.

In Warm Oceans. Anyone having to face a survival ordeal in the Arctic Ocean probably wishes fervently that he could at least be in the Indian

Ocean. Yet heat is as life-threatening as cold. The sun beats down unmercifully, hours on end. Unless you can protect yourself you will become sunburned, dehydrated, and demoralized.

Surviving in warm oceans presents challenges surprisingly similar to survival in deserts: lack of drinking water, sunburn, exhaustion.

Improvise a canopy, allowing for adequate ventilation. Deflate the floor of the raft. Bathe in the ocean, if it is safe. Keep clothes damp. Wear a hat, preferably one with a brim. Wear sunglasses. Protect your nose from sunburn. Did you include lip balm and sun screen lotion in your survival kit? If not, improvise with oils from fish or fowl.

Inflatable Craft. With inflatables, the object is to prevent chafing and punctures and to repair leaks promptly so as to prolong the life of the raft and, therefore, your own. Under particular stress are the areas around doors and handles; the juncture between the floor of the raft and the flotation chambers; and places where grab lines, towing lines, and sea anchor lines scour the fabric. Monitor the wear of the first two problems. Use plugs for external damage, patch holes on the inside of the raft. To ease the third problem, wrap lines in cloth or towels.

Marine life bumping into and rubbing against the underside takes a toll on the skin of the raft. Float a baffle sheet (a piece of material between the craft and the offender) or fender off to the side to foil any advances. If sharks or turtles persist in investigating your craft, a quick poke to the snout with an oar or a hold on a hind flipper will convince the offender that you are neither a meal nor a mate.

If you use spars or oars to rig up a sail or support an awning, be sure that the base does not scour the raft. Anything that might puncture the raft, such as knife or fish hook, must be handled thoughtfully.

Proper inflation is important. Use a pump or blow into a tube to keep the buoyancy chambers well-rounded but not stretched tight. On hot days, release air to compensate for the expansion of hot air. In cold oceans, keep

BOTTLE SIDE
OF RAFT

Figure 11-20. Correct way to right a raft

the raft well filled for insulation. If you have a favorable wind, inflate the raft fully and sit high.

In high seas, or because of a lack of balance, a raft or lifeboat may capsize or swamp. Secure important equipment, such as water containers and fishing tackle. To balance the craft, the heaviest person should sit in the middle. Keep low in the craft, do not stand, and do not move suddenly.

To right a capsized raft, fling the righting rope across the bottom; move to the other side; brace your foot against the raft and pull. If your raft has no righting rope, reach across the raft for the lifeline. Slide back into the water, pulling as you go. From the water, clamber aboard the raft at the narrow end, remaining as flat as possible.

Rigid Craft. Although not as apparently vulnerable to damage as a raft, a boat is subject to stress also, particularly at its seams. And the threat of capsizing or being swamped is still very real. Many of the same principles of weight and balance mentioned above also apply to rigid craft. If a heavy sea is following, you may want to proceed cut-away stern first, presenting the bow to the onrushing waves. A sea anchor attached to the bow adds to the stability of the craft by keeping the bow into the wave.

FOOD PROCUREMENT

You can live for about a month or so without food, only about a week without water. Providing you have plenty of drinking water, you can direct your efforts to obtaining food.

You should never be caught without fishing tackle. With it you are able to tap the vast food wealth of the sea, which in fact surpasses that of land or fresh water. If you should happen not to have fishing tackle, however, it is possible to improvise lines, hooks, and a bait grapple.

Fishing Lines

To make a fishing line cut a piece of canvas about a yard square, being careful to follow the weave of the fabric so the threads or ravelings may be drawn. Use dry canvas; wet canvas is difficult to unravel. Place eight or ten strands between the thumb and forefingers of each hand and roll or twist the thread clockwise, at the same time passing the right hand over the left counter-clockwise. This will form a small rope with a breaking point well over one hundred pounds. When about 18 inches of line is completed, cut off the strands at intervals of about 2 inches so that each thread will be progressively longer. As the end of each strand is reached, feed in a new strand, until fifty or more feet of line has been made. A two-strand line when made as described will have a breaking point well over twenty pounds. Fabric from clothing can be utilized in the same way.

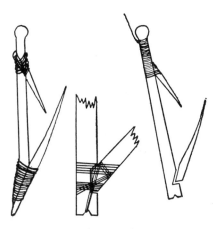

Figure 11-21. Construction of wooden fish hooks

Fishhooks

Fishhooks can be made from wood split from seat benches or gunwales. Shape the shaft and cut a notch near the end in which to seat the point. Sharpen the point so the hardest part of the grain will form the extreme tip as well as the barb. This section should form an angle of about 30 degrees with the longitudinal axis of the shaft and be lashed firmly in position, using single strands from the canvas. Make the line fast by binding it tightly to the shaft.

Bait Grapple

A grapple for collecting and pulling in seaweed can be made from four heavy slivers of wood cut from a raft or boat. Cut three notches near the end of the heaviest sliver of wood in which to seat three pieces and lash them in position. Make the line fast to the shaft by cutting three or four notches near the end and lashing it tightly with canvas threads.

Bait

Small forms of life drifting about in the sea furnish food directly or indirectly for all the larger forms of aquatic life. This drifting life is most abundant in northern seas, and in some areas is so dense that it colors the water. It can be gathered with a tow net or an improvised dip net. Use the small creatures as bait for fish, but don't eat them as they are salty and contain sharp spines that will injure the stomach and intestines. Likewise, don't eat jellyfish; they possess stinging cells that are poisonous.

Containers

You will have aboard the life raft many objects that can serve as containers. If you have to improvise water or fire buckets, however, you can make a bucket using a needle and some canvas. If the bucket is to be watertight, the seams must be reinforced with a narrow canvas binding and caulked with fish slime that is then allowed to dry into the seams.

The tail-half of a fish carefully skinned back, then scraped, stuffed with seaweed or rags and dried in the sun will make an oil or water container. Leave the tails and fins attached to the skin. The air bladder of large fish can be dried and used in the same way.

Fire Pots

The bottom of a canvas fire pot should be kept wet; the sides will act as wicks and prevent the pot from burning. Rags, a few seat shavings, and the oil from fish livers should be saved and lighted as a signal to attract rescuers. Extract the oil by placing the fish livers in the sun. A wick can be made from the canvas threads.

Fishing at Sea

Success with fishing equipment will depend on how it is used. Remember the following:

(1) Never fasten the line to something solid; it may snap when a large fish strikes.

(2) Try to catch small fish; large ones may destroy the tackle.

(3) Fish are more apt to see and strike a moving bait than a still one.

(4) Use part of any bird or fish caught for bait. It need not be fresh. Bird intestines threaded on a hook are excellent.

(5) Many species of fish are confined to certain depth zones by light, pressure, and food. Some range through a wide variety of depth zones while still others migrate from zone to zone at different times of the day. Try fishing at different times of the day and night at all depths. Don't give up; sea life is not evenly distributed; sooner or later a persistent survivor will catch a fish.

(6) When a large fish is hooked, keep a taut line and play him. Don't force him; the line may break or the hook may be torn loose.

(7) Watch for schools of fish breaking water. Schools of small fish are good indications of the presence of large fish and vice versa. Birds often follow schools of small fish.

(8) Many species of fish and drifting sea life come to the surface of the sea at night. Fish shallow and use a drag net.

(9) Many small fish are attracted by shade. Lower the sail or tarpaulin into the water, fish may gather under it.

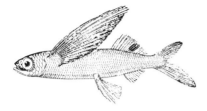

Figure 11-22. Flying fish

Fish

Fish caught at sea are good to eat—cooked or raw. None is likely to be poisonous. Flying fish are widely distributed, palatable, and probably the most available source of food if you have no equipment. Many survivors have lived on them alone. In time some may glide into the boat or against it. At night they are attracted by a light, become helpless within its radiance, and can be scooped in a net. Shine a light on the side of the boat or on any surface that will reflect it and the flying fish will often glide toward the light and in or against the boat.

The heart, liver, and blood of fish are good to eat, though in some fish they are less palatable than the flesh. Intestinal walls are edible, but the contents may be dangerous unless cooked. The stomachs of large fish may contain small fish partly digested; they are excellent. Fish eyes contain a high percentage of water.

Small fish can be caught with a skewer or gorge hook made of wood or metal and a short line improvised from shoe laces, canvas, or clothing. If you have a hook and line but no bait, fasten a strip of leather cut from the tongue of a shoe, a button, or a piece of canvas to the hook and troll it behind the boat. It must be kept moving so as to resemble a small fish.

If you have a knife, you may be able to stab large fish near the surface or spear them by tying the knife to the end of an oar. Slash with the knife in schools of small fish.

Fish spoil quickly in warm weather; therefore clean and eat them without delay and immediately dry what is left. If the sun is hot, fish can be partially cooked by cutting them into thin slices and placing them on a dry metal surface.

Seaweed

Raw seaweeds are tough and salty, absorb water from the intestines, and are difficult to digest. Eat them only if there is plenty of water. Small edible crabs, shrimp, and fish inhabit the seaweed along the coast and patches of sargasso weed far at sea. A grappler dragged behind the boat will collect seaweed. Shake it vigorously and examine carefully as the crabs, shrimp, and fish will be well camouflaged in it.

Birds

All seabirds are edible and nourishing, though they may have a fishy flavor and musty odor. Birds are relatively scarce on the open sea, but along coral islands and mid-ocean rocks thousands may be found. Three members of a torpedoed merchantman survived eighty-three days on a raft catching twenty-five or twenty-six birds during that time.

The number of birds one can expect to see on the open North Atlantic is comparatively small. In the North Pacific Ocean most of the seabirds are found near the coasts. Many tropical seabirds breed throughout the year and eggs and young can be found at all times. In the southern oceans many species of birds may be seen and caught hundreds of miles from shore. Land birds migrate miles over water; they often alight on boats to rest and at such times exhibit little fear of humans.

Gulls, albatross, terns, gannets (boobies) can be caught by dragging a baited fishhook behind a boat, or lured within shooting distance in the same manner. A flat, sharp-edged, triangular-shaped piece of metal or shell, dragged behind the boat, will attract gulls and albatross. A shiny or colored object is effective and a bait of fish or intestines adds to its attractiveness. The bird dives, seizes the lure, and the sharp points catch in its bill and hold fast.

Gannets once settled on a boat or raft will often allow themselves to be captured without attempting to fly away. If they are shy they may be caught in the following manner: tie a loose knot with two pieces of line, fastening two of the free ends of the knot to the boat. Place some fish entrails or similar bait within the loop. When a bird is attracted to the food, pull the knot together about its legs. A simple overhand knot can be used for the same purpose. Whatever bird that is caught, use all of it. The smaller feathers can be used to make a fly or lure. A spinner can be fashioned from the long plates of the bill. The bones can be utilized for skewer or barbed hooks and the quills stripped to make string. The skin is highly nutritious, but if you need warm clothing, skin the bird down the back, dry in the sun, and use the thick downy breast feathers for a cap, ear muffs, scarf, or shoe lining.

NAVIGATION

In most situations, it is better to try to stay in the area where your boat or plane went down. If you were able to get off an emergency signal or MAYDAY message, searchers will probably be sent out quickly to your last reported position. If help has not arrived within, say, twenty-four hours or so, chances are something has gone wrong. Your emergency message did not get transmitted, or it was not received, or your position was incorrectly reported.

At this point, you must decide whether to continue streaming your sea anchor or drogue, in an attempt to remain in the vicinity or, instead, hoist an improvised sail, if possible, in hopes of reaching either a more heavily traveled sea lane or a safe haven ashore. Many variables come into play in this decision. You must take into account the available supplies of food and water, the equipment on hand, and the condition of yourself, your fellow survivors, and your craft. Equally important are the level of navigational knowledge you and other members of your party possess and the inventory of your navigational tools. This section cannot substitute for a course in navigation, but we do include it as guidance for those familiar with basic principles of navigation, and in the hope that it may point out to those who are not the risks of going to sea without a life raft properly equipped and a mind properly educated for pathfinding at sea.

To be well prepared, you should have tucked away in your survival craft the following:

- a timepiece (for example, a stopwatch or wristwatch of chronometer quality)
- a magnetic compass
- a nautical chart of the area
- a seasonal pilot chart of the area
- a sextant
- either a *Nautical Almanac* or an *Air Almanac*
- a set of sight reduction tables
- a speed log
- a supply of sharpened pencils
- a nautical protractor or plotter.

All these should be stored in waterproof containers, such as plastic freezer bags.

If no one has even basic knowledge of navigation or you don't have the equipment, your best chance for survival is probably to attempt to stay as near your crash or sinking site as possible, and let rescuers find you. If you are drifting away despite your streaming a sea anchor or drogue, at the least you will eventually come within reach of the nearest land downwind and downcurrent from your initial position. Always overestimate the length of time it will take to reach your projected landfall. Having an idea of how long you will be at sea before making a landfall is helpful in allocating supplies. You might choose to rig a sail to increase your drift speed in order to reach land sooner.

If you or someone in your group knows how to navigate and you have the necessary equipment on board, you may elect to try to voyage to safety. The established rule of thumb, when chances for rescue at your present position are small, is to choose to sail to a probable landfall—downwind and downcurrent.

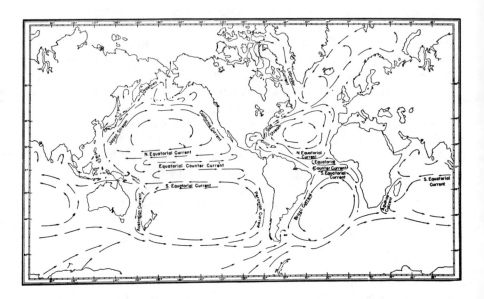

Figure 11-23. Primary current systems of the world. Because these basic patterns can often be somewhat altered by seasonal winds and local storms, it is important to maintain a good dead reckoning plot by means of which actual course and speed over the ground between fixes can be calculated. Seasonal pilot charts are of great assistance in determining the normal currents and winds.

Your options of where to head are limited by the prevailing winds and currents (see Figure 11-23). A life boat or raft can often make from one to three knots in the direction of the wind and current, but even one rigged with a sail can make virtually no headway upwind or against the current. You must, therefore, choose your destination carefully. It is far better to decide on a destination several hundreds of miles downwind in the direction the current is flowing than one much closer but in the opposite direction. Because navigation under survival conditions can only consist of rough estimations, you should in most cases head for a large, mountainous island or a continental land mass rather than any small low-lying islands that could too easily be missed.

If you have opted for an extended voyage, your first task is to establish your present position, if you do not already know it. Then you must determine your destination and your route and record your progress.

Determining Position and Direction
Normally you, or someone in your group, will have a fairly good idea of the position of your plane, ship, or boat just before the emergency. This in

most cases can be used as your initial position. If it is unknown, however, it can be estimated.

Position-fixing is done by determining your latitude and longitude, and then plotting these coordinates on your nautical or pilot chart or whatever you have improvised. The position thus plotted is termed a *fix*. A standard plastic or metal sextant or one improvised from a protractor, from a piece of plotting sheet paper, or from a chart compass rose is necessary to determine latitude; in addition, an accurate timepiece is needed for determining longitude. Remember that in a pitching boat in stormy seas, the accuracy of any sextant observations you make will be significantly affected.

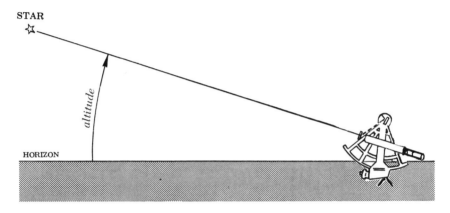

Figure 11-24. Altitude of a celestial body is the vertical angle measured from the horizon to the line of sight to the body.

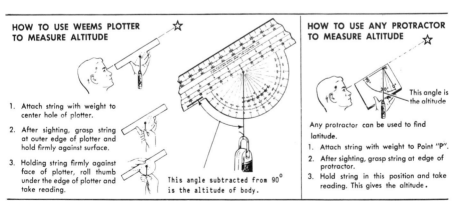

Figure 11-25. (*left*) How to use a Weems plotter to measure altitude; (*right*) How to use any protractor to measure altitude

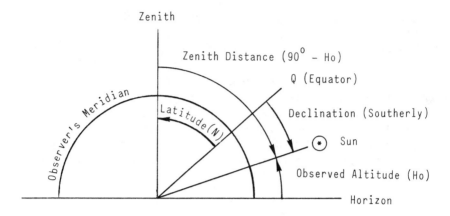

Figure 11-26. Sketch of the relationships among the zenith of an observer in northern latitudes, the equator, and a celestial body with south declination (the sun in this case) at meridian transit. Here, the observer's latitude is equal to the zenith distance (90 degrees − the observed altitude [Ho]) minus the sun's declination. There are five other possible relationships among the observer, the equator, and a celestial body. In each case, the observer's latitude will be equal to the sum or difference of the zenith distance and the declination of the body when it is at meridian transit. Whether to add or subtract can be determined by drawing a similar diagram of the relationships in each case.

Determining Latitude. In the northern hemisphere, one of the easiest ways to determine latitude is simply to take an altitude observation of the pole star Polaris with either a standard or improvised sextant (see Figures 11-24 and 11-25). The observed altitude of Polaris is approximately equal to the latitude of the observer. If you have a *Nautical Almanac*, you can check the back of the book to find a set of small corrections that will allow you to be accurate to the nearest half degree of latitude or better. If you haven't an *Almanac*, an uncorrected observation will usually yield your latitude to within 1½ to 2 degrees (equivalent to ninety to one hundred twenty miles) under most conditions.

A second way to find latitude if Polaris is not visible is to take an altitude observation of any other navigational star or planet whose declination (position north or south of the equator) is known at meridian transit, that is, when the body passes over your meridian and hence bears due north or south. Declinations for these bodies are listed in the *Nautical* and *Air Almanacs*. After recording the altitude, the zenith distance (90 degrees minus observed altitude) is either added to or subtracted from the declination, depending upon the relationship of the body and the observer with the equator at the time of observation, to yield the latitude. Draw a picture like that in Figure 11-26 to help visualize the relationships involved and determine whether to add or subtract in each case. The sun is, of course, the most readily observable body for this purpose (be sure to protect your eyes if you observe the sun).

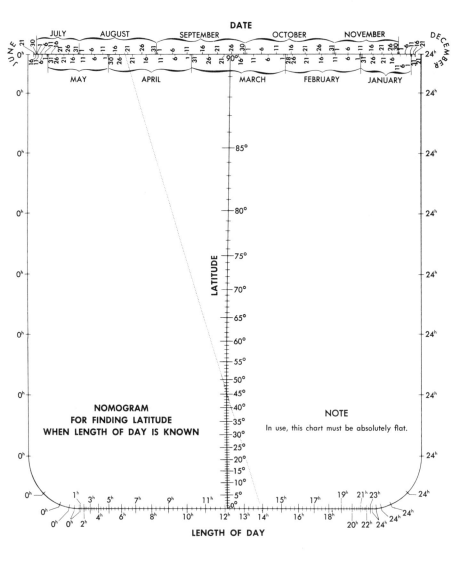

DATE

NOMOGRAM
FOR FINDING LATITUDE
WHEN LENGTH OF DAY IS KNOWN

NOTE
In use, this chart must be absolutely flat.

LATITUDE

LENGTH OF DAY

INSTRUCTIONS

To find your latitude:

In Northern Latitudes:

1. Find length of the day from the instant the top of the sun appears above the ocean horizon to the instant it disappears below the horizon. This instant is often marked by a green flash.
2. Lay a straight edge or stretch across the Nomogram, connecting the observed length of the day on the Length of Day Scale with the date on the Date Scale.
3. Read your latitude on the Latitude Scale.

EXAMPLE: On August 20, observed length of the day is 13 hours and 54 minutes. Latitude is 45°30′N.

In Southern Latitudes:

Add six months to the date and proceed as in northern latitudes.

EXAMPLE: On 11 May observed length of day is 10 hours and 4 minutes. Adding 6 months gives 11 November. Latitude is 41°30′S.

Figure 11-27. Nomogram

There is a third method of determining latitude that is independent of a celestial altitude observation. If you can time the exact length of the day from first appearance of the sun at dawn to its disappearance at sunset, you can use the nomogram of Figure 11-27 to determine latitude. Because of the annual migration of the sun above and below the equator, caused by the tilt of the earth's axis, there is a definite relationship between the length of the day for each date and latitude. Line up a straightedge over the recorded length of day on the left side with the date on the right side (if in south latitudes, subtract six months from the date first). You can then read the latitude to the nearest degree from the scale in the middle.

Determining Longitude. You must have a timepiece if you are to be able to estimate longitude, as you must be able to determine the correct Greenwich mean time (GMT). Your timepiece can either be set directly on GMT—the standard time kept in the Greenwich, England, time zone—or on your local zone time, as indicated in Figure 11-28. GMT can easily be

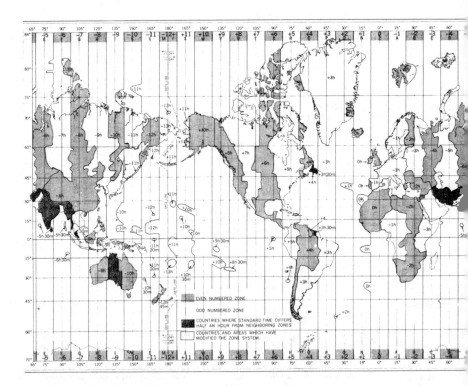

Figure 11-28. Standard time zone chart of the world. Standard times can be converted to GMT by application of the zone difference indicated to the standard zone time.

Day	SUN Eqn. of Time 00ʰ	12ʰ	Mer. Pass.
	m s	m s	h m
25	03 13	03 10	11 57
26	03 07	03 03	11 57
27	03 00	02 57	11 57

Figure 11-29. A sample equation of time, *Nautical Almanac*, 25–27 May 1973

determined from the latter by applying the zone difference. Knowing the correct GMT will allow you to find how far you are from the Greenwich (prime) meridian, on which both mean time and longitude are based.

At noon each day, record the GMT of the meridian transit of the sun at your location, perhaps by noting the moment when a northerly or southerly shadow is cast by an improvised plumb line or vertical stick or spike. Then refer to the tabulated three-column *equation of time* in the *Nautical Almanac*, an example of which is shown in Figure 11-29, to obtain the time of meridian passage of the apparent sun at Greenwich for this date (from the column marked *Mer. Pass.*). This time can also be used with minimal error as the *local zone time* (that is, standard time) of meridian passage at all other locations on the same day. It is necessary to obtain this time because the apparent sun will often either lead or lag the theoretical mean sun by which standard time is reckoned by several minutes; for each four minutes of error in time, a longitude error of one degree (equivalent to sixty miles at the equator, about thirty miles in mid-latitudes) will result. In the equation of time in Figure 11-29, for instance, the GMT of meridian passage of the apparent sun on 26 May is 1157.

After recording the exact GMT of local apparent noon at your location, find the difference between this time and the tabulated GMT of meridian transit at Greenwich. Then use the rate of travel of the mean sun—15 degrees of longitude per hour—to determine the longitude of your position by converting the observed time difference to an arc difference. You can do this either mathematically or by use of an arc/time conversion table contained in the *Nautical Almanac*.

For example, if your observed GMT of local noon on 26 May was 2019, the time difference between the GMT of noon where you are and noon at Greenwich (from Figure 11-29) would be 2019 − 1157 = 8 hours 22 minutes. Using the conversion factor of 15 degrees per hour, this time difference converts to an arc difference of 125½ degrees, or a longitude of 125° 30′ W ($15° \times 8^{22}\!/_{60} = 125\frac{1}{2}°$). The longitude is *westerly*, because the GMT of noon where you are is *later than* the GMT of meridian transit (noon) at Greenwich. In east longitudes, the Greenwich time of local meridian transit will be earlier than the GMT of apparent noon at Greenwich.

If you have had prior training in navigation, you can also obtain longitude from an observation of the sun in morning or evening hours, or during twilight from an observation of any other celestial body to the west or east, by the process of celestial sight reduction. To do this you will need to have with you a timepiece, a *Nautical* or *Air Almanac*, and a sight reduction table.

Direction determination. The best reference for determining direction is, of course, a magnetic compass. To use it properly, you will need to convert its magnetic directions to true directions by adding or subtracting the variation (that is, the difference between magnetic and true north) for the area in which you are adrift. The variation is obtainable from the nautical chart of your area. You will need to add the amount of any easterly variation to your compass bearings to get true bearings, or subtract if variation is westerly.

If you do not have a compass, you can still make rough estimates of your direction of travel. Use the relationship of the prevailing wave pattern of the sea, which does not change much over time, with any or all of the following: (1) the direction of the sun at sunrise and set (use Figure 11-30);

Latitude	5 Feb.	20 March	6 May	21 June
60°N	124°	090°	056°	037°
45°N	113°	090°	067°	055°
30°N	109°	090°	071°	063°
15°N	107°	090°	073°	065°
0°	106°	090°	074°	067°
15°S	107°	090°	073°	065°
30°S	109°	090°	071°	063°
45°S	113°	090°	067°	055°
Latitude	7 Aug.	22 Sept.	6 Nov.	21 Dec.
60°N	056°	090°	124°	143°
45°N	067°	090°	113°	125°
30°N	071°	090°	109°	117°
15°N	073°	090°	107°	115°
0°	074°	090°	106°	113°
15°S	073°	090°	107°	115°
30°S	071°	090°	109°	117°
45°S	067°	090°	113°	125°

Figure 11-30. True bearing of the sun at sunrise (when lower edge of the sun is half the sun's diameter above the horizon). For dates and latitudes between those tabulated, interpolate between the given bearings. For sunset, find the difference between the listed bearings and 90°. If the listed bearing is greater than 90°, subtract this difference from 270° to find the bearing at sunset; if the listed bearing is less than 90°, add the difference to 270°.

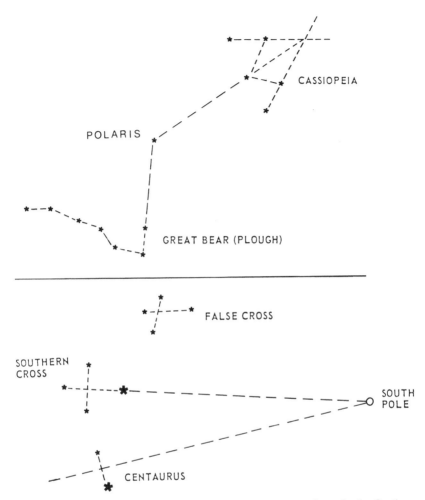

Figure 11-31. Polaris in the Northern Hemisphere; the Southern Cross in the Southern Hemisphere.

(2) local noon when the sun is either due north or south; or (3) the star Polaris in the northern hemisphere or the Southern Cross in the southern hemisphere, which bear approximately due north or due south, respectively (see Figure 11-31). Be sure not to confuse the direction of the primary wave pattern with cross-patterns caused by local wind variations. In most cases, you should be able to distinguish the one from the other by a few minutes' careful observation.

Signs of Land

Large numbers of birds indicate some kind of land nearby. Most of the tropical seabirds do not range far from their breeding grounds. This is particularly true of the "boobies" or gannets which are found throughout tropical seas within fairly close proximity to land. Their habit of diving into the sea for food is in itself a characteristic almost sufficient to distinguish the bird as a gannet. The only other seabirds that dive from the air are the brown pelicans, also seen close to land, and the much smaller terns and the long tail-feathered tropic birds which may or may not be far from land. Note the path of flight of seabirds, for in some species it will be an indication of the distance to and direction of land. Frigate birds are easily distinguished from any other seabird. When survivors see them in the evening, they can be reasonably sure that land is not too far away on their line of flight. Gulls are primarily birds of the shorelines and are not found in the open ocean. In northern seas, especially in the Bering Sea, adjacent parts of the North Pacific Ocean, and in parts of the North Atlantic and Arctic Seas, various species of auks are a good indication that land is near. The very distinctive tufted and horned puffins and the common murre are generally not seen very far out to sea, and their flight at dawn and dusk shows the direction of land.

Fixed cumulus clouds in an otherwise clear sky are likely to have been formed over high or mountainous land. Take note of any stationary cloud especially where moving clouds are passing by, for it is an indication that land lies beneath it beyond the horizon. Lagoon glare, a greenish tint in the sky or on the underside of a cloud, is caused by the reflection of sunlight from the shallow water of coral reefs. The reflection of light from any surface such as sand, shoal water, ice, or snow may be reflected in the sky or on clouds and is an indication of land. Drifting wood or vegetation is an indication that you are approaching land.

If you take full advantage of all available means of navigation, use common sense, keep track of your position, and above all, don't panic, you will find yourself approaching an hospitable shore. With a little luck, a seaworthy craft, and determination, land is seldom beyond attainment.

CHAPTER 12

Abandoning Ship and Survival Swimming

"Abandon ship!" With this cry, your world is totally and immediately transformed. Your once idyllic existence (or if not actually idyllic, it will seem so after a few days afloat in a life raft) becomes a thing of the past as you are thrust into a desperate struggle for survival.

It is impossible to predict the conditions under which you may have to abandon ship. It could be in daylight, dusk, or darkness; in high seas or on a mirrorlike surface; in a matter of minutes or with hours of warning. Despite the variables, one absolute emerges: Abandon ship *only* if there is no other recourse.

After abandoning ship, you will either enter a life craft, in which case the first part of this chapter is pertinent, or you will have to enter the water—with or without a PFD. The second section of the chapter addresses that situation.

Abandoning ship is not the only way of finding yourself having to swim. "Man overboard" is another dreaded cry. Knowing such techniques as survival floating, treading water, and HELP (heat escape lessening posture) may make a difference in those crucial moments before rescue.

ABANDONING SHIP

The way a vessel is operated, even long before an accident occurs, can affect the outcome of a survival situation. Keeping a good lookout will prevent collisions or runnings aground. The boat's position should be noted at least every watch, preferably at two-hour intervals. Drills give crew members a chance to practice their duties in case of an emergency.

Aboard the Parent Craft

You should make every effort within your power to keep your vessel afloat or your plane airborne (the "parent craft"). Attempt repairs, or try to ride out the storm. Use all the skill you possess to avoid leaving a larger craft

IF YOU ARE IN DISTRESS SEND

1. 'MAYDAY, MAYDAY, MAYDAY'
2. NAME OF VESSEL AND CALL SIGN
3. WHERE YOU ARE (POSITION IN RELATION TO A
   KNOWN POINT OR AREA, LATITUDE AND
   LONGITUDE OR LORAN READINGS)
4. WHAT THE TROUBLE IS
5. NUMBER OF PEOPLE ON BOAT
6. DESCRIPTION OF BOAT (LENGTH AND COLOR,
   TYPE OF FISHING RIG)
7. WEATHER WHERE YOU ARE
8. OTHER RADIO FREQUENCIES YOU HAVE

REMEMBER – IF YOU DON'T HAVE TIME FOR ANYTHING ELSE,
GET ON YOUR RADIO AND SAY – 'MAYDAY, MAYDAY, MAYDAY,
AND THEN TELL WHO YOU ARE AND WHERE YOU ARE.

IF YOU NEED MEDICAL HELP SEND

1. NAME OF VESSEL AND CALL SIGN
2. WHERE YOU ARE
3. INJURED PERSON'S NAME AND AGE
4. DESCRIBE ILLNESS OR INJURY AND WHEN IT HAPPENED
5. WHAT KIND OF HELP DO YOU NEED
6. CAN PATIENT WALK
7. TEMPERATURE AND PULSE READINGS
8. ANY VOMITING OR DIARRHEA
9. ANY SWELLING OR PAIN – IF SO – WHERE?
10. WHAT MEDICINE HAVE YOU GIVEN
11. WHAT YOU HAVE DONE FOR THE PATIENT AND WHAT FIRST
    AID MATERIALS AND MEDICINE DO YOU HAVE ABOARD?

DISTRESS SIGNALS

1. FIRING A GUN ABOUT EVERY MINUTE
2. CONTINUOUS SOUNDING OF A FOG HORN
3. A RED FLARE
4. AN ORANGE COLORED SMOKE SIGNAL
5. DRAPING OR FLYING A RECTANGULAR FLAG COLORED INTERNATIONAL ORANGE
6. SLOWLY AND REPEATEDLY RAISING AND LOWERING ARMS OUTSTRETCHED TO EACH SIDE
7. FLAMES ON THE BOAT (AS FROM A BURNING TAR BARREL, OIL BARREL, ETC.)
8. HOISTING A SQUARE FLAG WITH A BALL ABOVE OR BELOW IT
9. ROCKETS OR SHELLS, THROWING RED STARS, FIRED ONE AT A TIME AT SHORT INTERVALS
10. HOISTING THE INTERNATIONAL CODE FLAGS N. C.

NOTE – WHEN AN AIRCRAFT WANTS YOU TO FOLLOW HIM TO THE SCENE OF A DISTRESS, HE WILL FLY OVER THE BOW OF YOUR BOAT
OPENING AND CLOSING THE THROTTLES OR CHANGING HIS PROPELLER PITCH (NOTICEABLE BY A CHANGE IN SOUND) AND
THEN GO OFF IN THE DIRECTION HE WANTS YOU TO FOLLOW. IF THE AIRCRAFT NO LONGER WANTS YOU TO FOLLOW HE
WILL FLY OVER THE STERN OF YOUR BOAT OPENING AND CLOSING HIS THROTTLES OR CHANGING PROPELLER PITCH.

Figure 12-1. Signaling for help (Courtesy of the U.S. Coast Guard)

for a smaller one. Even as you attempt to save your boat, or plane, you should have someone radio for help. Figure 12-1 contains U.S. Coast Guard instructions on signaling for aid.

Abandoning ship is an action of last resort, but it should be done in as orderly a manner as possible. Only the captain should give the order to abandon ship, and he or she should delay as long as the parent craft remains afloat and escape routes are clear. Generally speaking, the following procedure is recommended:

(1) sound the alarm throughout the craft
(2) take charge, organizing and directing the crew and passengers regarding the following priorities
    (A) don PFDs
    (B) send distress signal (EPIRB)
    (C) attempt to save parent craft
    (D) prepare survival craft
    (E) gather survival equipment and other supplies
    (F) turn propeller off
    (G) drink water that you cannot take with you.

The smaller the craft, the faster it usually sinks. If you don't have time for the above sequence, try this:

(1) make radio distress signals
(2) gather people (wearing PFDs)
(3) throw EPIRB and water cans (tethered, if possible) into the life craft or into the sea.

If you have only a minute or two, think of PFDs, portable radio or signaling mirror, water cans, knife, and fishing tackle.

Launching the Life Craft

Do not inflate the life raft until just before you intend to use it. Launch the life craft from the lee side of the parent boat. This offers you some protection from the weather and positions you well to retrieve other survivors or useful floating debris. Before boarding, remove shoes and any sharp objects that may endanger an inflatable life raft. Fend off large floating objects.

If you must enter the sea rather than a survival craft, try to do so on the weather side of your yacht to preclude it bearing down on you. If possible, enter cold water slowly as the shock of sudden immersion weakens the body's defenses against hypothermia.

Do not swim, unless for a very short distance to life rafts or to something you can hold onto. Swimming, especially in cold water, will cause further loss of heat.

Aboard the Life Craft

Fight the mental or physical collapse that may threaten after transferring to the life craft, for now your work really begins. It is very important that someone assume command or leadership of your group. That person may be the captain of the parent craft, the first mate, or another who is both knowledgeable and capable. This has proven to be the single most important factor in the survival of a group at sea. This person sets priorities and assigns tasks. We list the tasks that confront you alone or your group in the first few minutes after gaining the life craft. Some may be done concurrently:

(1)   move away from sinking or burning ship
(2)   stream sea anchor or drogue
(3)   check buoyancy of craft
(4)   collect swimming survivors
(5)   collect other inflatables or dinghies
(6)   tie up with other survival craft
(7)   tend to first aid needs
(8)   set up radio
(9)   collect available debris
(10)   make inventory of equipment
(11)   arrange survivors in craft and secure equipment
(12)   rig shelter, if necessary
(13)   establish a lookout
(14)   start a log
(15)   rig sail and set course, if desired
(16)   read survival manual.

Some of the above are self-evident, other points can benefit from a few comments.

Collect Swimming Survivors. Have those boarding the lifeboat from the water clamber aboard from the upwind side. Those already in the craft should prepare to help pull fellow survivors aboard. If some are injured and cannot pull themselves aboard, then turn their back to the craft, push them down slightly to get the benefit of buoyancy, and then haul them aboard.

Tie-up with Other Survival Craft. The line holding the life rafts or boats together should be long enough to allow for the motion of the sea. A line of twenty-five feet is usually sufficient. The rafts should be connected only at the life line, which encircles the outside of the raft. Watch for chafing. A group of rafts or boats is more likely to be spotted than a single craft. Also resources can be pooled, and tasks shared.

Establish a Lookout. As soon as possible, watches should be arranged.

The watchstander should be tied to the craft, and if the weather is cold, he ought to be given extra clothing. Watches should be of short duration, no more than two hours, especially if labor, such as bailing out or blowing up the raft, is involved.

As a lookout in a life craft, you are a very busy person. You must keep an eye on the craft's buoyancy and seaworthiness. You must make sure lines are not chafing the craft and that leaks are located and repaired promptly. You must wield an oar or paddle to ward off predatory or inquisitive sea life. You must attend to the fishing requirements of the craft. At night, you must watch that your companions sleep safely—no trailing of arms or legs over the side. You must take account of the craft's direction and speed and of the weather conditions. Finally, you will probably be the first to spot the lights of a passing ship or signs of land. Always sound an alert, but be aware that some, even most, will be false.

Start a Log. Keeping a log is useful for recording navigational data (see the section on Navigation), the number of days afloat, the number of survivors, first aid treatment, supplies and issuance of rations, amount of water and rainfall, numbers and types of fish caught, condition of craft, and so forth.

Rig a Sail and Set Course. In most cases you will want to use a sea anchor or drogue to stay in the vicinity of the accident in order to increase your chances of rescue. If, however, rescue is not likely and you know your position, you may want to consider sailing. Some rafts and lifeboats are equipped with sails. If yours isn't and you have determined that sailing will help you reach land or travel lanes, erect a square sail in the bow of the craft. Use oars as mast and crossbar. Sails can be made of sailcloth salvaged from the parent craft, tarpaulin, or parachute cloth. Be sure to protect the raft where the mast rubs against it by padding the bottom of the mast. The lower corner of the sail should not be tied firmly, or you risk a ripped sail or a capsized raft. Hold the lines in your hands. Consult the section on Navigation to help plan your course to safety. Be realistic about the number of days it should take you to reach your destination, whether it be rain-likely latitudes, commercial sea or air lanes, or land. It is better to overestimate rather than underestimate your travel time, for disappointment is a draining emotion.

No matter how savage the sea, your greatest enemy lurks not in the wild vicissitudes of nature but within yourself. The tendency to panic will be most strong in the first twenty-four hours after abandoning ship. But if you can exercise control over yourself you will inevitably come in time to exercise some measure of control over your environment. The experience of Maurice and Maralyn Bailey, as told in their book, *Staying Alive!* bears this out. To the first ship they had seen in forty-three days, Maralyn shouted,

"Please come back. . . . Please. . . . I [Maurice writes] was oblivious now to the ship's movement as I knelt in the dinghy. Maralyn was still imploring it to return. Let it go on, I thought, this is our world now on the sea, amongst the birds and the turtles and the fish.

Human beings may be limited physiologically in their ability to adapt to some environments and climates, but the human will, intangible and mysterious, insistent on the survival of its flesh and bone casing, refuses to recognize the possibility of defeat.

Maralyn had suddenly stopped her entreaties but continued to wave her jacket quietly. I looked up and stared for some time at the ship. I looked long and hard at it in disbelief. Was it returning or was it a trick of my eyes? Maralyn looked across at me, her eyes moist and gleaming. "It's coming back," she said

of the eighth ship they had seen in almost four months under survival conditions.

SURVIVAL SWIMMING TECHNIQUES

Cold water, darkness, rough seas, bulky or restrictive clothing, and injuries are all factors that survivors may have to deal with. Survival swimming is the art of staying afloat or traveling with the least possible expenditure of energy. You may have to tread water, swim along the surface, swim underwater, or just float. These skills must be developed by considerable practice in a controlled, comfortable environment. There is no substitute for taking a good swimming course. The first thing to learn is to "adapt" to the water—that is, to be comfortable and capable of solving problems and thinking rationally. Whenever the body is immersed in water, especially the face, the normal reaction is to tense up and assume a vertical position, attempting to get the head out of water. This tendency must be suppressed. Tenseness must be replaced with confidence. The second step is to learn to breathe properly. The natural impulse is to inhale large breaths of air and to exhale small amounts or none at all. Proper breathing is especially important in cold water. The initial reaction of the body when suddenly thrust into cold water is to gasp convulsively. Controlling these tendencies and preventing aspiration of water requires considerable practice. The third thing to learn is to keep the body in the proper position to conserve energy. If the situation requires swimming along the surface, you must assume a near horizontal position keeping most of the body underwater. The position of your head controls the rest of the body. When your head is raised, your feet will sink. Propelling the body with minimum effort requires proper coordination and mechanics of arms and legs.

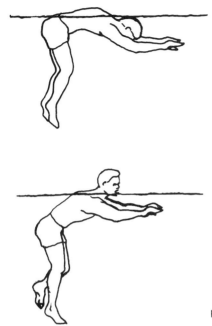

Figure 12-2. Survival floating

Survival Floating

Many survival situations will require that you simply remain afloat for some time. Survival swimming skills are particularly designed to help you survive for a long time without a PFD. Assume a face-down position with your waist slightly bent and your chin resting on your chest. (Floating on the back allows water to run into the mouth and nose.) Let your legs dangle beneath you. The arms are kept at the surface, palms down. This position will be restful because most of the body is in the water. Breathe rhythmically by raising your head, while keeping your chest in the water. Raise your head high enough to allow one quick "explosive" exhalation through the mouth and nose followed by deep inhalation through the mouth only. Inhaling through your mouth and nose immediately after clearing the water may result in choking on water trapped in the many small nose hairs. You must practice to become proficient. To support your head while breathing, use your arms in a broad sculling motion, keeping them near the surface with elbows slightly bent and sculling the hands. Do not press downward. The legs should be used only if additional support is needed. The most

Figure 12-3. Another view of survival floating. (Courtesy of the U.S. Navy, Naval Aviation Water Survival Training Program Model
Manager)

Figure 12-4. Survival swimming, traveling
stroke. (Courtesy of the U.S. Navy, Naval
Aviation Water Survival Training Program
Model Manager)

efficient kick is the modified or shortened frog kick. To begin the kick, the
knees are drawn up in a manner similar to a sitting position and separated
comfortably. The feet are turned outward with toes pointed up. The lifting
action is derived by stepping down on the water with the soles of your feet
and extending your ankles. The knees, however, move downward very
little. At the end of the kick, the feet are separated and the toes are pointing down. Most of the action is in the knee and ankle, with little action in
the hips or waist. After inhaling, lower your face into the water and resume
the relaxed position. This survival floating skill is designed to conserve energy, prevent aspiration of water, and provide time to resolve problems
with equipment or to implement auxiliary flotation devices. Provided the
water is warm, survival floating will keep you alive with as little expenditure
of energy as possible. With practice, this skill can be accomplished with
legs only, arms only, with neither arms nor legs, with clothes on, in rough
seas, and so on.

Treading Water

There is one important caveat to the survival floating process. Submerg-
ing the head in cold water (72°F or less) will rapidly cool the body and
could possibly lead to hypothermia. Survival floating in cold water should
be attempted only when there is no other way of keeping your head out of
water. Without a PFD or other flotation device, supporting the head above
water for any length of time will be exhausting. The most effective way to
tread water is to assume the breathing position of survival floating. With

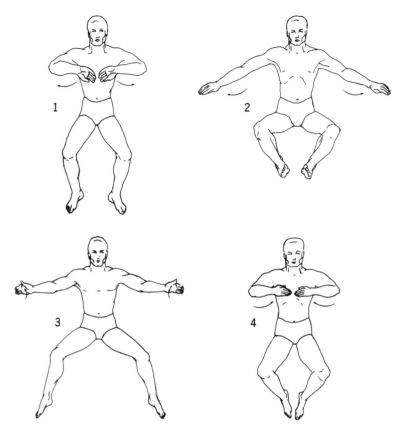

Figure 12-5. Treading water

the head held above water, the legs and arms must continually work to support it. The action of the arms and legs is the same.

Traveling Stroke

The survival floating skill can be modified to provide propulsion along the surface. To move forward, the swimmer extends the arms to the front as the face is lowered into the water following inhalation. As the face enters the water, the waist is straightened as the legs follow through with a full frog kick. In the full frog kick, the legs completely extend, pressing backward with the soles of the feet as the ankles are extended. Complete the kick with the feet and legs together and toes pointing backward. The travel or glide position should be maintained until forward motion almost stops. At the end of the glide the head should be raised for breathing as the arms scull to support it and the legs are recovered for the next kick.

Figure 12-6. Another view of treading water. (Courtesy of the U.S. Navy, Naval Aviation Survival Training Program Model Water Manager)

Figure 12-7. H. E. L. P. (Heat Escape Lessening Posture)

Figure 12-8. Huddle (Courtesy of the U.S. Coast Guard)

Additionally, poor recovery techniques create problems. Do not kick the legs to complete extension. Instead, they maintain a separate relationship and finish their downward stroke still bent at the knee and hip. The feet follow through with an ankle extension as in a frog kick. Most of the kick action should be in the ankle (very little in the hip and knee).

Arm Action. The tendency of poor swimmers is to push directly downward with the palms of the hands. This provides far too much downward force. The proper action is a sculling motion. The hands should be tilted 45 degrees into the direction of the scull; degrees of 90 or more pull the swimmer down. The elbow should be bent through a proper sculling motion. Most of the action is in the elbows and wrists, and not at the shoulders. The hands shift angles according to the direction of the sculling motion to continuously provide positive lift.

Leg Action. The frog kick is the most efficient kick for treading water. Think of the kick as a step to the side. Turning the toes outward, lift your leg by the knee with your toes pointed. Then flex your ankle and "step out on the water," pushing downward with the sole of your foot. After a short distance, the thighs extended at about 135 degrees, the foot follows through by ankle extension to the pointed toe position. The kick should not raise the body out of the water but just maintain it at the proper level.

Timing. Alternate the arms and legs so that the arms are recovering while the legs are kicking; and while the legs are recovering, the arms are sculling. Do not pull and kick together. This only increases the tendency to bob in the water.

HELP and Huddle

The Heat Escape Lessening Posture, known as HELP, can help cut heat loss in half. HELP is only possible, however, when you are wearing a PFD, and even then some PFDs will merely roll you over face down in the water if you try to assume the full HELP position.

The full HELP position consists of keeping your head, including the back of it, out of the water, pulling your arms close to your sides and lifting the legs up to protect the groin. The idea behind this posture is that those high heat loss areas of the body—the head, trunk, and groin—are covered up and protected as much as possible. Even a partial covering is better than none, though, and covering up the head, neck, sides, and groin as much as possible will help extend your survival time.

When a group is involved, huddling can be quite effective. Again, keep heads out of the water, use your arms to hug one another over your PFDs. Hug close together, maximizing body contact, especially at the chest. Intertwine your legs as much as possible.

CHAPTER 13

Environmental Hazards at Sea

By being aware of the dangers that may beset you in the course of a journey by sea, you can at best avoid them or, if you must, handle them. Hazards come in many guises, but in talking about them here, we can divide them into three main categories. Two of the categories—physical and biological—also formed the basic distinction made in the chapter on land hazards. But the sea is a special place and for it we've created a third category, called "situational" hazards.

The definitions of physical or biological hazards in this section remain consistent with the interpretation that guided the land chapter. Physical hazards are those that arise out of the geographical nature of the setting: in the case of the sea, the height of the waves or the temperature of the water. Biological hazards continue to be these posed by the animal life of the environment: sharks, barracudas, and so forth. Situational hazards are those dangers to life or limb inherent in a situation or circumstance at sea: jumping from the deck of a ship, for example, or swimming through burning oil. Even as rescue or relief is near, situational hazards present themselves, as anybody who has attempted to swim through heavy surf to land can testify.

This chapter is not meant to frighten. Rather we wish to separate unnecessary fears from real dangers and to give you an inkling of how to conduct yourself so as to ensure a happy outcome.

PHYSICAL HAZARDS

Sea State

The sea mirrors the weather, as the Beaufort scale shows. In rough weather, signaling and rescue are much more difficult and the survivor is harder to see. In high seas, then, you must be extravigilant about signaling possible rescue craft. At the same time the very motion of the waves may make you clumsy when handling equipment. Take extra time, and control your frustration. (See Figure 6-7 for windchill when wind speed is measured in knots.)

BEAUFORT NUMBER	WIND SPEED knots	mph	SEAMAN'S TERM	Effects observed at sea	Effects observed on land
0	under 1	under 1	Calm	Sea like mirror.	Calm; smoke rises vertically.
1	1-3	1-3	Light air	Ripples with appearance of scales; no foam crests.	Smoke drift indicates wind direction; vanes do not move.
2	4-6	4-7	Light breeze	Small wavelets; crests of glassy appearance, not breaking.	Wind felt on face; leaves rustle; vanes begin to move.
3	7-10	8-12	Gentle breeze	Large wavelets; crests begin to break; scattered whitecaps.	Leaves, small twigs in constant motion; light flags extended.
4	11-16	13-18	Moderate breeze	Small waves, becoming longer; numerous whitecaps.	Dust, leaves and loose paper raised up; small branches move.
5	17-21	19-24	Fresh breeze	Moderate waves, taking longer form; many whitecaps; some spray.	Small trees in leaf begin to sway.
6	22-27	25-31	Strong breeze	Larger waves forming; whitecaps everywhere; more spray.	Larger branches of trees in motion; whistling heard in wires.
7	28-33	32-38	Moderate gale	Sea heaps up; white foam from breaking waves begins to be blown in streaks.	Whole trees in motion; resistance felt in walking against wind.
8	34-40	39-46	Fresh gale	Moderately high waves of greater length; edges of crests begin to break into spindrift; foam is blown in well-marked streaks.	Twigs and small branches broken off trees; progress generally impeded.
9	41-47	47-54	Strong gale	High waves; sea begins to roll; dense streaks of foam; spray may reduce visibility.	Slight structural damage occurs; slate blown from roofs.
10	48-55	55-63	Whole gale	Very high waves with overhanging crests; sea takes white appearance as foam is blown in very dense streaks; rolling is heavy and visibility reduced.	Seldom experienced on land; trees broken or uprooted; considerable structural damage occurs.
11	56-63	64-72	Storm	Exceptionally high waves; sea covered with white foam patches; visibility still more reduced.	Very rarely experienced on land; usually accompanied by widespread damage.
12	64 or higher	73 or higher	Hurricane	Air filled with foam; sea completely white with driving spray; visibility greatly reduced.	Violence and destruction.

ESTIMATING WIND SPEED

Figure 13-1. Beaufort Wind Scale

Water Temperature

In water, heat is lost about twenty-four times faster than in air of the same temperature. For this reason, hypothermia is a real danger. Preventing heat loss is of paramount importance in most waters. Do not swim, as this will increase the speed of body heat loss and the onset of hypothermia. Assume the Heat Escape Lessening Posture or huddle with fellow survivors.

BIOLOGICAL HAZARDS

Despite all the hoopla in films and bestsellers about great white sharks and killer whales, attacks by marine animals are rare. In dealing with sea creatures, use a little common sense.

Sharks

The danger of being attacked by a shark is greatly exaggerated. Sharks like warm water, and are usually found in subtropical and tropical waters. They are curious, so if you are in the water what you may think of as an attack may in fact be only an investigative foray. A sharp poke on the snout may send the shark on to less troublesome prey.

They are attracted by the smell of blood. Any flow of blood should be stopped quickly, but mainly for first aid reasons. Sharks do not go crazy at the smell of human blood. Be careful when cleaning fish at the edge of the life craft, and don't trail hands or feet in the water when sharks are present.

Stay with your companions, as groups are less subject to attack than lone individuals. Do not splash around. Flopping about on the surface could sound to a shark like a wounded fish. Making a fuss in the water will only quicken a shark's curiosity. Dark clothing seems to offer better protection than light. Do not bathe when sharks are following your craft.

Barracudas

Found in most tropical and subtropical seas, usually along coral reefs and near shoal waters, barracudas present a greater danger in murky water on reefs than in clear water. Stay away from schools of small fish on which barracuda feed. Under clouded conditions, they apparently have trouble recognizing their prey and are likely to attack indiscriminately. They are attracted to bright and shiny objects. Barracudas are seldom encountered in the open seas.

Electric Ray

The electric ray, or torpedo, lives in both open water and along sandy and muddy bottoms, both in tropical and temperate seas. It can give a paralyzing shock, but fortunately it is rarely encountered.

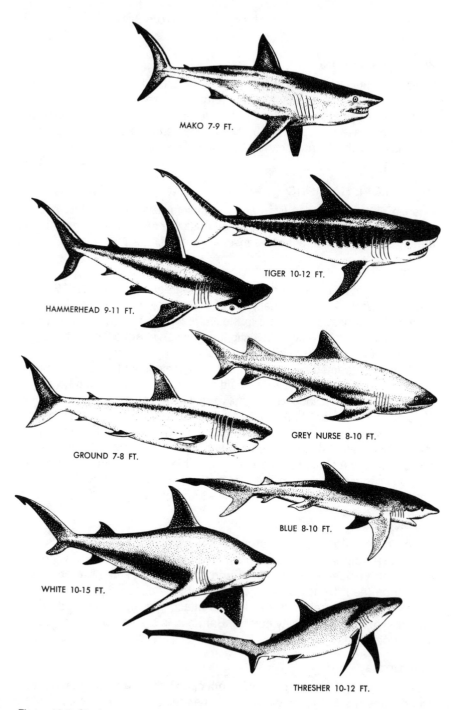

MAKO 7-9 FT.

TIGER 10-12 FT.

HAMMERHEAD 9-11 FT.

GREY NURSE 8-10 FT.

GROUND 7-8 FT.

BLUE 8-10 FT.

WHITE 10-15 FT.

THRESHER 10-12 FT.

Figure 13-2. Sharks

Figure 13-3. A giant ray (also known as a manta) is sometimes mistaken for a shark. Porpoises are also confused with sharks, but the jumping form is considerably different.

Jellyfish

Long, stinging tentacles produce painful stings and severe swelling which will last several hours. The greatest danger is not the sting itself but the fact that it may cause a swimmer to panic, cramp up, and lose energy, which may result in drowning. Wear clothing as a protection while swimming in areas where these animals are present, and avoid bubblelike objects on the water surface. If you are stung, make every effort to relax. If you're near a source, prompt application of ammonia will relieve the pain.

Stingrays

Stingrays are flat fish with a powerful, venomous tail stinger that can be driven through your foot, leaving a wound likely to become infected. They frequent sand or mud bottoms, and in warm seas they may grow to several hundred pounds. They are a danger only when you might step on them. To avoid that, shuffle your feet through the sand or poke ahead of you with a stick to frighten them out of your path. The sting of a large ray may be fatal, and a small one can put you in need of hospital treatment.

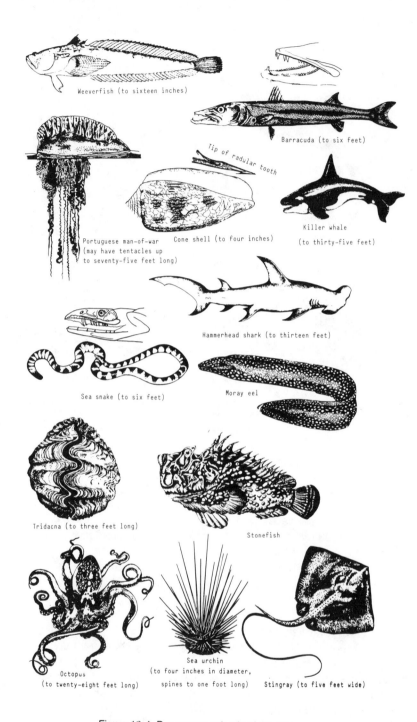

Figure 13-4. Dangerous animals of the sea

Other Marine Life

Whales, dolphins, and porpoises are large sea mammals, not dangerous to man. Cuttlefish, squid, and octopus have long, powerful tentacles but those large enough to be dangerous live in the depths of the ocean.

SITUATIONAL HAZARDS
AT THE BEGINNING OF AN ORDEAL

The aquatic survival situation presents some special problems. You may have to jump into the water from a high place such as a ship's deck or an oil rig. You may have to swim through surface oil and debris or even burning oil. You may be called upon to assist others in worse trouble than yourself. Ironically enough, being rescued or coming ashore has its dangers, too. These two sections will alert you to some of the obvious and not-so-obvious dangers and, by arming you with knowledge, give you confidence in overcoming them.

Jumping from a Height

You may choose to jump rather than suffer worse problems where you are. But if you can, it is far preferable, of course, to climb down into the water. Ships and oil rigs may be equipped with nets, ladders, and ropes

(A) Preparing to jump   (B) Preparing to enter the water

Figure 13-5. Jumping from a height

that you can use to lower yourself into the water, but here we discuss jumping, either with or without a PFD. (If you are wearing a PFD when you jump, you should hold it down.) Water entry must be correct or you may be injured. You have to time and place your jump to avoid debris in the water. Additionally, you have to watch out for being jumped upon once you're in the water. You should not, therefore, immediately attempt to regain the surface but rather swim as far away from the ship or platform as possible while still underwater.

The position of the body upon entry should be vertical. Your legs should be straight, crossed and locked at the ankles. If your feet are merely side by side, the soles of your shoes may act like miniature water skis and force your legs apart. If your legs are crossed and locked at the ankles, this can't happen. Also you are less likely to be injured by debris forcing its way up between your legs. Your head should be erect so that the spinal column is in a straight line. One hand should cover your mouth with the little finger tucked under the chin. You may pinch your nose with the thumb and first finger of this hand. The other arm should reach over this first one and grasp the opposing upper arm or shirt sleeve so that additional support is given to the first arm. This position protects your face and chest. Debris can't get under the chin, and the head and neck are given support during water entry. Because of winds and other problems, you may have to use your arms and legs for balance during descent and assume this position just before entry. This position is *only* effective when you enter feet first vertically.

Abandoning an Oil Rig

In response to increasing world demand, oil companies have tapped the petroleum deposits buried beneath the sea floor. Offshore platforms or oil rigs, which may be either fixed or floating, are the "islands" from which drilling is conducted. Many platforms are located in cold and stormy seas, such as the Bering Strait or the North Sea. As the offshore oil industry expands, more people are exposed to the dangers inherent in this work, and as they go about their everyday duties, there may arise a tendency toward complacency. Nevertheless, a hundred safe tours of duty or a hundred uneventful helicopter rides to the oil rig do not guarantee that the hundred and first will go as smoothly.

International guidelines and government regulations must ultimately be related to individual situations. You owe it to yourself to be aware of the dangers you could face and the course of action most likely to save your life.

Possible accidents include the collapse or capsizing of the rig itself, fire, collision, downing of a helicopter, or explosion. After the accident, the greatest danger comes from the environment: cold water; mountainous

Figure 13-6. If you work under hazardous conditions, wear suitable clothing and a flotation device.

seas; exposure to sun and wind. You may have to act on various survival principles presented in this book: jumping from a height; swimming through burning oil; or, as discussed below, abandoning a helicopter.

Your company may offer training sessions in survival techniques, and if so we recommend you take advantage of them. Whether you have the benefit of formal classes, there are certain measures you can take that will increase your chances.

As an emergency develops, be aware of its nature and probable course. Look around and note escape routes. Have alternatives if one becomes blocked. Know the locations of important equipment such as PFDs, life boats or capsules, and survival suits. Collect the gear you will need to survive—PFD, exposure suit, extra clothing, particularly hats, gloves, and boots. Attend to your assigned duties; working can keep your speculations from fanning into panic, and you set an example of courage for others. If you must work under dangerous conditions and run the risk of falling over-board, wear protective clothing and a flotation device.

Once the order comes to abandon the rig, board the survival craft. You must be familiar with boarding and launching the life craft. Some emergency craft provided for workers may be quite sophisticated and, although offering excellent protection, they require special training to operate. Again, try to see to it that you are taught how to operate life-saving equipment. If you must enter the water rather than a survival craft, practice the HELP technique or assume the huddle position with fellow survivors. At this stage, the general principles of survival begin to apply: move out of the area of the wrecked rig but try to remain in the general vicinity; signal for help; and attend to first aid and other survival needs.

Abandoning a Helicopter

As a passenger or crew member of a helicopter you should be thoroughly familiar with emergency exit procedures and able to follow them whether the aircraft is floating upright or sinking upside-down. You must be able to do so without visual references because it will be difficult if not impossible to see. You must know how to work the emergency exit doors.

As the helicopter submerges, water will rush in with a great force. Because this inrushing water can wash you to unfamiliar places inside the aircraft, you should keep strapped in and hanging on until all the violent motion stops. Additional problems such as difficulty releasing the lap belt, confusion, getting lost, difficulty in operating the emergency exits, and being bumped by other passengers have all been reported by people who have experienced a helicopter ditching at sea. The following are the recommended procedures for an open-water helicopter ditching.

(1) Upon boarding any aircraft, note the emergency exits and procedures. Mentally plan an escape route with references that can be felt and recognized whether right side up or upside down. Admit that there is a possibility that the aircraft might go down at sea and be prepared for it.

(2) When flying, remain strapped in the seat as much as possible.

(3) Upon hearing the warning or noting any unexplained pitching of the helicopter, sit down and fasten seat belt immediately. Hang on with both hands and brace for impact. If facing forward, lean forward with head low. If not, sit upright with head against seat back.

(4) Don lifevest but do not inflate it.

(5) After impact, open an exit within reach of your strapped-in position.

(6) If the helicopter is floating upright, calmly leave through the nearest exit or as directed by the crew. If the helicopter is moving, do not exit. Do not inflate your lifevest until outside the aircraft.

(7) If the helicopter begins to roll, remain calm and strapped into the

seat. Grasp the emergency exit frame or a reference point. As the fuselage submerges, the passenger compartment will fill with water pouring in through the open exits with a heavy force.

(8)   When the compartment has filled with water, the violent motion will subside. Ensure that one hand is on the emergency exit frame or other reference point and release your lap belt with the other hand. If you cannot hold onto a reference point near the exit, hold on to any reference point and pull yourself hand over hand to the exit.

(9)   Move to the exit pulling yourself along from one reference point to another. Be sure to have a firm grip on the next reference point before releasing the last one.

(10)   At the exit, pull yourself clear of the aircraft with your arms. Do not attempt to swim out an exit on the bottom side of a sinking helicopter. Swimmers can not move as fast as a metal aircraft can sink.

(11)   Once clear of the wreckage, inflate your PFD.

Swimming through Surface Oil and Debris

Water may have oil, fuel, or debris floating on the surface. In these instances, use a modified breaststroke to avoid getting the mouth and eyes contaminated. Alter (radically) the usually somewhat flat breaststroke alignment by holding your head high and clear of the water while keeping your feet very low. If your feet are near the surface, then it is difficult to keep your head high enough. The body should make roughly a 45 degree

Figure 13-7. Swimming through surface oil and debris

angle with the water's surface. The arm pushes out in a sweeping motion in front of the body, moving the water, and any fuel, oil, or debris that may be floating on it, forward and sideward. With the elbows bent at the beginning of the stroke, use the elbow and wrist in a sweeping motion. The hands should scull during the recovery for lift. (*Scull* means that the hands are tilted 45 degrees to provide lift while moving horizontally.) The splash produced by the hands in this stroke should be in the front of the swimmer's path and at least as wide as his or her shoulders. Repeat splashes until you are clear of the contaminated water. Remember, you are using your arms to clear a path, not for propulsion. Trying to do both results in doing neither well. Swim into the wind, because then the wind will blow the oil and debris past you.

Swimming through Burning Oil

Swimming through burning oil is not really a skill in itself, but a series of smaller skills, such as underwater swimming, vertical movement through the water, and splashing. You should try to totally avoid burning oil. It is obvious that the surface is not the best place to be if the surface is engulfed in flames. In such a situation, swim underwater to safety. A problem arises if you run out of air before you run out of fire on the surface. Catch-

Figure 13-8. Sea on fire

ing a breath amidst the flames is possible by splashing from an under water position to create a clear space and then breathing within that space. By so breathing at regular intervals, you can proceed through burning oil to safety, regardless of the distance involved. Do not try to hold your breath for too long or the urge to breathe will perhaps hinder the proper execution of the technique. Two methods of swimming through burning oil—one from underwater and the other from the surface of the water—are discussed here.

From underwater. The preferred method of swimming through burning oil is underwater. When you have to breathe, follow these four steps:

(1) Stop—look: When it is time to breathe, stop moving forward and look up at the surface. If there are flames, they will be visible. If there is any doubt, assume fire is present.

(2) Splash: While still looking up from underwater, splash the surface, throwing the burning oil clear of the area until you can see that flames are not present.

(3) Surface and breathe: Once the area is clear, stop splashing and use your hands to surface vertically. With eyes closed, turn your head to one side when surfacing and grab a quick breath (one exhalation, one inhalation) with the head turned and the mouth tucked just in front of the shoulder. You may use one hand to protect the exposed side of the mouth.

(4) Feet-first surface dive: Immediately following the breath, make a feet-first surface dive to a point where underwater swimming may be resumed. The *feet*-first surface dive is made by keeping the body vertical and sweeping the arms from the sides upwards (palms toward the surface) to an overhead position. A *head*-first surface dive prolongs body exposure to the burning oil.

From the Surface of the Water. There may be situations where you are unable to get under the surface of the water and must remain amid the flames on the surface, such as when, for instance, you are wearing a PFD. In such a case, you must splash the oil away from your body continuously. Spin around so that you keep the oil away on all sides and not just in front of you. To progress through the water, imagine yourself rolling continuously from the breaststroke to the backstroke and back again to the breaststroke in a spiral. One hand should be continuously splashing while the other protects the face from the flames. Splash to the front and one side, and then turn toward that side and repeat the action.

Being in the middle of a burning oil slick in the open ocean is not exactly the situation that brings life insurance agents clamouring for your policy. But your plight isn't as hopeless as it seems. The action of the waves breaks up the oil slick very quickly and patches of clear water will begin to appear.

Assisting Others

In any survival situation, others may be injured or less aquatically able than you. For the very reason that they need your help, you must first provide for your own survival before assisting others. If the others could not survive without your assistance and you die in the effort, they will die anyway. After you have ensured your own flotation, you should help others by coaching, lending a hand, or rescuing unconscious victims.

Coaching. The person in the water who is not prepared for such an emergency has a tremendous urge to panic. A strong authoritative voice may be all that is needed to get that individual to provide for his or her own survival. It is not always the most experienced traveler, or the most mature individual in a group of survivors, who is best able to assume the leadership role. If you see another who is allowing a floating object to get out of arms' reach, or just seems to be giving up, you should "bark" an order to that individual to perform the necessary action. In other cases, it is necessary to keep the spirits of others up by encouraging them with comments such as, "We're going to make it," "Just a little farther," and so forth.

Lending a Hand. If you can assist someone else in getting a PFD on properly, without endangering yourself, you should do so. You may be able to help others by pushing a floating object toward them. You may be able to toss a line from a raft and pull someone to safety. There are many ways for one survivor to assist another without greatly endangering his or her own life.

If you are a good swimmer, you might assist someone by holding on to his or her arm. In most open ocean survival situations, however, this is risky. The risk is somewhat lessened if you have completed a life saving and water safety course, but you should still be aware that you may be very fatigued, be much more taxed in a survival situation than in the recreational setting, and may be endangering your own life. In the ocean, there is simply no place to go. The most you can do is await rescue. It is usually more beneficial for both if you help your companion get flotation or attain a raft, rather than attempt to hold him or her up for hours and exhaust yourself in the process.

Rescuing an Unconscious Person. Remember the priorities of survival in water? If you are to help an unconscious or injured person, you must first provide that individual with flotation. You may administer mouth-to-mouth resuscitation in the water and tow the victim to a raft when breathing is restored. Do what is in your power, but don't overestimate your strength. See the instructions for giving mouth-to-mouth in the first aid section of the Preparedness and Priorities chapter.

SITUATIONAL HAZARDS WHEN RELIEF IS NEAR

Swimming through Surf and Rough Water

In rough seas, you don't have the luxury of breathing whenever you desire. You must hold your breath when a wave is crashing overhead and breathe in the trough. It is important, therefore, that you be able to control your breathing whenever necessary. In rough water and heavy surf, you may want to go underwater to reach calmer water, for it is much easier to go underwater or dive into waves than to allow them to hit you.

Swimming in Currents

The currents that may affect you as you attempt to swim ashore are rip currents, along-shore currents, and undertows.

Rip Currents. Rip currents run for a short distance straight out to sea, and are caused by water that has been temporarily dammed up on the beach by strong winds. This water attempts to flow back out to sea along the course of least resistance such as in a channel between two sandbars. These currents may be very strong, and you should not attempt to reach shore by swimming against them. If caught in a rip current, allow the current to carry you out until it looses strength, then swim parallel to the shore until you reach a point where the water is traveling toward the shore.

Figure 13-9. Mouth-to-mouth resuscitation can be administered in the water. Time is crucial and minutes may elapse before the victim is hauled aboard the rescue craft.

Some seaward currents at the mouths of rivers extend for a short distance out to sea and may catch swimmers unaware. Incoming and outgoing tides at the mouths of bays generate very strong currents. You can't fight them but you can beat them by swimming parallel to the shore until you are free of the current and then swimming to shore.

Along-shore Currents. Running parallel to the shoreline, along-shore currents can carry you past the small island or point of land you are trying to reach. They sometimes flow at an angle away from the shore because of the contour or slope of the land mass. If you are caught in an along-shore current, swim with the current but at an angle toward the shore. It is very important not to fight a current.

Undertows. One wave running back to sea underneath the next wave coming in creates a current known as an undertow. Although much has been made of undertows, they are not as treacherous as many claim. They will not grab a victim, pull him or her down, and carry him or her out to sea. It is true that an undertow may be very strong in some places, but it is always shortlived. It can knock you off your feet, but it will not carry you far. If you are knocked down by an undertow, go with the flow for the few feet that it may travel and then return to the surface.

In general, you can cope with a current if you know it's there. You must not under any circumstances, however, try to swim against the current. The fastest swimmers in the world can just hit five miles per hour on a short sprint. The average swimmer cannot move faster than about two miles per hour. A survivor who is clothed and weak may not even manage one mile per hour. Currents, though, can easily get up to five miles per hour or faster.

Being Rescued by Helicopter

Shore-based helicopters have a range of fifty to one hundred nautical miles, but at such a distance cannot remain long on site because of limited fuel. Many survival tasks can be prepared for, practiced, or simulated, but rescue by helicopter is not one of them. About the only time you will have the experience of grabbing and getting into a hoisting device is when that swaying object seems to mean the difference between life and death. By the time you get to the point of reaching for the strop, you will already have been through a great deal. You should be confident that you have managed this far. Remain calm, control frustration, do not panic. Helicopters cannot usually effect rescues at night or in very high seas, but even a temporarily failed effort means you have been located, and search and rescue craft will be able to estimate your drift. Be assured that they will not give up until they see you to safety.

If you have signaled distress from the parent craft, you may receive a radio message such as this:

SUGGESTED STANDARD HOIST BRIEFING MESSAGE

To insure that a vessel will be adequately prepared for a hoist, the SAR Mission Coordinator, if in communication with the vessel, should send a briefing message as early as possible before the helicopter arrives on scene. The following is a sample.

"A Coast Guard helicopter is enroute to your position. Request that you make the following preparations for hoisting. Lower all masts and booms that can be lowered. Provide a clear area for hoisting, preferably on the stern. Keep all unnecessary personnel out of the way. When the helicopter arrives in your area, change course to place the wind 30 degrees on your port bow and continue at standard speed. This may be modified on request from the helicopter pilot. The helicopter will provide all of the required equipment. The rescue device should be guided to the selected location on deck by the ship's crew by means of the steadying line. On each approach, allow the rescue device to touch your vessel, to discharge any static electricity. If the rescue device has to be moved to the person being evacuated, unhook it from the hoist cable. Do not move the rescue device from the hoisting area with the hoist cable still attached. If the cable is unhooked, do not, I repeat, do not attach the cable to any part of your vessel. For safety the helicopter may move to one side while the patient is being prepared for hoisting. Ensure that the person being hoisted is wearing a lifejacket, if his condition permits. The patient should be made as comfortable as possible, and if conscious, should be informed of the instructions on the rescue device. Upon signal from your vessel, the aircraft will move back over the vessel and lower

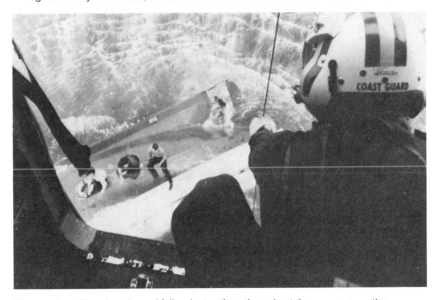

Figure 13-10. Remain calm and follow instructions throughout the rescue operation.

the hook. Allow the hook to touch your vessel to discharge static electricity. Then refasten the hook to the rescue device. When the vessel is ready to hoist, a "thumbs up" signal should be given to the aircraft. Ensure that personnel are tending the steadying line to prevent the rescue device from swinging excessively. During the hoist, strong gale force winds may be developed by the helicopter. These winds may make it difficult to steer your vessel. Ensure that all loose gear on the vessel is securely tied down. Attempt to contact Coast Guard rescue helicopter (*number*) on (*frequency*) at (*time*)."

Follow instructions, but always remember to allow the rescue device to contact the water before you touch it. This grounds it, preventing shock caused by static electricity build up. There are two main methods of lifting people into the helicopter.

Rescue Basket. A rescue basket is usually open on one side. When the basket is in the water, grab hold of it and turn the open side to you. Climb into the basket, sit still, and hold on.

Rescue Strop. Rescue *strops* (the approved international term) can be lowered to people either in a boat or in the water. If you are in a life craft and helping a companion into the rescue strop, hold it as if you were holding a coat for someone. Have your fellow survivor back into the strop, putting one arm and then the other into it. He or she should then drop the arms to the waist. The strop should be around the back and under the arms "high up." Keep the yoke of the strop and the hoist cable to the front, and remember that the strop is not designed to be sat in.

If you are in the water, avoid the cable as you approach the strop. Put one arm up under the strop. Lower your head and other arm under the

Figure 13-11. Anybody can find himself in a life-threatening situation. Twenty-four passengers and seven crew members were out of the plane and safe aboard a rescue ship within twenty minutes of the crash and one minute before the plane sank.

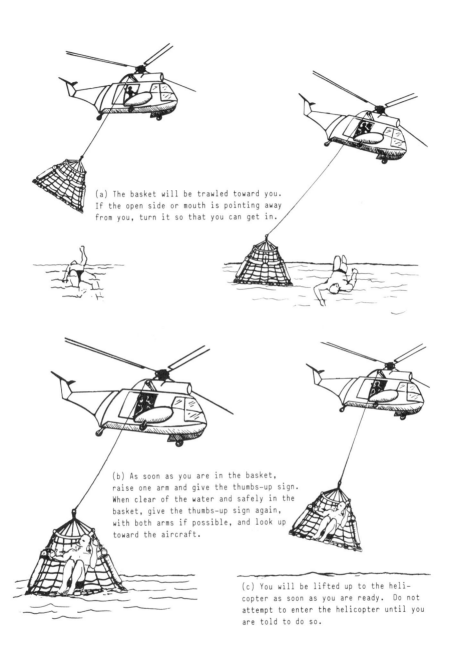

(a) The basket will be trawled toward you. If the open side or mouth is pointing away from you, turn it so that you can get in.

(b) As soon as you are in the basket, raise one arm and give the thumbs-up sign. When clear of the water and safely in the basket, give the thumbs-up sign again, with both arms if possible, and look up toward the aircraft.

(c) You will be lifted up to the helicopter as soon as you are ready. Do not attempt to enter the helicopter until you are told to do so.

Figure 13-12. Helicopter rescue by basket from the sea

(a) Grasp the strop with one hand.

(b) Always hold on to the strop with one
hand until it is fitted.

(c) Slip the other arm and the head
through the loop and arrange the strop
so that it fits under the armpits.

(d) Pull the webbing loop down so that
it is as close as possible to the chest.
Cross the arms, grasping the strop, and
give the thumbs-up sign. Look up toward
the helicopter.

Figure 13-13. Helicopter rescue by strop from the sea

water and bring them up inside the strop. Your armpits are then atop the loop, which runs across your back.

To signal "Ready to Hoist," raise your hand and give a thumbs up sign. Once hoisting has started, bear hug the strop and keep your head turned to the side so that the cable won't hit your face. If not ready to hoist, extend an arm horizontally, clench fist, and hold thumbs down.

Do not get out of the hoisting device until you are assisted by the helicopter crew. Follow their instructions.

Being Rescued by Boat

Searches are mainly conducted by air, but rescues are most often accomplished by other boats or ships in the area. This can be quite a dangerous operation, depending on weather, light, seas, and craft involved. Although you may be weak, you need to keep your wits about you.

Ships may launch lifeboats to retrieve survivors, throw a line down, send swimmers to fetch you, or tow you to a more sheltered place.

PART 3

Natural Disasters Survival

CHAPTER 14

Natural Hazards

Viewed from space, our planet seems serene, with earth and water in their proper places below a cushioning atmosphere. Such appearances are deceiving. The unstableness of the earth's crust; the risings and fallings of the oceans, rivers, lakes, and streams; the frequent turbulence of the air—all these constitute a truer picture of our unquiet earth.

The ancient Greeks, who placed great store in direct observation of nature, thought that the world was composed of four elements: air, water, earth, and fire. When we consider the natural phenomena that animate our planet, we see that each makes its force felt through one of these four elements.

Our atmosphere, churned by the ceaseless circulation of air currents over both sea and land, produces thunderstorms—almost two thousand somewhere on earth at any time. The tornado, fearsome but short-lived, can touch down in the American Midwest up to a thousand times a year and has been seen in every state of the Union. Hurricanes, also called typhoons, are perhaps the most awesome windstorm of all. Forming throughout the world fifty or sixty times a year, it is likely that during their most prolific season—from June to November in the Northern Hemisphere—at least one is bearing down on a populated coastline.

Water, earth's most common substance, seeks to expand its bounds continuously. At any particular moment somewhere in the world, someone's house and crops are underwater. People are displaced every year by floods, and today flash floods are the number one natural hazard killer in the United States. Tsunamis, giant seismic sea waves sometimes reaching great heights and carrying an immense weight of water, are unwelcome but unfortunately not infrequent visitors to Japan's shores and occasionally also to those of, among other states, Hawaii and California.

At least, one would hope, the ground beneath us would be firm. But earthquakes—perhaps the most terrifying if not the deadliest of natural catastrophes—outrage our very idea of stability. Each year more than three thousand tremors roll through the earth's rock. Hundreds produce discernible changes in the land's appearance. Somewhere on earth twice each day the tremors are strong enough to damage property. And from twenty or more times a year earthquakes cause widespread death and destruction.

How does fire, the fourth element according to the ancients, fit into this? Fire can be a primary hazard in its own right, such as when it ravages thousands of acres of brush or forest and threatens human communities. More often it is a secondary hazard, resulting from, say, an earthquake, volcano, or, ironically, a flood.

A natural disaster occurs when a hazard, that is, a threat or risk, becomes an actual event that results in the death and injury of many people and in the destruction of property. A hurricane at sea where no ships are involved is merely a spectacular storm, not a disaster. A volcanic eruption on an uninhabited island is merely a pyrotechnic display, not a disaster.

With population increasing around the world, land formerly shunned, such as floodplains and unstable hillsides, becomes liable to development. With changes in national economies, people migrate in search of jobs to areas subject to natural phenomena they have no experience with. Thus, natural hazards and human communities are set on a collision course.

How can you protect yourself and your family? When the elements rage, we are brought face to face with the power of nature and the fragility of the human body—a dichotomy we normally prefer to ignore. In this struggle between unequals, the balance wheel is scientific understanding of the hazard and technological advances in prediction and protection. By educating yourself regarding the latest developments in these areas, you equip yourself to act wisely when you must make life or death decisions in a matter of minutes or even seconds. Because it is important to "know your adversary," the first chapter of this section will be devoted to various types of natural hazards—their causes, likelihood of prediction, areas of possible devastation, frequency, measurements, and secondary dangers. The second chapter, "When Disaster Strikes," describes what to do before, during, and after a disaster and how to interact with various relief agencies so as to bring the greatest help to you and your family.

Much of the information in this book would be useful in fighting not only natural but also man-made disasters. The myriad aspects of man-made disasters (train wrecks, chemical poisonings, air crashes, and so forth) preclude, however, accounting for all situations. Natural hazards, on the other hand, can usually be reckoned as earthquakes, volcanoes, tsunamis, tornadoes and waterspouts, fires, floods, hurricanes, blizzards, thunderstorms, and avalanches and landslides. It is these we shall discuss in this chapter.

EARTHQUAKES

At dawn on 9 February 1971, an earthquake of magnitude 6.6 on the Richter scale struck California's highly developed San Fernando Valley. Heavy overpasses collapsed on freeways below, but because of the early hour few commuters were on the roads. The near-by Van Norman Dam held, thereby saving an unsuspecting eighty thousand people from possible death by drowning. Not so fortunate was the Olive View Hospital which, although recently built to exacting earthquake engineering regulations, was completely destroyed. All told the shuddering of the earth for a mere ten seconds took sixty-four lives and caused $500 million of property damage.

For the individual, the terror of an earthquake is twofold: the seconds or minutes of the tremors themselves, and the aftermath, when the extent of the damage becomes obvious. After the San Fernando earthquake, seismologists, or earthquake scientists, studied intensely the effects of the shaking on urban structures such as reinforced concrete buildings, elevated roads, gas and water mains, and electricity grids. Certain ideas emerged as to the most appropriate measures to be taken should a de-

Figure 14-1. Collapsed overpasses and shattered roadworks are the result of an earthquake that struck San Fernando, California, at dawn on 9 February 1971. (Courtesy of the U.S. Geological Survey)

structive earthquake be forecast early enough. Also certain types of areas were identified as especially dangerous.

If adequate warning is possible—and that is the catch—highrises and hospitals would be evacuated, nuclear power plants would be shut down, oil pipelines turned off, and water levels in local dams would be lowered. The San Fernando earthquake showed that single-story, timber-framed houses withstand tremors well. Houses at greatest risk are those built upon alluvial, or loose, soil and those perched on hills where landslides could result from the shaking. Ironically, one area of San Francisco that is highly at risk is the land-filled Bay area, created largely from the debris of the 1906 earthquake. Computer-based calculations suggest that large bridges such as the Golden Gate would probably survive but that many highway overpasses would not outlast even a moderate tremor. Glass would fly like shrapnel from the windows of office buildings, causing an airborne hazard. Aged, crowded, wooden buildings, such as those of San Francisco's Chinatown, could contribute to a secondary danger—fire. The term *secondary danger* refers to a life-threatening force that occurs after and because of the primary disaster. A secondary danger could, in fact, take more lives and destroy more property than the triggering event.

If an earthquake equal in strength to the 1857 Los Angeles (probably about magnitude 8.0 on the Richter scale) or the 1906 San Francisco (8.3 Richter) quake were to strike either of today's great cities, it could be the worst natural disaster the United States could experience. Estimates have been made that twenty-three thousand people could lose their lives, and damage to property could amount to $70 billion (1980 dollars).

Figure 14-2 shows the tectonic, or crustal, plates of the world. Most earthquakes occur along the edges of the plates. Some earthquakes, however, have shaken places far from plate boundaries: Boston, Massachusetts, in 1755; New Madrid, Missouri, 1811-12; and Charleston, South Carolina, 1886.

The field of earthquake prediction is in its infancy. The first successful short-term prediction was made in 1975 by Chinese scientists. The town of Haiching was evacuated hours before it was razed by an earthquake. The Chinese acted on indications from sophisticated instruments as well as on such old-fashioned clues as dogs howling; horses pacing nervously; mice, rats, and snakes emerging from their holes; and fish, especially the normally sleepy catfish, thrashing about in ponds and rivers. However, a terrible earthquake months later in Tangshan, China (magnitude 8.0)—the world's most deadly in more than four hundred years—put an end to any premature excitement that the time of reliable short-term earthquake prediction had arrived.

You will probably not, therefore, receive much warning of an impending earthquake. The following chapter describes how to prepare in advance

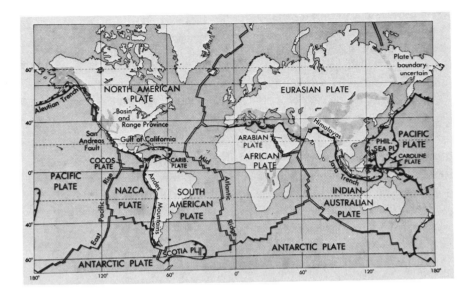

Figure 14-2. Earth's major crustal plates, along which most earthquakes occur. (Courtesy of the U.S. Geological Survey)

and what precautions to take at the time of an earthquake. After the tremors have ceased, and as you begin to assess your situation, word will filter back to you, perhaps via yours or a neighbor's portable radio, of the magnitude of the shock. This is important because it will give you some idea of the extent of devastation and how long you may have to wait for rescue. A few words, therefore, are in order about the primary method of measuring earthquakes, the Richter scale. Another system of measurement, the Modified Mercalli Intensity scale, also discussed below, is descriptive rather than quantitative. As such it gives you a means of measuring the size of the earthquake by observing the damage around you.

The Richter Scale

Named after seismologist Charles F. Richter, the Richter scale is the yardstick by which earthquakes around the world are measured. The Richter scale measures the *magnitude* of an earthquake by calculating the size of the tremors, represented by the highest crest or deepest trough of an individual shock wave recorded on a seismograph. An increase of one in the scale indicates a tenfold increase in the strength of the seismic waves. An earthquake that measures 8.0 on the Richter scale, therefore, releases ten times the energy of one registering 7.0.

The Modified Mercalli Intensity Scale

Devised in 1902 by Italian seismologist, Guiseppe Mercalli, and modified in 1931 by American scientists, the Modified Mercalli Intensity scale describes qualitatively the damage done by earthquakes. It does not account for special conditions that affect the level of destruction, for example, the kind of groundsoil or type of building construction. Nevertheless, a reading of the Modified Mercalli Intensity scale provides some inkling of the secondary hazards posed by an earthquake.

Secondary Hazards

After an earthquake hits a large modern city, the entire infrastructure of communications, public services and utilities, food delivery, medical services, and so forth is disrupted. If there is fire, there will be no water to put it out. If there is a seismic sea wave, there will be little warning. If there is ground subsidence, even more damage will occur. If there are aftershocks, still more destruction. Garbage will be uncollected, sewer lines will be broken, water sources may be polluted, epidemics may break out. In some parts of the world, earthquakes often accompany a volcanic eruption. The following chapter discusses in detail how to survive an earthquake and avoid succumbing to its resulting ravages.

VOLCANOES

On 18 May 1980 at 8:32 A.M., Mount St. Helens in Washington state's Cascade Range exploded with the force of five hundred Hiroshima-size

Figure 14-3. Mt. St. Helens, 1980. (Courtesy of the American Red Cross and the U.S. Geological Survey)

atom bombs. The cataclysm was preceded by an earthquake, magnitude 5.0, which sent two million cubic kilometers of debris tumbling toward a river valley some fifteen miles distant. Searing gases and steam shot out horizontally from the flank of the mountain, flattening forests of Douglas fir as far off as seventeen miles. From the top of the mountain issued a roiling cloud of ash, reaching twelve miles into the atmosphere. Day turned to night in Yakima, Washington, eighty-five miles away as the ash cloud blocked out the sun's rays. Ash was soon falling on much of eastern Washington, northern Idaho, and western Montana. Within days the dust cloud had traveled over the continent to the oceans.

In the face of such awesome natural forces, your best chance for survival is to stay out of the hazard area in the first place. Of those sixty-one who died in the Mount St. Helens blast, some were residents who had refused to leave after local government officials ordered their evacuation. Others were hikers and campers, attracted to the beauty of the setting and unaware of the might of the forces mounting against them. In many places twenty miles was not a wide enough margin of safety. Still others were people whose work brought them into the area—loggers, scientists, photographers. When a hazard like a volcano is expected, if you don't have to be on the mountain, don't be.

Provided you have the good sense or good fortune not to be within the blast zone, you will be fighting not so much for your life as for your health and for a limit to your property damage. Your enemies: tons of ash—in the air and on the ground—which abrades bronchial tubes, clogs machinery, and suffocates crops; floods, which may come as late as the following spring as streams silt up; and mudflows, which historically have caused the greatest loss of life and damage to property.

The most deadly volcanic mudflow, engulfing fifty-five hundred people, occurred during the eruption of Kelut volcano, Java, in 1919. Mt. Rainier, Washington, last active one hundred fifty years ago, was the site of some of the world's largest mudflows some five thousand years ago. Today, a string of towns between the mountain and Puget Sound could be threatened.

Predicting Volcanic Danger

One evening in 1973 tourists observing the activity of a relatively small vent of the Kilauea volcano in Hawaii were suddenly told to leave. Seismographs at the nearby Volcano Observatory had recorded a strong tremor, and tiltmeters, which measure changes in the slope of a mountain, showed that the summit was deflating—classic signs of impending eruption. Four hours later an explosion cut off all access roads to the mountain.

Predictions of volcanoes are by no means infallible, as the 1976 non-explosion of La Soufrière in Guadeloupe showed. Based on persuasive evidence, authorities evacuated seventy thousand people. But after a few flashes and rumblings, the volcano quieted down with no further ado.

Different circumstances prevailed before the recent eruption in Mexico of El Chichón. Until quite late, the government, on the advice of scientists, urged waiting, not evacuation. The mountain erupted first on 28 March 1982, after which most fled. Official evacuation orders were not issued until the countryside was in the grip of the second and worse eruption a week later—too late for many.

Tilt measurement and seismic monitoring can help evaluate the likelihood of volcanic eruptions. Of general use are maps depicting areas of volcanic risk. Most striking is the Pacific's "Ring of Fire"; but also of major significance are the Mid Atlantic Ridge, the West Indian arc, and the eastern Mediterrean, all of which coincide with plate boundaries. Hawaii's volcanoes, an exception to the pattern, are thought to be caused by a fixed "hot spot"—a magma source rising from the earth's interior—over which the tectonic plate carrying the floor of the Pacific Ocean moves as it advances slowly northward.

The purpose of accurate prediction is to save lives by warning people. Some people in the Mount St. Helens eruption died because they did not heed the warnings of scientists and government officials. As you weigh their warnings and decide whether to leave or stay, keep in mind that it is always better to err on the side of safety.

TSUNAMIS

Tsunamis, Japanese for *harbor waves*, is the name given to the giant waves that can result from earthquakes, deep sea avalanches, or volcanoes. Although they may be a secondary hazard, they can be exceptionally destructive.

The seismic sea waves generated by a volcanic explosion in 1400 B.C., perhaps even greater than the great Krakatoa volcano of 1883, might have fatally weakened the flourishing pre-Greek Minoan civilization on the island of Crete. Seventy miles south of the eruption, Crete could have been hit by two hundred-foot waves within half an hour of the explosion. Minoan civilization is known to have declined after this time, and historians have speculated that the tsunamis played a role in its fall and in the rise of the legend of Atlantis.

Today, if a series of tsunamis were to hit the cities of the West Coast or the islands of Hawaii, the Tsunami Warning System would sound the alert. But would it be heeded?

The warning of a probable series of seismic sea waves, produced by a magnitude 8.5 earthquake in Chile in May 1960, had given residents of Hilo, Hawaii, more than six hours to evacuate to safe ground, but many had ignored the prediction. Sixty-one people were swept away by the

Figure 14-4. Hilo, Hawaii, 1 April 1946. A lone figure faces the sea that is about to engulf him. Originating in the Aleutian Islands near Alaska, this tsunami killed 159 persons in Hawaii, including this man. (Courtesy of the Water Resources Center Archives, University of California at Berkeley)

fifteen- to thirty-five–foot waves, one of the most destructive tsunamis of recent history. In Japan, commonly plagued by tsunamis, no warning was issued because no one expected an earthquake so far away could cause tsunamis to hit the shores of Japan. One hundred eighty persons were killed in northern Japan and Okinawa, and the tsunamis claimed another twenty in the Philippines.

If a tsunami warning is issued for your area, do not let the apparent calm mislead you. By the time you see a seismic sea wave approaching, it is probably too late to flee. And remember they often come in a series, each separated by perhaps an hour. Return to your home only after the authorities say that it is safe to do so. In 1964, five of seven people who returned early to clean up a tavern in Crescent City, California, were over-whelmed by the third wave generated by the great Alaska earthquake (magnitude 8.5). It had enough power to inundate thirty city blocks.

TORNADOES AND WATERSPOUTS

On 3-4 April 1974, an unprecedented number of tornadoes swept across thirteen states, killing 315 persons, injuring 6,142, and destroying 9,600 houses. Ten states were declared disaster areas, and property damage was tagged at $600 million. In terms of total number of tornadoes (148, several extremely powerful), total land covered (2,598 miles), and total damage, this was truly a "superoutbreak," as tornado experts labeled it.

People took some actions that saved lives and property. Students caught in a school bus as a tornado approached persuaded the driver to let them abandon the bus and seek shelter in a nearby ravine. They survived; the bus, however, was demolished. At a local high school, teachers who had remained after the students were sent home moved to a pre-determined central hallway as the tornado bore down. They survived; the rest of the school was destroyed.

After much study of the effects of this superoutbreak, T. Theodore Fujita of the University of Chicago and Allen Pearson, then director of the National Severe Storms Forecast Center, developed a six-point scale to measure a tornado's intensity, path length, and width. In the superout-

Figure 14-5. Grand Island, Nebraska, June 1980. When a tornado bears down, cars should be left for more secure shelter or for a ravine. (Courtesy of American Red Cross)

Figure 14-6. Mammatus clouds forming beneath anvil-shaped thunderclouds often presage tornadoes. (Courtesy of R. K. Pillsbury)

break, five tornadoes had an intensity of F 5, or "incredible damage" (F 0 is "light damage").

Studies confirmed some beliefs about tornadoes and debunked others. Mobile homes and automobiles are indeed dangerous places to be caught during a tornado. On the other hand, many people believe tornadoes are propelled by winds of astronomical speed. Most scientific measuring of tornado wind speed indicates wind rarely exceeds 250 or 275 miles per hour. Although wind speed is not as great as commonly supposed, wind blast, not a precipitous decrease in air pressure, causes the worst effects on buildings. Another misleading notion is that in houses without basements the southwest corner is the safest. This is not true. Most tornadoes in the United States approach from the southwest, and above ground the most dangerous place to be is that which receives first and maximum impact. The safest place to be in nonbasement houses is on the ground floor in a small interior room with nonload-bearing walls. Put as many walls between you and the tornado as possible. A small interior closet or bathroom is usually the safest place. The following chapter discusses precautions more fully.

Nobody understands exactly how tornadoes form. It is recognized that tornadoes occur in association with thunderstorms. If it's late afternoon in spring or summer in the American Midwest, if the day has been hot and thunderstorms are brewing, a tornado could also be forming. A *tornado watch*, announced over the local media and NOAA Weather Radio, means that current weather conditions are conducive to the formation of tor-

Figure 14-7. Waterspout, Yangtze-kiang, China, 21 July 1928

nadoes. A *tornado warning* means that a tornado has been sighted, and you should find shelter immediately.

Waterspouts are simply tornadoes over water, although they can move onshore and cause damage. At sea, they do little damage, although they are a vivid element in sailors' stories. Statistically there is a very low chance of ever encountering a waterspout, but that is little consolation for the unfortunate crew that does. Always maintain a good lookout, and if a waterspout is spotted, move away from it at right angles.

FIRE

Each fall, in the chaparral country bordering Los Angeles, the dessicating Santa Ana winds blow in from the desert. They cross the coastal ranges through such passes as the Cajon and the Santa Ana to reach the shore as dry hot winds often laden with stinging dust particles. If that were their only drawback, residents of the hill country would suffer them gladly for the pleasure of living in the beautiful, smog-free mountains. Unfortunately they blow over easily ignited brushwood known as chapparal. A single spark—caused by snapping electrical wires, a carelessly tossed cigarette, even arson—and the winds whip the flames into a fast-traveling, all-devouring fire.

As more and more people move into houses strung along the narrow ridges or clustered on the canyon floors, the juxtaposition of residences and brush sets the scene for disastrous conflagration. A fire chief has called it a fire control problem possibly without equal in the world.

Although the high-hazard month is usually October, fires have begun in the summer months. In August 1980 a fire storm concentrated in the San Bernadino area claimed four lives. It devastated 323 homes, 150 other buildings, and 84,000 acres. Structural damage was put at $42 million, while watershed damage reached another $40 million.

Three counties were declared disaster areas, thus allowing residents to apply for low-interest government loans. Many chose to rebuild on the site of their leveled houses, despite the fact that each year they not only have to face the recurring threat of fire but also of landslide, as the hillsides, stripped of their vegetative cover, become unstable.

The chaparral fires, fanned by violent Santa Ana winds that can exceed 60 mph, have been known to move so fast that minutes after sighting, people must flee for their lives. To protect yourself, listen to the radio for fire

Figure 14-8. Fighting forest fires is hard, dangerous, dirty work despite such modern weapons as bulldozers and chemical-bombing aircraft. (Courtesy of National Park Service, Fred Mang, Jr.)

alerts when you think weather conditions are likely to spread a fire and be prepared to evacuate quickly.

Fire departments have devised methods of combating these fires. They have constructed fire breaks into the mountains, helicopter pads, and strategically placed water tanks. To control a fire in progress, helicopters spray water and chemical retardants on the vegetation. One man, in a 1979 fire, told of a helicopter appearing out of the smoke and dumping a full load of water on him as he stood surrounded by flames, the heat searing his lungs. The true aim of the pilot saved his life, but don't count on such good luck. The next chapter will discuss ways of avoiding being trapped by a brushfire, be it in settled areas or in wilderness.

FLOODS

In April 1927, the Mississippi River burst through some 120 of its levees and inundated 16.5 million acres in seven states. A result of an unusually heavy rainy season that had begun the previous August, the Mississippi flood of 1927 may have taken as many as 500 lives, cast some 650,000 from their homes, and cost more than $230 million. Flood waters of the lower Mississippi did not recede until July. New Orleans was saved only by sacrificing two sparsely populated parishes below it. The 1927 Mississippi flood marked a turning point in flood control theories and practices.

Figure 14-9. The 1927 flooding of the Mississippi River changed forever flood-control practices on the river. (Courtesy of the U.S. Army Corps of Engineers)

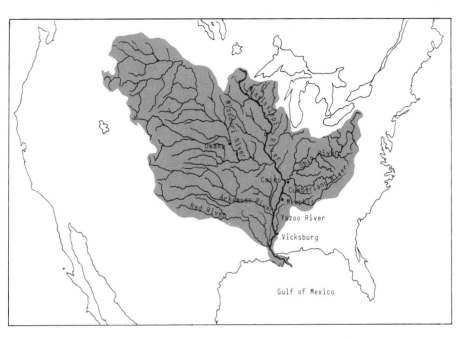

Figure 14-10. Mississippi drainage system. (Planet Earth/*Flood* drawing by Bill Herlep and John Britt © 1982 Time-Life Books Inc.)

Today the Mississippi receives no less than 73 percent of the funds allocated for river-channel improvement. And 65 percent of expenditures on embankments and floodwalls also go to the Mississippi and its major tributaries, the Missouri and Ohio rivers.

Almost fifty years after the pivotal 1927 flood, another flexing of the Mississippi's might showed the wisdom of putting money into controls and warning systems rather than clean-up. After a 1973 flood, engineers estimated that 14.5 million acres were saved from inundation by flood control measures and although damage costing $1 billion was incurred, without controls, the damage may have reached $15 billion. Most important, the death toll plummeted. Only twenty-three persons were killed compared with hundreds in the earlier floods, and although sixty-nine thousand persons, still a significant number, had to flee their homes, hundreds of thousands had to evacuate in the 1920s. These figures have fallen even as population and industry have increased along the Mississippi and its tributaries. For those who live and work within the Mississippi drainage basin, structural controls have so far proved invaluable. Flood forecasts and warnings, and wise zoning in floodplains, are equally important.

The Mississippi is one of the world's great water systems (only the Amazon and Congo basins are larger), but every stream, no matter how humble, is susceptible to flooding if certain conditions exist. Throughout the world, no hazard exacts as high a toll in lives lost or property damaged as floods. One international study estimated that of the more than 250,000 persons who died in natural disasters between 1947 and 1967, 64 percent died in river floods. In the United States alone, 3,800 settlements of at least 2,500 residents are prone to disastrous flooding. Eighty-five percent of federal disaster declarations are issued in response to flood and flash flood damage.

Hydrologists, those scientists who specialize in the study of water, rate floods on the basis of past performance of a particular stream or river. Thus a flood of a given magnitude is reckoned to be expected every ten years or every hundred years. This is not to say that floods occur at these regular intervals. It does, however, assess the chances of, for example, a ten-year flood occurring in any specific year as one in ten.

This rating system can be applied to both the slow, inexorable rise of

Figure 14-11. The Big Thompson flash flood of 1976 showed with what swiftness—and deadliness—such floods can strike. (Courtesy of the American Red Cross)

Figure 14-12. Flash flood warning signs in Big Thompson valley. (Courtesy of the State of Colorado Highway Department)

major rivers as well as to the raging wall of water that comes in a flash. With the first, although the area of devastation is usually much greater, the warning period is often long enough to allow for evacuation. Flash floods happen so quickly, however, that forecasting their arrival and warning the residents of the threatened valleys are major challenges.

Flash floods have become the number one weather-related killer in the United States. Since the 1940s, the number of deaths due to flash flooding has tripled to an average of two hundred persons annually. Property damage now exceeds more than $1 billion a year.

One reason for the increased costs of floods is the spread of urban development. Almost half of Los Angeles can be said to be flood-prone—mainly to flash floods. Another reason is the greater accessibility of formerly remote wilderness regions. The tragic 1976 Big Thompson flash flood occurred during a holiday weekend when the canyon's normal population of about six hundred had swelled to thirty five hundred. One hundred thirty-nine persons lost their lives in the flood. Today signs along the roadway picture a person scurrying up a slope as water laps at his feet; the message says, "Climb to safety in case of a flash flood."

Most flash floods occur in conjunction with thunderstorms but they can also result from dam breaks and massive landslides. On occasion and for various reasons, thunderstorms become stalled. The clouds, carrying enormous amounts of moisture, drop their load over one area, which cannot absorb the extraordinary downpour. Such were the weather conditions that caused the Big Thompson disaster. The difficulty for forecasters is in predicting which thunderstorms will stall and what areas, because of geography, soil type, vegetation, and other factors, will be swept by flash floods.

The weather service issues flash flood watches and flash flood warnings. A *watch* means that weather conditions could produce heavy rain and resulting floods. A *warning* means that flash floods are either imminent or have already begun. We cannot stress enough how important it is that you take the announcements seriously.

Despite faultless forecasting of a September 1977 flash flood in Kansas City, some residents ignored the warnings and at one restaurant customers actually raised their glasses to toast the awesome sight. Their attitude changed quickly, however, when rushing waters smashed through the

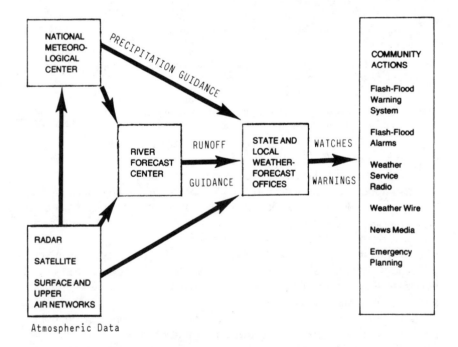

Figure 14-13. The U.S. flash flood warning system

glass front of the restaurant, and they had to scramble out the back for their lives.

HURRICANES

On 17 August 1969, Hurricane Camille, one of the fiercest storms ever to strike the United States, roared ashore at Pass Christian, Mississippi. Directly in its path were the Richelieu Apartments, where twenty-four people, twelve of whom had gathered for a hurricane party, had stayed behind despite evacuation recommendations. The weather service was predicting an "extremely dangerous" storm, estimating landfall about a hundred miles to the east of Pass Christian.

No doubt the party-goers expected to share food, drink, and—in safety—exhilarating views of the storm's majestic fury. Instead all but one of the twenty-four shared death in a maelstrom of 200 mph winds and a storm surge nineteen feet above the usual high tide line.

The tragedy at the Richelieu apartment complex could have been averted if fundamental precautions had been taken into account. Although weather satellites, a complex communications system, and computer-based analyses of data help meteorologists track hurricanes and estimate their strength, it remains a difficult challenge to predict what a particular storm will do in the immediate future.

Today forecasters can project the route of a hurricane within a 100-mile margin of error when the storm is about twenty-four hours from landfall. You should keep those hundred miles in mind when you hear a projected landfall point. Also, local and state government officials, guided by weather service

Figure 14-14. Storm surge of Hurricane Hilda, New Orleans, Louisiana, 1964. (Courtesy of the American Red Cross)

predictions, will urge evacuation of threatened areas. As the lone survivor of the ill-fated Richelieu Apartments said, "Whenever's there's a hurricane warning now, I get out with all the rest."

Deaths during hurricanes are generally due to one of three forces: high winds, riverine flooding following heavy rain, or coastal flooding caused by storm surges, erroneously called "tidal waves." Of the three, storm surges—battering mountains of seawater that accompany every hurricane—take as many as nine lives out of ten.

Innately destructive, storm surges become even more so if (1) the hurricane coincides with high tide; (2) a concave coastline or a barrier island prevents the water from spreading out; or (3), worst of all, the coastal shelf rises gradually, causing a swirling dome of water to concentrate beneath the eye of the storm. The sea may surge as much as twenty-five feet above its normal level.

Before a storm smashes ashore, it has had a long and tumultuous life at sea. *Tropical cyclones*, the generic name for vortices of wind and rain that originate over tropical waters, are the greatest storms on earth in terms of force, duration, and size. Their extreme forms, called *hurricanes* in the West and *typhoons* in the Pacific and Indian oceans, are also the deadliest, taking more lives worldwide—usually by flooding—than tornadoes, thunderstorms, blizzards, and hailstorms combined. A tropical cyclone in Bangladesh in 1970 may have claimed as many as a million lives.

Tropical cyclones normally form between June and November in the

Figure 14-15. In one of the worst natural disasters of the twentieth century, a tropical cyclone slammed into Bangladesh in 1970, inundating thousands of square miles, taking millions of lives, and devastating crops.

Northern Hemisphere when the equatorial ocean waters are warm and the air humid. The evaporation of water from the sea's surface fuels the storm, so that when hurricanes advance inland they generally lose their energy source and weaken. (Hurricane Camille was an exception, remaining strong as it moved over land, its rains causing severe river flooding in Richmond, Virginia vicinity, and in the mountains of Virginia and West Virginia.

In a *tropical depression*, winds are less than 39 miles per hour; a depression becomes a *tropical storm* when winds reach gale force, 39 miles per hour. At 74 mph, the clouds—as seen from a weather satellite—have taken on the characteristic spinning-top appearance of a fully fledged *hurricane*. The earth's rotation helps nudge the clouds into a counterclockwise swirl in the Northern Hemisphere, clockwise in the Southern. The tighter the coil of clouds, the more concentrated the storm.

The National Weather Service tracks the cyclonic mass, predicting its likely path. As with other natural hazards, watches and warnings are issued. A *hurricane watch* means a hurricane may threaten an area. You should be aware that you may be in danger and listen for further advisories on the radio. A *hurricane warning* means that a hurricane is expected to strike within twenty-four hours.

BLIZZARDS

Buffalo, New York, is used to harsh winter weather. Situated on the eastern end of Lake Erie and exposed to the moisture-laden winds blowing in from the lake, Buffalo receives some of the worst winter weather of any American city. The winter of 1976-77 was especially cold and snowy throughout the country, but the blizzard that struck Buffalo on 28 January 1977 was a milestone.

Figure 14-16. Buffalo, New York. Red Cross volunteers on snowmobiles search for persons trapped in their cars after record snowfall. (Courtesy of the American Red Cross)

Although thirty-five inches already lay on the ground, the blizzard added another foot. Contributing most to the city's paralysis, however, were the 70 mph winds that picked up and blew the snow into thirty-foot drifts and cut visibility to near zero. The wind-chill factor was an incredible −60°F.

When a blizzard or heavy snowstorm barrels into a city, transportation systems succumb quickly. Cars and trucks are stopped in their tracks by the poor visibility, drifts, and sheer volume of snow. Of the twenty-nine persons killed in the Buffalo blizzard, nine either froze to death or were asphyxiated by carbon monoxide in their stranded vehicles.

In a record-setting Ohio blizzard a year later, a trucker whose tractor-trailer was immobilized and then buried beneath a snow drift managed to survive for six days by eating snow and huddling beneath his only blanket. In another 1978 blizzard in New England, perhaps the worst in that region's history, three-thousand cars were abandoned on the beltway encircling Boston. Understandably, clean-up operations are immensely hindered by stranded cars.

As transportation—the life-flow of a city—comes to a standstill, other vital services are affected. Doctors and nurses cannot reach hospitals to relieve their overworked colleagues. When communication and power lines go down, crews cannot get out to make repairs. Food and heating supplies dwindle as deliveries are impeded. Transportation not only within the city but also between the stricken area and outside points ceases as railroads, airports, and bus services are shut down. When federal troops were airlifted to aid New Englanders in the aftermath of the 1978 blizzard, there was at first no place for them to land.

A *blizzard* is a life-threatening winter storm in which winds exceed thirty-five miles per hour and visibility is frequently near zero in the heavily falling and blowing snow.

In Buffalo's 1977 blizzard, nine counties were declared disaster areas—the first time in history that a blizzard earned this official label.

THUNDERSTORMS

At any given moment, about two thousand thunderstorms rage through the earth's atmosphere, each one containing the energy of ten or more Hiroshima-size nuclear bombs. Averaging forty-five thousand a day or more than 16 million a year worldwide, the commonplace thunderstorm is in fact a complex system of up-and-down drafts of air, and precipitation.

Thunderstorms bring with them harmless thunder as well as deadly lightning and destructive hail. In the United States alone, nearly two hundred persons are struck and killed by lightning each year. Only in the last decade have flash floods outstripped lightning as the main weather-related killer. Hail accounts for a loss of one billion dollars a year to crops and a further $75 million due to livestock deaths and property damage. Among thun-

Figure 14-17. Lightning strikes the ground. (Courtesy of the American Red Cross)

Figure 14-18. The starburst pattern of lightning striking the ground explains how members of a group, although standing apart, can be killed or hurt by the same lightning bolt. (Courtesy of NOAA)

derstorms' other rampageous offspring are tornadoes, flash floods, and landslides, all discussed elsewhere in this chapter.

At sea, the approach of either a single towering thunderhead or a row of thunderstorms, known as a *squall line*, sends sailors scurrying for port with many a nervous look over their shoulders at the looming black wall. In 1977, on the Chesapeake Bay, a squall line overtook a 42-foot fishing boat. Of the twenty-seven persons on board, thirteen drowned when the boat capsized.

If you are out on the water, have a NOAA weather radio. When a thunderstorm or squall line approaches, head for a safe harbor immediately. A small craft in open water during a thunderstorm, with its lightning, torren-

Figure 14-19. A squall line

tial downpour, and unpredictable wind shifts, is an extremely dangerous place.

Being on land, in or close to shelter, is no guarantee of safety either when lightning is flickering through the air. People have often been killed while standing under a tree during an electrical storm—a classic mistake. Some have been struck while running to shelter across exposed flat land, such as a beach. Others have been struck down in the doorways of their own homes as they watched the storm. Walking beneath electrical wires is daring fate, while people talking on telephones whose lines have been hit have suffered shocks and burns and have even died. Death by lightning to users of CB radios during storms has increased as the radios have increased in popularity. Still, most people killed by lightning have been caught outdoors and most of those while standing under trees or engaging in water-centered activities.

AVALANCHES AND LANDSLIDES

On 31 May 1970 a massive ice and rock slide disaster, the greatest ever known, was triggered by a magnitude 7.7 earthquake. In less than four minutes it traveled the nine miles from its origin on the north peak of Peru's highest mountain to the ski-resort town of Yungay. Of the 18,000 residents, only 92 survived. They had literally run for their lives to, ironically, Cemetery Hill, the only land to remain above the all-engulfing mass.

Avalanches and landslides, defined as slippages of snow or of soil, rock, and mud down a slope, are second only to earthquakes in their suddenness and lack of warning. They generally accompany seismic tremors, volcanic eruptions, heavy rainfall, frost, or flooding. Your best protection is to be aware of the possibility of a debris flow in the wake of another cataclysmic event.

While often triggered by natural causes, landslides and avalanches also occur where humans have altered the land. The chapparal country of Los Angeles is an example of a region where housing development—with its alterations of slope gradient and protective ground cover—has exacerbated a difficult natural situation where spring mudflows are common on slopes denuded by autumnal fires.

The American city that seems most at risk for an avalanche disaster is Juneau, Alaska, where one subdivision has been built directly in the path of previous avalanches. Fortunately, none has struck in the last twenty years, although one study estimated that a house with a forty-year life span had a 96 percent chance of an avalanche knocking at its doors.

Prediction is the key to preserving lives threatened by avalanche or landslide. If the hazard can be identified, the likely area of damage delineated, and the schedule of the event estimated, then evacuation is possible. Much progress has been made recently in predicting and controlling avalanches. At the same time, avalanche deaths have quadrupled in the past thirty years in the United States as more and more people take to the backcountry for winter recreation.

If you use the high mountains in winter, learn to recognize the makings of an avalanche. The worst combination is a blizzard followed by warm, springlike days. Stay on windward slopes as overhanging cornices build up on the lee side. The aspect or orientation of a slope seems to figure in the likelihood of avalanches. In the Alps, for example, about 90 percent of avalanches that bury skiers occur on north- and east-facing slopes. In the spring, southerly slopes can become unstable. Check the lie of the land and avoid locations where you could be swept over a cliff or into water or buried in a gully. Most important, obey posted avalanche warning signs.

CHAPTER 15

When Disaster Strikes

Stranded in the wilderness or cast away at sea, you and perhaps a few companions battle feelings of isolation as well as physical hardships as you struggle to survive. A natural disaster, in contrast, usually involves not only yourself and your family but also your neighbors, the community, perhaps your entire region of the country. A natural disaster is a social event—an experience that unites people. Because the social aspects of natural disasters provide the context in which an individual makes life or death decisions, we will first discuss how humans behave en masse when danger looms. We will then focus on the steps you can take to protect life, limb, and property.

SOCIAL ASPECTS OF NATURAL DISASTERS

Time and time again, people choose, for a variety of reasons, to locate their homes, businesses, and farms on floodplains, on the flanks of volcanic mountains, in seismically active zones, on beaches within reach of storm surges, in fire-prone hill country. Some may not realize they are in a hazard zone. Others gamble on having enough warning or on the periodicity of the event. Still others feel the benefits of a particular area outweigh the potential disadvantages. Some may be lulled into a false security, believing technology will in all cases mitigate the consequences. This is especially likely to be the common belief when the hazard is flooding.

Natural disasters affect more people more dramatically than do individual survival episodes. Ironically, the "it can't happen to me" mentality seems even more set when it comes to considering oneself a possible victim of nature's extremes.

To protect yourself and your family from disaster, you must first perceive the danger. Many Midwesterners, for example, are willing to invest money in modifying their houses to make at least one small interior room more resistant to tornadoes. The way people respond to disaster, then, begins long before the wind begins to howl, the first tremor is felt, or the first drops of rain begin to fall. It begins with where you choose to live and, given the

Figure 15-1. The effects of forty-four inches of rain in forty-two days on slopes denuded by fires the previous fall are fought with sandbags and a touch of humor. (Courtesy of the National Geographic Society)

constraints usually inherent in that decision, what general safeguards your community has identified, preliminary precautions you have taken, and, in particular, what you do when you hear the weather service warning.

The conditions under which people first hear a warning influence their reactions to it. For instance, if you are with friends when the announcement comes over the radio or television station, you may tend to shrug it off. Peer pressure seems to encourage a certain bravado. If, on the other hand, you are with your family, your concern will be much greater and you are more likely to react in a way that will ensure their safety.

Upon hearing a warning, most people will seek independent confirmation. They may switch to another radio or television station, ask neighbors, or check weather conditions themselves. A violent thunderstorm may verify the danger of possible tornadoes, but the "calm before the storm" could be deceptive if the threat is a hurricane or tsunami. Similarly, the conditions producing a flash flood upstream are not always visible from down the valley.

Past experience with the accuracy of predictions also figures. And herein lies a conundrum for forecasters: whether to issue warnings liberally in the interest of safety or whether to hold back for fear of "crying wolf" too often.

For your own benefit, heed all warnings. Listen for subsequent an-

Figure 15-2. Houses on left, built before Los Angeles tightened its building code, cling precariously to slide-prone slopes. Development on right presents graded lots well provided with storm drains. (Courtesy of the National Geographic Society)

Figure 15-3. The owner of this automobile has parked it on high ground in response to flash flood warnings. (Courtesy of NOAA)

RESPONSIBILITIES IN NATURAL DISASTERS

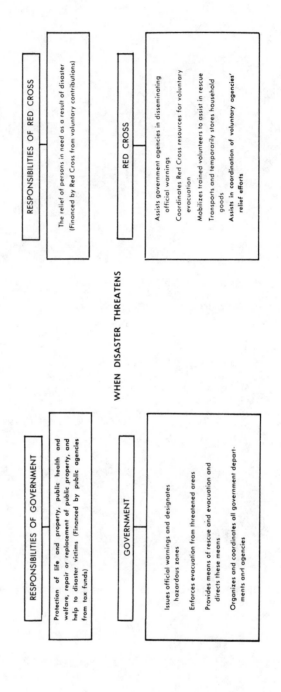

RESPONSIBILITIES OF GOVERNMENT

Protection of life and property, public health and welfare, repair or replacement of public property, and help to disaster victims (Financed by public agencies from tax funds)

RESPONSIBILITIES OF RED CROSS

The relief of persons in need as a result of disaster (Financed by Red Cross from voluntary contributions)

WHEN DISASTER THREATENS

GOVERNMENT

Issues official warnings and designates hazardous zones

Enforces evacuation from threatened areas

Provides means of rescue and evacuation and directs these means

Organizes and coordinates all government departments and agencies

RED CROSS

Assists government agencies in disseminating official warnings

Coordinates Red Cross resources for voluntary evacuation

Mobilizes trained volunteers to assist in rescue

Transports and temporarily stores household goods

Assists in coordination of voluntary agencies' relief efforts

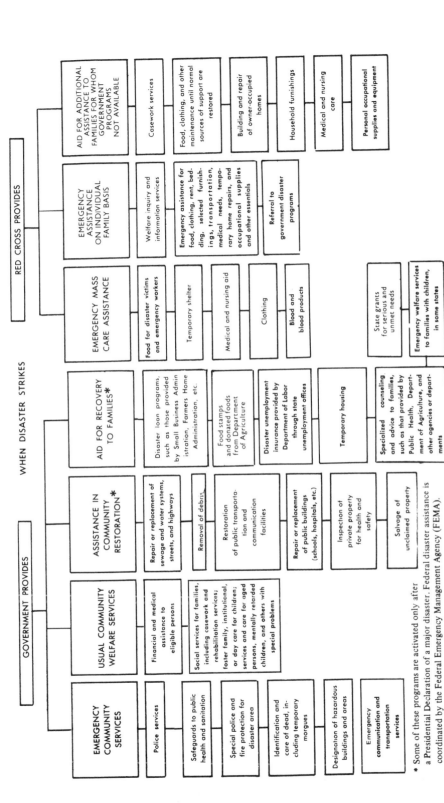

Figure 15-4. Responsibilities in natural disasters. (Courtesy of the American Red Cross)

nouncements that will give further details. If, on occasion, you have heard no warning but you think weather conditions are ripe for a disaster, trust your own judgment and seek safety. Warnings in the case of the Big Thompson flash flood came too late to save most lives.

Depending on the hazard, you will prepare either to evacuate or to dig in upon hearing a forecast of an extreme natural event. If floods threaten, those in low-lying districts should seek the safety of high ground. Hurricanes, nature's largest and fiercest windstorm, often necessitate the evacuation of thousands from coastal settlements threatened by the storm's sea surge.

In 1979, on the basis of satellite reports, radar, aerial reconnaissance, and computer data that indicated a likely storm surge of twelve feet in Mobile Bay and vicinity, 125,000 persons were evacuated. When Hurricane Frederic hit, the storm surge averaged twelve feet—as predicted. The United States's most costly hurricane in economic terms claimed only five lives, thanks to superb forecasting and public observance of the warnings.

Disaster, strangely enough, seems often to bring out the best in human nature. Mass panic in the face of impending disaster is in fact extremely rare. Most people evacuate calmly and in an orderly manner with their families. As long as there is enough warning and escape routes remain open, people will react reasonably.

The difficulty for those in charge of evacuations is not keeping crowds in control but convincing people to leave home. In 1961 Hurricane Carla caused one of the largest evacuations in American history, yet the majority of residents in the threatened areas never left. In a deadly Rapid City flood

Figure 15-5. Rescuers aid victims of a flash flood in Montgomery County, Maryland, 1975. (Courtesy of NOAA)

in 1972 the residents thought the mayor was kidding when he warned people to leave the area.

When disaster strikes, people usually begin helping one another as early as possible. Family members are the first helped, then neighbors and friends, finally strangers. The Red Cross and other disaster relief agencies are of tremendous value, especially in devastating disasters, but people usually seek aid from organizations only as a last resort. Many more people find shelter in the homes of more fortunate neighbors or with family members outside the stricken area than in organized camps or designated shelters.

The spectre of looting accompanies every disaster, yet it is apparently more a spectre than reality. In a study of a Xenia, Ohio, tornado, more than 60 percent of those asked said they had heard reports of looting, but less than 8 percent were able to say they knew of actual looting.

People sometimes fear that police officers, fire fighters, medical personnel, and others in the front lines of disaster relief will leave their posts to see to the security of their own families. Various studies have shown that almost invariably these people carry on responsibly and selflessly.

Another myth has it that in the aftermath of a disaster, people are stunned, apathetic, unable to fend for themselves, in need of direction. This condition, called *disaster syndrome*, has proven to afflict only a small minority of victims, and, then, for most it is short-lived. One survey of tornado victims, for example, revealed that a majority felt they had coped better than they would have expected.

Outlook for the long-term mental health of disaster victims seems favorable also. Generally, following a disaster, admissions to local mental hospitals drop, crime levels decline, and people say they feel optimistic about their own and their neighborhood's future. Only in two cases did researchers find community mental health adversely affected. Both were mining-related accidents, one in Wales (landslide) and the other in West Virginia (flash flood) where nearly every family in a small town lost at least one family member.

For most survivors of natural disaster, feelings of fear and dismay are balanced by a heightened morale and a sense of unity with fellow sufferers. People perform deeds of heroism and compassion they would not have dreamt themselves capable of in the normal course of events. Despite batterings from nature, the human spirit shows itself to be amazingly resilient.

INDIVIDUAL RESPONSES TO DISASTER

Know the dangers to which your area might be vulnerable. And carry that knowledge one step further by learning what precautions your community has taken to protect its residents against the assaults of nature.

NOAA WEATHER RADIO NETWORK

Legend—Frequencies are
identified as follows:
(1)—162.550 MHz
(2)—162.400 MHz
(3)—162.475 MHz
(4)—162.425 MHz
(5)—162.450 MHz
(6)—162.500 MHz
(7)—162.525 MHz

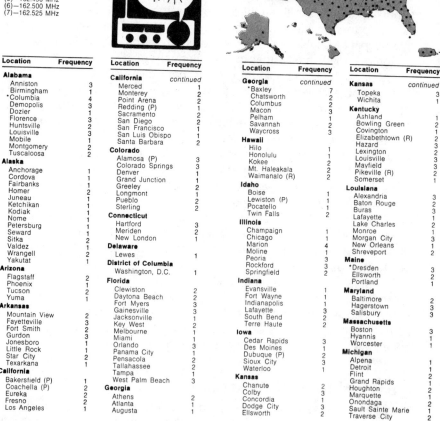

Location	Frequency
Alabama	
Anniston	3
Birmingham	1
*Columbia	4
Demopolis	3
Dozier	1
Florence	3
Huntsville	2
Louisville	3
Mobile	1
Montgomery	2
Tuscaloosa	2
Alaska	
Anchorage	1
Cordova	1
Fairbanks	1
Homer	2
Juneau	1
Ketchikan	1
Kodiak	1
Nome	1
Petersburg	1
Seward	1
Sitka	2
Valdez	1
Wrangell	2
Yakutat	1
Arizona	
Flagstaff	2
Phoenix	1
Tucson	2
Yuma	1
Arkansas	
Mountain View	2
Fayetteville	3
Fort Smith	2
Gurdon	3
Jonesboro	1
Little Rock	1
Star City	2
Texarkana	1
California	
Bakersfield (P)	1
Coachella (P)	2
Eureka	2
Fresno	2
Los Angeles	1

Location	Frequency
California	*continued*
Merced	1
Monterey	2
Point Arena	2
Redding (P)	1
Sacramento	2
San Diego	2
San Francisco	1
San Luis Obispo	1
Santa Barbara	2
Colorado	
Alamosa (P)	3
Colorado Springs	3
Denver	1
Grand Junction	1
Greeley	2
Longmont	1
Pueblo	2
Sterling	2
Connecticut	
Hartford	3
Meriden	2
New London	1
Delaware	
Lewes	1
District of Columbia	
Washington, D.C.	1
Florida	
Clewiston	2
Daytona Beach	2
Fort Myers	3
Gainesville	3
Jacksonville	1
Key West	2
Melbourne	1
Miami	1
Orlando	3
Panama City	1
Pensacola	2
Tallahassee	2
Tampa	1
West Palm Beach	3
Georgia	
Athens	2
Atlanta	1
Augusta	1

Location	Frequency
Georgia	*continued*
*Baxley	7
Chatsworth	2
Columbus	2
Macon	3
Pelham	1
Savannah	2
Waycross	3
Hawaii	
Hilo	1
Honolulu	1
Kokee	2
Mt. Haleakala	2
Waimanalo (R)	2
Idaho	
Boise	1
Lewiston (P)	1
Pocatello	1
Twin Falls	2
Illinois	
Champaign	1
Chicago	1
Marion	4
Moline	1
Peoria	3
Rockford	3
Springfield	2
Indiana	
Evansville	1
Fort Wayne	1
Indianapolis	1
Lafayette	3
South Bend	2
Terre Haute	2
Iowa	
Cedar Rapids	3
Des Moines	1
Dubuque (P)	2
Sioux City	3
Waterloo	1
Kansas	
Chanute	2
Colby	3
Concordia	1
Dodge City	3
Ellsworth	2

Location	Frequency
Kansas	*continued*
Topeka	3
Wichita	1
Kentucky	
Ashland	1
Bowling Green	2
Covington	1
Elizabethtown (R)	2
Hazard	3
Lexington	2
Louisville	3
Mayfield	3
Pikeville (R)	2
Somerset	1
Louisiana	
Alexandria	3
Baton Rouge	2
Buras	3
Lafayette	1
Lake Charles	2
Monroe	1
Morgan City	3
New Orleans	1
Shreveport	2
Maine	
*Dresden	3
Ellsworth	2
Portland	1
Maryland	
Baltimore	2
Hagerstown	3
Salisbury	3
Massachusetts	
Boston	3
Hyannis	1
Worcester	1
Michigan	
Alpena	1
Detroit	1
Flint	2
Grand Rapids	1
Houghton	2
Marquette	1
Onondaga	2
Sault Sainte Marie	1
Traverse City	2

Figure 15-6. NOAA Weather Radio Network

Location	Frequency
Minnesota	
Detroit Lakes	3
Duluth	1
International Falls	1
Mankato	2
Minneapolis	1
Rochester	3
Saint Cloud (P)	3
Thief River Falls	1
Willmar (P)	2
Mississippi	
Ackerman	3
Booneville	1
Bude	1
Columbia (R)	2
Gulfport	2
Hattiesburg	3
Inverness	1
Jackson	2
Meridian	1
Oxford	2
Missouri	
Columbia	2
Camdenton	1
Hannibal	3
Joplin/Carthage	1
Kansas City	1
St. Joseph	2
St. Louis	1
Sikeston	2
Springfield	2
Montana	
Billings	1
Butte	1
Glasgow	1
Great Falls	1
Havre (P)	2
Helena	2
Kalispell	1
Miles City	2
Missoula	2
Nebraska	
Bassett	3
Grand Island	2
Holdrege	3
Lincoln	3
Merriman	2
Norfolk	1
North Platte	1
Omaha	2
Scottsbluff	1
Nevada	
Elko	1
Ely	2
Las Vegas	1
Reno	1
Winnemucca	2
New Hampshire	
Concord	2
New Jersey	
Atlantic City	2
New Mexico	
Albuquerque	2
Clovis	3
Des Moines	1
Farmington	3
Hobbs	2
Las Cruces	2

Location	Frequency
New Mexico	*continued*
Ruidoso	1
Santa Fe	1
New York	
Albany	1
Binghamton	3
Buffalo	1
Elmira	1
Kingston	3
New York City	1
Rochester	2
Syracuse	1
North Carolina	
Asheville	2
Cape Hatteras	3
Charlotte	3
Fayetteville	3
New Bern	2
Raleigh/Durham	1
Rocky Mount	3
Wilmington	1
Winston-Salem	2
North Dakota	
Bismarck	2
Dickinson	2
Fargo	2
Jamestown	2
Minot	2
Petersburg	2
Williston	2
Ohio	
Akron	2
Caldwell	3
Cleveland	1
Columbus	1
Dayton	3
Lima	2
Sandusky	2
Toledo	1
Oklahoma	
Clinton	3
Enid	3
Lawton	1
McAlester	3
Oklahoma City	2
Tulsa	1
Oregon	
Astoria	2
Brookings	1
Coos Bay	2
Eugene	2
Klamath Falls	1
Medford	2
Newport	1
Pendleton	1
Portland	1
Roseburg	3
Salem	3
Pennsylvania	
Allentown	2
Clearfield	1
Erie	2
Harrisburg	1
Johnstown	2
Philadelphia	3
Pittsburgh	3
State College	1
Wilkes-Barre	3
Williamsport	2

Location	Frequency
Puerto Rico	
Maricao	1
San Juan	2
Rhode Island	
Providence	2
South Carolina	
Beaufort	3
Charleston	1
Columbia	2
Florence	1
Greenville	1
Myrtle Beach	2
Sumter (R)	3
South Dakota	
Aberdeen	3
Huron	1
Pierre	2
Rapid City	1
Sioux Falls	2
Tennessee	
Bristol	1
Chattanooga	2
Cookeville	1
Jackson	3
Knoxville	3
Memphis	1
Nashville	3
Shelbyville	3
Waverly	2
Texas	
Abilene	2
Amarillo	1
Austin	2
Beaumont	3
Big Spring	3
Brownsville	1
Bryan	1
Corpus Christi	1
Dallas	2
Del Rio (P)	2
El Paso	3
Fort Worth	1
Galveston	1
Houston	2
Laredo	3
Lubbock	2
Lufkin	1
Midland	2

Location	Frequency
Texas	*continued*
Paris	1
Pharr	2
San Angelo	1
San Antonio	3
Sherman	3
Tyler	2
Victoria	3
Waco	3
Wichita Falls	3
Utah	
Logan	2
Cedar City	2
Vernal	2
Salt Lake City	1
Vermont	
Burlington	2
Windsor	3
Virginia	
Heathsville	2
Lynchburg	2
Norfolk	1
Richmond	3
Roanoke	3
Washington	
Neah Bay	1
Olympia	3
Seattle	1
Spokane	2
Wenatchee	3
Yakima	1
West Virginia	
Beckley	6
Charleston	2
Clarksburg	1
Gilbert	7
Hinton	4
Romney	7
Spencer	6
Sutton	5
Wisconsin	
La Crosse (P)	1
Green Bay	1
Madison	2
Menomonie	2
Milwaukee	3
Wausau	
Wyoming	
Casper	1
Cheyenne	3
Lander	3
Sheridan (P)	3

Notes:

1. Stations marked with an asterisk (*) are funded by public utility companies.

2. Stations marked (R) are low powered experimental repeater stations serving a very limited local area.

3. Stations marked (P) operate less than 24 hours/day; however, hours are extended when possible during severe weather.

4. Occasionally the frequency of an existing or planned station must be changed because of unexpected radio frequency interference with adjacent NOAA Weather Radio stations and/or with other government or commercial operators within the area.

Does your town have an effective warning system? Are public shelters well marked? Do the local radio stations receive the National Weather Wire Service? To develop or improve the Emergency Broadcast System in your community, contact the local National Weather Service Office or the civil preparedness director.

Are evacuations planned and allowances made for breakdowns and traffic jams? Has your town prepared a postdisaster plan delineating responsibilities of various officials and providing for basic services—health care, water, shelter, and food—despite disruption to the usual systems?

Has your child's school identified and designated safety areas? Are drills conducted? Do school bus drivers know what to do in an emergency?

Is your house constructed to take into account, not confront, the extremes of nature? In hazardous areas, houses and other buildings should be built with safety in mind. They can be examined by engineers who will recommend special techniques that offer protection against earthquake, tornado, hurricane, and so forth. All members of a household or office force should know the safest and nearest areas.

Figure 15-7. Take a close look at your own house to see how it might withstand an earthquake. *Roof:* Lightweight roofs of wood or composition shingles do not add an extra load during a quake. Tile roofs may need extra bracing; *Chimney:* Masonry chimneys—particularly those over four weight tall—may need extra support; *Doors:* Crookedly hanging doors may indicate significant settling and possible foundation problems; *Walls:* Large solid areas strengthen the house if firmly tied to roof and foundation. Masonry walls may want reinforcement; *Remodeling:* Replacing large areas of wall with glass may weaken the house's resistance, unless carefully engineered; *Trees:* Have weakened, looming trees removed professionally; *Property site:* Geological maps will alert you to hazards from faults, landslides, and floods; *Foundation:* Cracks of more than ⅛ inch wide may indicate that the foundation needs further support. (Courtesy of Darrow Watt)

Figure 15-8. Local Red Cross volunteers process disaster claim forms, more than five thousand in the first few days following a flood in Rapid City, South Dakota, in June 1972. (Courtesy of the American Red Cross)

Does your community have stringent tie-down regulations for mobile homes? Even if tied down, they should be left for more substantial shelters. Mobile home parks should have a good warning system and storm shelters for their residents.

Safety in the face of a natural hazard is a combined effort between yourself and your community. On a larger scale, the well-being of yourself and your family may rest to a certain extent on the efficiency and cooperation of relief agencies such as the Federal Emergency Management Agency (FEMA) and the Red Cross. In the final analysis, though, it is your own grasp of survival know-how that will bring you safely through most disasters.

General Precautions

The survival kit described in the land survival section would serve you well whether you were stranded in remote regions or trying to cope with a natural disaster in your hometown. In either case, the priorities of survival remain much the same.

Keep a first aid kit handy. Plenty of bottled drinking water is important as public water mains may be disrupted or the supply polluted. Figure on 4 gallons for drinking per person per week. Change your stored water every six months to keep it fresh. Before the disaster hits, fill your bathtub with water. A portable radio with spare batteries will keep you informed. Try to judge what sort of special clothing you might need—rain slickers, boots, warm sweater and hat, even, in the event of hail, a football helmet. Keep a stock of food at hand, things that need little cooking and no refrigeration. Don't forget pet food—and a can opener. Electric power may be interrupted. Candles, matches, flashlights, and fresh batteries should be in good supply.

Keep your valuables and copies of important papers in a metal, fireproof box. Do not open it soon after a fire as the intense heat inside could cause the papers to burst into flame when oxygen hits them. It is preferable, if you must leave home, to take your important papers with you.

Know how and where to turn off your electricity, gas, water, and central heating oil. Discuss disaster risks with your family and make advance arrangements to reunite if you're apart at the time of the disaster. In other words, have a family disaster plan. Chances are that your family will not be together if the disaster is of sudden onset, such as an earthquake or tornado. Learn the locations of shelters accessible to you during your daily rounds and point out to your children designated shelters near their schools and playgrounds.

Take a first aid course for the benefit of yourself, your family, and others. If you are skilled in first aid, you may be valuable to the relief effort. But unless you are qualified and have been allocated specific tasks, stay away from the disaster area. This is no time for sightseeing.

After dealing with matters requiring immediate attention, make an inventory of your losses. Keep listening to the local media for directions on where and how to report problems or unsafe conditions. Try to stay off the telephone during this period.

Figure 15-9. Red Cross first aid classes can equip you to deal with many emergencies. (Courtesy of the American Red Cross)

Figure 15-10. Some two hundred volunteers handled the phones round-the-clock in the after-math of the Good Friday earthquake in Alaska, 1964. (Courtesy of the American Red Cross)

Disaster is an apparently simple word that in reality carries a multitude of meanings. It can refer to the type of environmental disruption, its extent, or the numbers of people involved. We will look at disaster in terms of its chronology—before, during, and after—and discuss how you can survive each phase until you achieve the final goal of restoration.

The Warning Period

A National Weather Service *watch* for a particular hazard means that pre-vailing conditions are right for the formation of such a hazard. You should listen for further advisories. A National Weather Service *warning* means that the threatened hazard has materialized, and you should follow the in-structions of authorities.

Earthquakes are difficult to predict in the short-term, although some earthquake hazard zones are well-identified. The first things to look at are the location of your house and the soil underlying it. Do you live near an active fault? Is your house built on loose, porous soil liable to landslide? Are you in the flood plain of a burst dam or overflowing river? Are you near the coast and vulnerable to a tsunami? Geological maps will help you an-swer these and other questions. Consult the U.S. Geological Survey and city or county planning offices.

We saw from the previous chapter that wood-frame houses generally stood up well to earthquakes. All elements of the house, however, such as roof, ceiling, walls, and foundation, must be tied firmly together. A structural engineer could evaluate your house; a soil engineer or a geologist would be able to advise you on the nature of the ground beneath it. Support local land-use regulations and building codes designed to limit earthquake damage.

Anchor firmly all heavy appliances, furniture, lamps, picture frames, and so on that could fall during a big shake. Do not cover stairs or hardwood floors with rugs that could cause you to slip. Protect against the secondary hazard of fire. Secure flammable liquids and propane gas cylinders against falls. Keep a fire extinguisher of the proper type on hand.

Like earthquakes, volcanoes may show signs of activity months and weeks ahead of the actual devastating event, which is difficult to predict exactly. By heeding official warning of imminent volcanic eruptions, you can ensure that you are not on the mountain when it blows. Ashfall can affect communities many miles away. If a heavy ashfall is predicted, close all windows, doors, and dampers in your home. Put cars and farm machinery into garages and barns. Bring pets and livestock in under cover.

Tsunamis, which strike with tremendous force, are capable of drowning many people and causing widespread property damage. There is, however, an effective warning system in place along the Pacific Coast and the Hawaiian islands. If you hear a tsunami warning, evacuate immediately. If water recedes suddenly, it is because of the draw of the big wave that is imminent. Seek high ground immediately. Do not wait around to see the tsunami. If you're close enough to see it, you're probably close enough to drown in it. Await official clearance before returning, as tsunamis usually occur in a series.

In tornado-risk country, shelters prepared beforehand offer the best protection. An in-residence shelter consists of a small interior room, such as a closet, bathroom, or study, that has been reinforced to counter the effects of wind, atmospheric pressure change, and wind-borne debris. Those who do not have a cellar to their house should have an in-residence shelter, which is better than an outdoor cellar. There are companies and research institutes that specialize in in-residence shelters.

You should include in your tornado shelter a lantern, shovel, pick, crowbar, and other tools that might help you dig out.

Upon hearing a *tornado watch* for your area, continue to listen to the radio for further developments. Move loose objects indoors or tie them down. Call children in from play. A *tornado warning* means a funnel has been spotted.

Tornado/At Home. Stay away from windows. Go to the basement, to a reinforced interior room, or to an outdoor root cellar. Get under something sturdy. Take a portable radio and batteries with you.

Tornado/At Work. In office buildings, stand in an interior hallway on a

Figure 15-11. When a tornado threatens, seek shelter not on the top floor of a building but in its basement or predesignated hall. (Courtesy of NOAA)

lower floor, preferably the basement. In factories, post a lookout. Move quickly to the area of the plant offering the greatest protection (this should be determined by engineers beforehand). Stay away from windows.

Tornado/At School. Go to the school's basement or to a predesignated interior hallway. The interior hallway should not be parallel to the tornado's path, which in the United States is usually from the southwest. Never use gymnasiums, auditoriums, or other rooms with wide, free-span roofs as they may collapse. Stay away from windows. Both students and teachers should know in advance their assigned shelter. If a tornado catches students on the school bus, they should leave the bus and seek shelter in a nearby building or, if no other recourse, in a nearby ditch or ravine. Lie down and put your hands over your head. The same holds true if you're in a car as a tornado approaches.

Tornado/Mobile Homes. Appoint members of the community to listen for watches and warnings during stormy weather. If a notice is issued, leave your mobile home for a stronger shelter. If no shelter is nearby, lie flat in the nearest ditch or ravine with your hands shielding your head. Most deaths occur because of head injuries. A hard hat or football helmet kept near the door so you could grab it easily on your way would be a good safety measure.

Tornado/In Open Country. Leave your car. Seek shelter in a ditch or ravine.

In areas where forest or brush fires are common, be alert for the signs and warnings of fires during the dry season. Emergency phone numbers for the civil defense, ambulance service, forest service, and fire department should be posted near each phone. If you detect a fire, notify authorities immediately. If officials inform you of a fire, follow their instructions. Wetting down houses and property will keep sparks from igniting them easily. Prepare to evacuate if authorities recommend it.

If you are on foot in the backcountry, do not try to outrun the fire. It can travel very quickly. Instead, search out streams or rivers or an outcropping of rocks and bare ground—anyplace that offers little fuel for a fire. Wet your clothing and put a wet jacket over your head. Panicky forest animals fleeing the fire may come close but they have more on their minds than you and will not harm you unless you impede their escape.

Each year some 200,000 Americans are driven from their homes by floods. Annually during the past decade 200 persons were killed and more

Figure 15-12. A stream offers some protection from a forest fire. (Courtesy of the National Park Service)

Figure 15-13. Wheel chocks and tie-downs are precautions against high winds. (Courtesy of NOAA)

Figure 15-14. Pleasure boats are moored in canals, ready for the hurricane. (Courtesy of NOAA)

than $2 billion worth of property was damaged. In flood-prone areas, consider buying flood insurance. Keep on hand sandbags, plywood, plastic sheeting, and lumber. Sandbags should not be stacked directly against the outer walls of a house because they do create added pressure when they become wet. Keep your car fueled as filling stations may not be able to operate for several days if electric power is cut off. Follow general precautions regarding first aid, water, and food supplies. Know your elevation above flood stage (check with your Department of Public Works). Have a safe route planned from your home or business to the nearest high ground. Move to a safe area before flood water prohibits access. Be sure children are not playing near streams, culverts, or in low-lying fields. Flash floods come very quickly. If you are not threatened by a flash flood but by a slowly rising river flood, and only if you have time, move essential items to higher ground and grease immovable machinery. Keep insurance policies and a list of personal property in a safe place, such as a safe deposit box.

Hurricanes usually give more warning than floods, although flooding—in the form of the storm surge—accounts for most of a hurricane's fatalities. When a hurricane is forecast for your area, your first decision will be to stay or to leave.

In general, plan to leave if you live on the coast or on offshore islands; if you live in a mobile home; or if you live on or near a floodplain. Consider staying if you live on high ground away from coastal beaches. However, always follow the advice of local officials.

Be prepared at the beginning (June) of each hurricane season. Recheck your supply of boards (to cover windows), tools, batteries, nonperishable foods, and other equipment. Trim back dead wood from trees. Learn the storm surge history of your area. Determine where to move your boat in an emergency.

When a hurricane watch is issued, fuel your car, moor small craft or move it to a safe location, and secure lawn furniture and other loose objects. A *hurricane watch* means a hurricane may threaten within twenty-four hours. When a warning is announced, board up doors and windows. Bring valuables to upper floors if there is a chance of flooding. Turn up the refrigerator to maximum and don't open it unless necessary. A *hurricane warning* means a hurricane is expected within twenty-four hours.

If you are leaving the area, leave early and in daylight if possible. Shut off water and electricity at main stations. Take small valuables and papers, but travel lightly. Bring pets indoors and leave food and water for them (shelters will not take them). Lock your house and, using recommended evacuation routes, drive to a friend's house or to a designated shelter.

If hurricanes are summer's big storms, then blizzards are winter's. The first line of protection against blizzards is to be alert to weather conditions. A *blizzard warning* is issued when the weather service expects consider-

Figure 15-15. Homeowners buy supplies to board up the doors and windows of their house. (Courtesy of NOAA)

Figure 15-16. Metal awnings offer protection from wind, rain, and flying objects. (Courtesy of NOAA)

able snow and winds of 35 mph or more. A *severe blizzard warning* means a heavy snowfall with winds of at least 45 mph and temperatures 10°F or lower. Be prepared to be snowbound.

Keep an adequate supply of heating fuel on hand and use it sparingly. Close off some rooms temporarily if you're not using them. Have some form of emergency back-up heating for at least one room. Take general precautions regarding medicines, water, food, a portable radio with batteries, and lighting.

At the beginning of winter, check your car. It should have chains or snow tires. Stock it with a container of sand, shovel, windshield scraper, tow chain or rope, flashlights, blankets or sleeping bags, extra clothing, and booster cables. If you are caught in a blizzard when traveling, seek shelter immediately.

In a thunderstorm, you may have to contend with a tornado, a flash flood, or lightning. We've discussed the first two, now we'll consider how to protect yourself from lightning.

When a thunderstorm rolls into your area, get inside a house, a large building, or an automobile (but not a convertible). Do not use the telephone except for emergencies.

If you are caught outside, do not stand under a natural lightning rod such as a tall isolated tree or a telephone pole. Avoid projecting above the

Figure 15-17. (*top*) Swimming pool area before hurricane preparation; (*bottom*) Chairs and umbrellas placed in the swimming pool to escape the high winds of a hurricane. (Courtesy of NOAA)

Emergency Supplies
KEEP IN THE CAR

Cars should be equipped with supplies which could be useful in any emergency. Depending on location, climate of the area, personal requirements and other variables, the supplies in the kit might include (but are not limited to) the following:

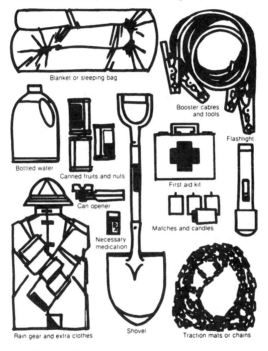

Blanket or sleeping bag

Booster cables and tools

Flashlight

Bottled water

Canned fruits and nuts

First aid kit

Can opener

Matches and candles

Necessary medication

Rain gear and extra clothes

Shovel

Traction mats or chains

Figure 15-18. Car emergency equipment. Never carry gasoline in containers other than the car's gas tank. (Courtesy of the Federal Emergency Management Agency)

surrounding landscape. Do not, for example, stand atop a hill. In a forest, seek shelter in a depression in the earth under a thick growth of small trees. In open areas, go to a ditch or ravine.

Move away from water, from tractors, other metal farm equipment, and metal fences, and from small metal vehicles such as golf carts, bicycles, or motorcycles. Put down golf clubs as the steel shaft can act as a conductor. If you are with a group in the open, spread apart.

Figure 15-19. The transceiver has led to the development of companion rescue. Each skier carries a transceiver, which can either give or receive signals. When caught in an avalanche, a skier switches to "transmit," and his companions to "receive." The intensity of the transmission reveals the location of the missing skier, who has a 50-50 chance if found in the first half hour. (Courtesy of Melanie Barocas)

If you feel your hair beginning to stand on end, lightning may be about to strike. Drop to your knees and bend over. Do not lie flat on the ground.

Avalanches and landslides will hurt you only if they can reach you. Avalanche hazard zones are usually posted. Obey warnings. For those, such as ski patrol members, who must work in avalanche territory, a device called a *transceiver* offers the best protection. Landslides usually occur as a secondary danger. You should know whether you're in a likely path. If the ground shakes and you hear a rumbling noise, head immediately for high ground.

The Disaster Strikes

When you feel the tremors of a major earthquake, try to stay calm and remember that the tremors are usually over in a matter of seconds or minutes.

Earthquake/At Home. Stay inside. Take cover under heavy furniture such as a desk or table or stand in a doorway or against the inner walls of a hall. Stay away from glass, chimneys, and furniture that might slide or topple.

Earthquake/At Work. If you're in a high-rise building, get under a desk. Restrain yourself from rushing for exits or stairways as they may be jammed with people. Do not get into an elevator.

Earthquake/Outdoors. Stay outdoors, but move away from buildings and power lines. Do not rush into or out of buildings as objects could be falling over passageways. (Deaths are often caused by falling debris.) Stay in an open area until the shaking stops.

Hazards within, say, twenty miles of a volcanic eruption include lava flows, rockfalls, earthquakes, mudflows, and flash floods. If caught in a small rock fall, roll into a ball and protect your head. Avoid streambeds and valleys as they may flood. If you feel the earth trembling, run uphill to high ground to avoid a possible mudflow.

Stay indoors during the passage of a tornado, hurricane, blizzard, or thunderstorm. Beware the "eye" of the hurricane, which is deceptively calm and may even show blue sky. Once the eye moves on, the storm will return with equal ferocity, this time the winds moving in the opposite direction. The eye may take from a few minutes to a half an hour or more to travel over your area.

During a period of heavy rains and flood warnings, avoid all areas subject to floods, especially to flash floods. Do not attempt to drive through a flooded road. It could be deeper than it looks, or flood water could rise quickly and carry you away. Do not attempt to cross a flowing stream if the water is above your knees. Avoid unnecessary exposure to the elements. Listen to your radio for further instructions. Be aware of the secondary dangers of fire and landslides and stay out of harm's way. If you do find yourself swept up in a flood, try to grab onto floating debris and make your way slowly to safe ground.

Aftermath

In the aftermath of an earthquake, your first act should be to protect against fire. Check around your house for fire hazards, and if one starts, put it out promptly. It is a good idea to keep a fire extinguisher handy. Do not use candles, matches, or other open flames either during or after

Figure 15-20. Flash flood waters can rise with incredible speed and force. Never attempt to drive through water; the car could be swept away or a part of the road may already be eroded. (Courtesy of the American Red Cross; photo taken by Jack Shaffer for the Arizona Daily Star)

the earthquake, because of possible gas leaks. If you are injured, seek medical help. Do not neglect your own injuries in your attempts to help others.

Check your utilities for breaks and leaks, but do not turn them on. The movement of the earth may have damaged gas, electrical, and water lines. If you smell gas, open the windows and shut off the main valve. Leave the building, and report the leak to the authorities. Stay away from the building until you are told it is safe to reenter.

If electrical wiring has been damaged, close the switch at the main meter box. If water mains are broken, shut off the supply.

Do not use the telephone except for emergency calls. Listen to the radio for further news. Do not eat or drink from open containers near shattered glass.

Avoid downed power lines. Beware of debris that may continue to fall. If you are in town stay away from large buildings. Do not go sightseeing, particularly in coastal areas where a tsunami may strike. Do not enter damaged buildings. Be aware of secondary dangers—fire, tsunami, landslide.

In a severe earthquake, roads will be broken up, traffic signals will not work, and confusion will reign. It is better to evacuate on foot. Rumors will circulate about further quakes to come. You should expect aftershocks, but listen to the radio for official information. Avoid walking along a wall, under a cliff, or by a river. In the city, take a cushion or helmet with you to protect your head from falling objects.

When it is safe to go home again, check your chimney from a distance for cracks and missing bricks. If it appears intact, then approach and check it carefully again. Look particularly in the attic and at the roofline. Call an expert in if you're uncertain. Undetected damage could cause a fire. Always approach chimneys with extreme caution. Examine also closets and storage shelves, being careful when opening doors. Have the damage to your home assessed by your insurance agent. Radio, television, newspapers, and disaster relief officials will have information on disaster assistance.

Following a volcanic eruption, ashfall will affect communities for miles downwind. The ash is actually pulverized rock, and as such it will be very heavy. It will clog waterways, reservoirs, and machinery, and its weight may cause roofs to collapse. Do not attempt to drive during a heavy ashfall; it will only stir up more ash and ruin your vehicle. Clear your roof of ashfall to prevent it collapsing. Cover your mouth and nose with a cloth to help filter the ash. Wear goggles over your eyes and keep your skin covered. Keep in mind that volcanoes can trigger earthquakes, mudflows, and flash floods, and their ash cloud can generate intense lightning storms.

Most tornadoes last only four or five minutes and travel on the ground for only about two miles before dissipating. After you emerge from your

Figure 15-21. Following a natural disaster, government and Red Cross relief information will be posted in the community and announced over local radio and television. (Courtesy of the American Red Cross)

shelter, having heard the all-clear signal on your radio, inspect your property, including automobiles, for damage. Check for disruptions to gas, water, and electrical connections. If you have extensive damage, get in touch with your insurance company. Have an agent assess your damage. Prompt assistance after a disaster is usually forthcoming. Secure your property from further damage; remember heavy rains may follow a tornado. Keep receipts—the cost of temporary repairs may be reimbursable under your policy.

Inventory your damage to speed your insurance settlement. Your policy may cover the cost of temporary housing and also the removal of debris. Do not contract with removal services before speaking to your insurance agent.

If you are already in the stricken area, help those you can, but do not travel to the disaster area. Use caution in entering a damaged building. Notify your relatives of your survival so that local officials do not waste time looking for you. Do not tie-up the telephone lines unnecessarily. Wear protective clothing—heavy boots, hat, and gloves—when cleaning up. Fiberglass insulation contains tiny shards of glass. Watch out that fragments do not get under your skin.

After a fire, secure the site against rain and unauthorized entry and call your insurance agent. If you need temporary housing, food, eyeglasses, or medicines destroyed in the fire, contact, for example, the Red Cross or the Salvation Army.

Upon revisiting the scene of the fire, watch that apparently dead ashes do not rekindle. Call your fire department for instructions. Do not reconnect any utilities. Roofs and floors may be weakened by the fire. Do not use food, beverages, or medicines that have been exposed to heat or smoke. Collect receipts for any fire-related costs.

Check your insurance policy, which may cover temporary housing and provide advance cash. Do not attempt to open your safe. Contact the police, who will keep an eye on things for you.

As floodwaters recede, contact the insurance agent who sold you your flood insurance policy. The agent will submit a loss form to the National Flood Insurance Program, and an adjuster will come out to survey the damage. As with other disasters, enter damaged buildings only with care and check on the supply lines. As a source of light, use a battery-powered flashlight, not a live flame. Cover broken windows and patch holes in the roof. Again, save receipts for temporary repairs.

Throw out any food or medicines that have come in contact with floodwater. Boil water, unless the public system has been declared safe.

The Red Cross can supply flood clean-up kits. Hose off appliances and furniture and keep them for the adjuster's inspection. To deodorize, use one teaspoon of baking soda to a quart of water. Air damaged items. Take pictures. The adjuster will make recommendations regarding their repair or disposal.

Take wooden furniture outdoors, but protect it from direct sunlight. Remove drawers, if necessary by *pushing* out from the back, not by *pulling* from the front.

Shovel out mud to give walls and floors a chance to dry. Once plaster walls have dried, brush off loose dirt and wash with soap. Rinse with clear, clean water. Start at the top and work down.

Remove mildew from dry wood with a solution of 4 to 6 tablespoons Trisodium Phosphate, 1 cup liquid chlorine bleach, and 1 gallon water. Clean metal and then wipe with a kerosene-soaked cloth to prevent rust. Scour all utensils. You can brighten aluminium by using a solution of vinegar, cream of tartar, and hot water.

Separate laundry to avoid running colors. Allow fabrics to dry before brushing off loose dirt. Send to a professional cleaner or rinse the items in lukewarm water with mild detergent. Dry in sunlight.

Drain flooded basements slowly as structural damage can result from too-fast drainage. After the surrounding floodwater has subsided, begin draining the cellar, about ⅓ of the water volume each day. After a hurricane has passed, seek medical attention if needed. Do not use the roads unless necessary. If you must drive, watch out for dangling wires, debris-filled or washed-out streets, and flooded low spots. Stay away from the stricken area so as not to hamper rescue and clean-up efforts. Take extra precautions to prevent fire. Lowered water pressure in town lines, blocked roadways, and rescue efforts elsewhere make the chances of the fire department getting to you slim. Together with neighbors, clear obstructions from your road.

Indoors, if you have suffered water damage, proceed as described above for floods. Document your losses with photographs. Losses not covered by insurance may be tax deductible. Check with a government representative.

Hazards to health may exist after a hurricane. Be prepared to store or bury garbage if collection crews cannot get around. Guard against spoiled food. If power went out during the storm you must not refreeze food once it has thawed. Conserve water for drinking and cooking until you are sure your supply is safe.

If the water in your cistern appears brownish, it is likely that mud has entered the cistern. It will settle in time. To clean your system, place one ounce of chlorinated bleach per 1,000 gallons of water in a bucket and lower it into the cistern. Agitate to promote distribution, or recirculate water by placing a hose in the cistern opening. Twelve or more hours later, take a sample of water to health officials for testing.

Digging out from under a blizzard has its own built-in danger. Avoid overexertion. Cold weather in itself puts a strain on the heart. Coupled with unaccustomed exercise, such as shoveling, pushing cars, or hiking through snow, the cold can be a deadly enemy.

Isolation is another aftereffect of a blizzard. Check on your neighbors to be sure they have enough heat, water, and food. Ask for help if you need it.

Contrary to popular belief, there may be life after an encounter with lightning. About two-thirds of the people involved in lightning accidents make a full recovery. Nevertheless, lightning remains a top weather-related killer in the United States.

Persons struck by lightning carry no electrical charge and can be safely handled. If the victim is not breathing, send someone for help and give mouth-to-mouth resuscitation immediately, once every five seconds to adults and once every three seconds to small children. If the victim is not breathing and has no pulse, administer cardiopulmonary resuscitation—a combination of mouth-to-mouth resuscitation and external cardiac compression. (See the first aid chapter). This should be given only by a properly trained person. If someone is unconscious but is breathing and has a pulse, he or she may recover spontaneously. Check victims for burns, especially at fingers and toes and next to buckles and jewelry. Get the person to medical help as soon as possible.

The struggle to survive against all odds—be it in the course of a natural disaster, at sea, or in remote corners of our earth—seems often to elicit the best in human nature. You may be thrown back on solitary resourcefulness or you may combine forces with friends and neighbors, but you will bring from your survival episode a surer knowledge of yourself and your abilities and, if this book has not already given some indication, a realization of the importance of being prepared.

Bibliography of Sources

We make available to our readers here a list of the books, articles, and reports we consulted in revising *How to Survive on Land and Sea*. Because we feel that readers of a survival manual—particularly those referring to it not from the comfort of an armchair by the fireplace—have a special need for quick access to information, we chose not to interrupt the text with notes. In the few places where we quoted directly or where attribution was necessary, we included names in the text that would facilitate reference to this list. Here we acknowledge the authors whose works guided us in a general way and suggest that readers may find many useful references relating to their own particular interests.

LAND SURVIVAL

Angier, Bradford. *Living Off the Country*. Harrisburg, PA., Stackpole Books, 1956.

——. *Feasting Free on Wild Vegetables*. Harrisburg, PA., Stackpole Books, 1972.

——. *Survival with Style*. Harrisburg, PA., Stackpole Books, 1972.

Appendix S. FASOTRAGRULANTDETBRUNSINST 3305.3. Survival, Evasion, Resistance and Escape School. *Courses and General Information, Student Handout*, Brunswick, ME.: U.S. Naval Air Station, January 1982.

Appendix T. FASOTRAGRULANTDETBRUNSINST 3305.3. *Cold Weather Survival School Student Handout for Cold Weather and General Survival Information*. Brunswick, ME.: U.S. Naval Air Station, March 1981.

Baird, Patrick D. *The Polar World*. New York: John Wiley & Sons, 1964.

Bangs, Cameron, M.D., and Hamlet, Murray, D.V.M. "Out in the Cold—Management of Hypothermia, Immersion, and Frostbite." *Topics in Emergency Medicine*, 2, no. 3 (October 1980): 19–37.

Basic Survival Medicine, rev. Maxwell Air Force Base, Alabama: Air Training Command, 1981.

Bernhartsen, J. C., and Schlenker, Richard. "Cold Water Fatalities: An Overview of Physiological Responses." *Current: The Journal of Marine Education* (Winter 1981): 6–9.

Brooks, Maurice. *The Life of the Mountains*. New York: The World Book Encyclopedia/McGraw Hill, 1967.

Brown, G. W., Jr., ed. *Desert Biology*. New York: Academic Press, 1968.

Bruemmer, Fred. *The Arctic*. New York: Quadrangle/New York Times Book Co., 1973.

————. "Eskimos Are Warm People." *Natural History* 90 (October 1981): 42–48.

Canby, Thomas Y. "The Search for the First Americans." *National Geographic* 156, no. 3 (September 1979).

Collis, M. L.; Steinman, Alan M.; and Chaney, R. D. "Accidental Hypothermia: An Experimental Study of Practical Rewarming Methods." *Aviation, Space, and Environmental Medicine* 48 (August 1977): 625–32.

Costello, David F. *The Seashore World*. New York: Thomas Y. Crowell, 1980.

Department of the Air Force, *Search and Rescue: Survival*. Washington, D.C.: U.S. Government Printing Office, 1969.

Department of the Army Field Manual. *Survival, Evasion, and Escape*. Washington, D.C.: U.S. Government Printing Office, 1969.

Findley, Rowe. *Great American Deserts*. Washington, D.C.: National Geographic Society, 1972.

George, Uwe. *In the Deserts of This Earth*. New York: A Helen and Kurt Wolff Book/Harcourt Brace Jovanovich, 1977.

Hansen, John V. E. "Clothing for Cold Climes." *Natural History* 90 (October 1981): 90–97.

Jaeger, Edmund C. *The North American Deserts*. Stanford, CA.: Stanford University Press, 1957.

Kaufman, W. C.; Bothe, D.; and Meyer, S. E. "Thermal Insulating Capabilities of Outdoor Clothing Materials." *Science* 215 (5 February 1982): 690–91.

Kimble, G. H. T., and Good, Dorothy. *Geography of the Northlands*. New York: John Wiley & Sons, 1955.

Krutch, Joseph Wood. *The Desert Year*. New York: William Sloane Associates, 1951.

Ley, Willy. *The Poles*. Life Nature Library. New York: Time Inc., 1962.

Merrill, W. K. *The Survival Handbook*. New York: Winchester Press, 1972.

NASA. *SARSAT: Search and Rescue Satellite-Aided Tracking: Space-age Technology for Rescue with Minimal Search*. Greenbelt, M.D.: Goddard Space Flight Center, 1983.

Naval Arctic Operations Handbook. rev. ed. Washington, D.C.: Department of the Navy, 1950.

Oliver, Douglas L. *The Pacific Islands*. Cambridge: Harvard University Press, 1951.

Paulcke, Wilhelm, and Dumler, Helmut. *Hazards in Mountaineering: How to Recognize and Avoid Them*. trans. E. Noel Bowman. New York: Oxford University Press, 1973.

Perry, Richard. *The Polar Worlds*. New York: Taplinger, 1973.

Price, Larry W. *Mountains & Man*. Los Angeles: University of California Press, 1981.

Proulx, Annie. "Clothes for the Cold." *Country Journal* (December 1980): 45–49.

"Ranges of Hypothermia Symptoms," Hypothermia card. Newport, R.I.: U.S. Yacht Racing Union.

Richards, Paul W. *The Life of the Jungle*. New York: The World Book Encyclopedia/McGraw Hill, 1970.

Richardson, Joan. *Wild Edible Plants of New England: A Field Guide*. Freeport, ME.: DeLorme Publishing Co., 1981.

Shell, Ellen Ruppell. "Engineering for Survival." *Technology Review* 85 (July 1982): 14–19.

Southward, A. J. *Life on the Sea-shore*. Cambridge: Harvard University Press, 1967.

Stefansson, Vilhjalmur. *Arctic Manual*. New York: Macmillan, 1945.

Steinman, Alan M. "Hypothermic Code." *Journal of Emergency Medical Services* 8 (October 1983): 32–35.

Strebeigh, Fred. "Frostbite and Hypothermia." *Country Journal* (December 1982): 80–91.

Sundt, Captain Wilbur A., USN (Ret.). *Naval Science*. vols. 2 and 3. Annapolis, MD., Naval Institute Press, 1981 and 1978 respectively.

Sutton, Ann and Myron. *The Life of the Desert*. New York: The World Book Encyclopedia/McGraw Hill, 1966.

Tobin, Wallace E., III. *The Mariner's Pocket Companion*. Annapolis, MD.: Naval Institute Press, 1974.

U.S. Coast Guard Commandant Instruction M3131.5. "A Pocket Guide to Cold Water Survival." October 1980.

Zimmerman, David. "The Mosquitoes Are Coming—and They Are among Man's Most Lethal Foes." *Smithsonian* 14 (June 1983): 28–37.

Zwinger, A. H., and Willard, B. E. *Land above the Trees: A Guide to American Alpine Tundra*. New York; Harper & Row, 1972.

WATER SURVIVAL

Bailey, Maurice and Maraly. *Staying Alive: 117 Days Adrift*. Lymington, U.K.: Nautical Publishing Co., 1974.

Boswell, John, ed. *The U.S. Armed Forces Survival Manual*. New York: Rawson, Wade, 1980.

Callahan, Steve. "Survival: Designing the Ultimate Liferaft." *Sail* (February 1983): 50–57.

Henderson, Richard; Dunbar, Bartlett S.; and Brooks, William E., III. *Sail and Power*. 3rd ed. Annapolis, MD.: Naval Institute Press, 1979.

Hobbs, Richard R. *Marine Navigation*. 2 vols. Annapolis, MD.: Naval Institute Press, 1981.

International Maritime Organization. "A Pocket Guide to Cold Water Survival." London, 1981.

Kotsch, William J. *Weather for the Mariner*. Annapolis, MD.: Naval Institute Press, 1977.

Maloney, Elbert S. *Dutton's Navigation & Piloting*. 13th ed. Annapolis, MD.: Naval Institute Press, 1978.

McMillan, Margaret. "Aquatic Survival in an Industrial Environment." In *Aquatics in the 80's*, ed. E. Louise Priest. A report of the 21st National Conference of the Council for National Cooperation in Aquatics, November 20–23, 1980, Atlanta, Georgia.

Nemiroff, Martin J., Cdr., USCG. "Survival following Cold Water Near Drowning." In *Aquatics in the 80's*. ed. E. Louise Priest. A Report of the 21st National Conference of the Council for National Cooperation in Aquatics, November 20–23, 1980, Atlanta, Georgia.

Robertson, Dougal. *Survive the Savage Sea.* New York: Praeger, 1973.
———. *Sea Survival: A Manual.* New York: Praeger, 1975.
Smith, David S., ed. *SASS Aquatic Safety, Cold Water Survival, Hypothermia Manual.* Imperial, MO.: Smith Aquatic Safety Services, 1982.
———. *SASS Hypothermia, Cold Water Survival, Critical Care Supplement.* Imperial, MO.: Smith Aquatic Safety Services, 1982.
Survival at Sea: Instruction Manual. Canberra, Australian Government Publishing Service, 1978.
Vignes, Jacques. *The Rage to Survive.* trans. Mihailo Voukitchevitch. New York: William Morrow, 1976.
Williams, Jerome; Higginson, John J.; and Rohrbough, John D. *Sea & Air: the Marine Environment.* Annapolis, MD.: Naval Institute Press, 1973.

DISASTER SURVIVAL

"Burning Hills, Southern California." *Newsweek* 94 (1 October 1979): 25.
Clark, Champ. *Planet Earth: Flood.* Alexandria, VA.: Time-Life Books, 1982.
Cupp, David. "Avalanche! Battling the Juggernaut." *National Geographic* 162 (September 1982): 290–305.
Ferguson, Edward W.; Schaefer, Joseph T.; Weiss, Steven J.; and Wilson, Larry F. "The Year of the Tornado." *Weatherwise* 36 (February 1983): 18–27.
Findley, Rowe. "Eruption of Mount St. Helens." *National Geographic* 159 (January 1981): 3–65.
"Fire Storm in California." *Newsweek* 96 (8 December 1980): 39.
Forrester, Frank H. "Winds of the World." *Weatherwise* 35 (October 1982): 204–10.
Frazier, Kendrick. *The Violent Face of Nature.* New York: William Morrow, 1979.
Fuchs, Sir Vivian, ed. *Forces of Nature.* New York: Holt, Rinehart and Winston, 1977.
Marrero, Jose. "Danger: Flash Floods." *Weatherwise* 32 (February 1979): 34–37.
Mitchell, J. Murray. "El Chichon: Weather-Maker of the Century?" *Weatherwise* 35 (December 1982): 252–62.
Moore, Gerald. "Los Angeles Is Burning." *Readers Digest* (August 1979): 173–80.
Neider, Charles, ed. *Man against Nature.* New York: Harper & Brothers, 1954.
Quarantelli, E. L. "Reality and Myth in Community Disasters." Office of the United Nations Disaster Relief Co-ordinator, *Undro News* (November–December 1982): 6–9.
Sunset Special Report. "Getting Ready for a Big Quake." *Sunset* (March 1982): 104–11.
Walker, Bryce. *Planet Earth: Earthquake.* Alexandria, VA.: Time-Life Books, 1982.
Waltham, Tony. *Catastrophe: the Violent Earth.* New York: Crown, 1978.
Weintraub, Boris. "Fire and Ash, Darkness at Noon." *National Geographic* 162 (November 1982): 655–84.
Whipple, A. B. C. *Planet Earth: Storm.* Alexandria, VA.: Time-Life Books, 1982.
———. "Storms the Angry Gods Sent Are Now Science's Quarry." *Smithsonian* (September 1982): 89–99.

White, Gilbert F., ed. *Natural Hazards: Local, National, Global.* New York: Oxford University Press, 1974.

Whittow, John. *Disasters: the Anatomy of Environmental Hazards.* Athens, GA.: University of Georgia Press, 1979.

"Winds of Autumn." *Time* 116 (8 December 1980): 37.

General Bibliography

Listed below are books for further reading. Some are general guides, others concern survival in specific areas or specific aspects of survival.

Acerrano, Anthony J. *The Outdoorsman's Emergency Manual.* New York: Winchester Press, 1976.

American Red Cross. *American National Red Cross Lifesaving, Rescue, and Water Safety.* Garden City, N.J.: Doubleday, 1974.

———. *Basic Rescue and Water Safety.* Washington, D.C.: American Red Cross, 1974.

Angier, Bradford. *On Your Own in the Wilderness.* New York: Hart, 1976.

———. *Bradford Angier's Backcountry Basics.* Harrisburg, PA.: Stackpole Books, 1983.

Assiniwi, Bernard. *Survival in the Bush.* Toronto: Copp Clark, 1972.

Beattie, John. *Lifeboats to the Rescue.* Newton Abbot, Great Britain, North Pomfret, VT.: David & Charles, 1980.

Berglund, Berndt. *Wilderness Survival.* New York: Scribner, 1972.

Boy Scouts of America. *Lifesaving.* Irving, TX.: Boy Scouts of America, 1980.

Bradner, Gary. *Living Off the Land.* New York: Galahad Books, 1974.

Brown, Tom. *Tom Brown's Field Guide to Wilderness Survival.* New York: Berkley Books, 1983.

Brown, Walter R. *Rescues.* New York: Walker, 1983.

Burch, Monte. *The Good Earth Almanac: Survival Handbook.* New York: Sheed and Ward, 1973.

Chartres, John. *Helicopter Rescue.* London: Ian Allan, 1980.

Dalrymple, Byron W. *Survival in the Outdoors.* New York: Outdoor Life, 1972.

Dickey, Esther. *Skills for Survival: How Families Can Prepare.* Bountiful, Utah: Horizon, 1978.

Doran, Jeffry. *Search on Mount St. Helens.* Bellevue, WA.: Imagesmith, 1980.

Dunlevy, Maurice. *Stay Alive.* Canberra: Australian Government Publication Service, 1978.

Family Home Preparedness. Los Angeles: Personal Welfare Committee, Los Angeles, California, Santa Monica Stake, Church of Jesus Christ of Latter-day Saints, 1976.

Fear, Gene. *Surviving the Unexpected Wilderness Emergency.* Tacoma, WA.: Survival Education Association, 1975.

Fleming, June. *Staying Found.* New York: Vintage Books, 1982.

Fry, Alan. *Wilderness Survival Handbook.* New York: St. Martin's Press, 1981.

Ganci, Dave. *Hiking the Desert*. Chicago: Contemporary Books, 1979.

Gearing, Catherine. *A Field Guide to Wilderness Living*. Nashville, TN.: Southern Pub. Association, 1973.

Gibbons, Euell. *Stalking the Good Life*. New York: D. McKay Co., 1971.

Gonzales, Ellice B. *Storms, Ships, & Surfmen*. Patchogue, N.Y.: Eastern National Park and Monument Association, 1982.

Graves, Richard H. *Bushcraft*. New York: Schocken Books, 1972.

Harlow, William Morehouse. *Ways of the Woods*. Washington, D.C.: American Forestry Association, 1979.

Henderson, M. A., ed. *The Survival Resource Book*. New York: St. Martin's Press, 1980.

Hildreth, Brian. *How to Survive in the Bush, on the Coast, in the Mountains of New Zealand*. Wellington: Government Printing, 1970.

How to Survive in the Wilderness. New York: Drake Publishers, 1975.

Howarth, Patrick. *Life-boats and Life-boat People*. New York: White Lion Publishers, 1974.

IMCO Search and Rescue Manual. London: Intergovernmental Maritime Consultative Organization, 1980.

International Conference on Maritime Search and Rescue. Final Act of the Conference, with attachments, including the International Convention on Maritime Search and Rescue. London: Intergovernmental Maritime Consultative Organization, 1979.

Knap, Jerome J. *The Complete Outdoorsman's Handbook*. Toronto: Pagurian Press, 1974.

Kraus, Joe. *Alive in the Desert*. Boulder, CO.: Paladin Press, 1978.

Lacefield, Eric M. *Survival in the Marsh*. New Orleans: Louisiana Wildlife & Fisheries Commission, 1975.

Lewis, Thomas R. *Organization, Training, Search, and Recovery Procedures for the Underwater Unit*. Marquette, MI.: Northern Michigan University Press, 1979.

Lifesaving and Marine Safety. Piscataway, N.J.: Association Press, New Century Publishers, 1981.

MacInnes, Hamish. *International Mountain Rescue Handbook*. New York: Scribner, 1973.

Manual of U.S. Cave Rescue Techniques. Huntsville, AL (Cave Ave., Huntsville 35810): National Cave Rescue Commission of the National Speleological Society, 1981.

Mason, Rosalie. *Beginners Guide to Family Preparedness*. Bountiful, Utah: Horizon, 1977.

Merchant Ship Search and Rescue Manual (MERSAR). London: Intergovernmental Maritime Consultative Organization, 1980.

Moir, John. *Just in Case*. San Francisco: Chronicle Books, 1980.

Morton, Julia Frances. *Wild Plants for Survival in South Florida*. Miami: Fairchild Tropical Gardens, 1982.

National Lifeguard Manual. New York: Association Press, 1974.

National Science Foundation, Division of Polar Programs. *Survival in Antarctica*. Washington, D.C.: U.S. Government Printing Office, 1979.

Nault, Andy. *Staying Alive in Alaska's Wild*. Washington, D.C.: Tee Loftin Publishers, 1980.

Neimark, Paul G. *Survival*. Chicago: Children's Press, 1981.

Nelson, Dick. *Desert Survival*. Glenwood, N.M.: Tecolote Press, 1977.

The NSPS Ski Mountaineering Manual. Denver (2901 Sheridan Blvd., Denver 80214): National Ski Patrol System, 1982.

Nuttle, David A. *The Universal Survival Handbook*. Latham, Kan.: David A. Nuttle Survival Association, 1979.

Olsen, Larry Dean. *Outdoor Survival Skills*. Provo, Utah: Brigham Young University Press, 1973.

————. *Wilderness Survival*. North Brunswick, N.J.: Boy Scouts of America, 1974.

The Outdoors Survival Manual. New York: Drake Publishers, 1978.

Patterson, Craig E. *Mountain Wilderness Survival*. Berkeley, CA: And/Or Press, 1979.

Petzoldt, Paul K. *The Wilderness Handbook*. New York: Morton, 1974.

Plate, M. W. *Australian Bushcraft*. Melbourne: Lansdowne Press, 1971.

Platt, Charles. *Outdoor Survival*. New York: Watts, 1976.

Platten, David. *The Outdoor Survival Handbook*. Newton Abbot, Great Britain, North Pomfret, VT: David & Charles, 1979.

Pond, Alonzo William. *Afoot in the Desert*. Maxwell Air Force Base, Ala.: Air Training Command, 3636th Combat Crew Training Wing Environmental Information Division, 1974.

Poynter, Margaret. *Search & Rescue*. New York: Atheneum, 1980.

Rile, Michael J. *Don't Get Snowed*. Matteson, Ill.: Greatlakes Living Press, 1977.

Salisbury, Barbara G. *Just in Case*. Salt Lake City: Bookcraft, 1975.

Schuh, Dwight R. *Modern Outdoor Survival*. New York: Arco, 1983.

Self, William L. *Survival Kit for the Stranded*. Nashville, Tenn.: Broadman Press, 1975.

Setnicka, Tim J. *Wilderness Search and Rescue*. Boston: Appalachian Mountain Club, 1980.

Shanks, Bernard. *Wilderness Survival*. New York: Universe Books, 1980.

Simer, Peter. *The National Outdoor Leadership School's Wilderness Guide*. New York: Simon and Schuster, 1983.

Staender, Vivian. *Our Arctic Year*. Anchorage, Ala.: Northwest Pub. Co., 1983.

Sweeney, James B. *Disasters*. New York: McKay Co., 1981.

Szczelkun, Stefan A. *Survival Scrapbook*. New York: Schocken Books, 1973.

Temple, Ernest. *Survival*. Aldergrove, British Columbia: Frontier Pub., 1978.

Thygerson, Alton L. *Disaster Survival Handbook*. Provo, Utah: Brigham Young University Press, 1979.

Torney, John A. *Teaching Aquatics*. Minneapolis, Minn.: Burgess Pub. Co., 1981.

Tucker, John. *A Jungle Handbook*. Singapore: Donald Moore for Asia Pacific Press, 1970.

U.S. Coast Guard. *Air Search and Rescue*. Washington, D.C.: Dept. of Transportation, Coast Guard, 1978.

Welch, Mary Scott. *The Family Wilderness Handbook*. New York: Ballantine Books, 1973.

Wilson, Jack. *Australian Surfing and Surf Life Saving*. Adelaide, Rigby, 1979.

Winkelman, Jack L. *Essentials of Basic Life Support*. Minneapolis, Minn.: Burgess Pub. Co., 1981.

Index

ABOUT THE AUTHORS

Frank and John Craighead are world-recognized ecologists and survival experts who pioneered survival training for the armed services and in World War II set up the U.S. Navy's first land/sea survival training program for aviators. After the war, the two brothers continued work on the development of survival techniques for the U.S. Strategic Air Command and became extensively involved in field studies of wildlife and wilderness areas for the National Geographic Society, the New York Zoological Society, the U.S. Forest Service, and the Department of Interior. Their research, writing, and photography on wildlife has taken them all over the world, from the deserts of Africa to the icebergs of Alaska.

The Craigheads are perhaps best known for their definitive research on the biology of the grizzly bear. They are also known for pioneering radio-tracking and satellite biotelemetry techniques and for their leadership in originating the National Wild and Scenic Rivers System in the United States. They have co-authored four books, scores of articles, and numerous educational films and documentaries.

ABOUT THE REVISORS

Ray E. Smith is a retired U.S. Navy survival training expert, with more than twenty years experience in both land and sea survival training. He is presently coordinator for the Naval Aviation Water Survival Training Program. He is also the diving officer for Naval Aviation Schools Command and a diving instructor for the National Association of Underwater Instructors. He has served many years as instructor/trainer for the American Red Cross in first aid, water safety, and CPR training programs. In his present position, he is responsible for analyzing the survival requirements of naval aviators and developing appropriate training programs. He has co-authored one book and has written numerous articles on survival and diving techniques.

D. Shiras Jarvis, a lieutenant commander with the U.S. Naval Reserves, is senior instructor, Swim Division, School of Survival, Naval Aviation Schools Command. He, too, is a qualified water safety instructor of the American Red Cross and is certified by that organization to teach first aid and cardiopulmonary resuscitation techniques. He is studying for a doctorate in motor learning at Florida State University and has written the instructor's manual for use in the Naval Aviation Water Survival Training Program.